IBM® PC COBOL

William J. Atkinson, Jr.
Paul A. DeSanctis

Reston Publishing Company, Inc.
A Prentice-Hall Company
Reston, Virginia

Library of Congress Cataloging in Publication Data

Atkinson, William J.
  IBM PC COBOL.

  Includes index.
  1. IBM Personal Computer--Programming. 2. COBOL
(Computer program language) I. DeSanctis, Paul A.
II. Title. III. Title: I.B.M. P.C. C.O.B.A.L.
QA76.8.I2594A85 1984   001.64′2   84-8318
ISBN 0-8359-3051-3

Production supervision/interior design: Tally Morgan

© 198.5 by Reston Publishing Company, Inc.
A Prentice-Hall Company
Reston, Virginia 22090

10 9 8 7 6 5 4 3 2 1

Printed in the United States of America

CONTENTS

PREFACE

Our aim in this book is to present a variant of COBOL specially designed for use in microcomputer systems, particularly the IBM® Personal Computer (IBM PC). We have selected two COBOL packages upon which to base this book: MICROSOFT COBOL-80 and MICRO FOCUS CIS COBOL.—e.g., the self-documenting feature using ordinary English words to perform complex business problems—and features that allow COBOL to function interactively in a conversational mode. Users can communicate with their files directly through the terminal keyboard and the video display screen. These features are not always found in COBOL for large-scale systems, and when they are, it is difficult to find references to them in standard COBOL texts. Therefore, much of the emphasis in this book focuses on their use.

IBM® PC COBOL assumes no particular background in data processing, although some general knowledge of computers and programming languages would be helpful. For the reader with no previous programming experience, we have included in Chapter 1 a discussion of business data processing concepts and microcomputer systems, presenting these in sufficient detail to form a good foundation for the more advanced work that follows. The reader with a computer background may skip the introductory chapter and begin with Chapter 2, where we begin COBOL and its usage in applications.

Our approach to the subject is practical, involving numerous examples and exercises. In the first chapters we present an overview of COBOL, focusing on the syntax and grammar of the language. In succeeding chapters, we center on the various functions of the language, showing how they are used. Since computer programming is largely an applied science, particular emphasis has been placed on technique rather than theory. Following each chapter is a set of review questions and exercises intended to test the reader's knowledge and skills. The questions, which are broad in scope, require a bit more thought than the questions found in many programming texts. The problems, which begin after Chapter 6, are intended to build specific coding skills. As many of them as possible should be done.

All problems in this text use the data file shown in Appendix B. The reader should create this file using a text editor, or should write their own program using the screen formatting techniques shown in Chapter 7 to create this file. As the reader progresses through the text, this file will be the input file for all programs.

Years of teaching computer languages and working with them in industry have convinced us that the best way to impart programming principles is by frequent examples. With this thought in mind, we have included several fully coded COBOL programs in the appendix that incorporate all of the techniques discussed and illustrated in the main body of the test. From time to time you will be asked to refer to these sample programs. Please be sure to do so, for nothing will speed your progress more than studying techniques from within the context of a complete working program.

We wish to thank our editors Tom Fay and Tally Morgan at Reston Publishing Company, and Brian Baker, for their valuable suggestions and advice for improving the manuscript. Most of all we would like to thank our wives, Maria Atkinson and Marguerite DeSanctis, and our children, Tracey Atkinson and Paul DeSanctis, for their support and patience during the many long days that went into the preparation of this book.

1

INTRODUCTION TO THE PROCESSING OF DATA

DATA PROCESSING CONCEPTS

Data processing is a distinctly human function. As long as people have had minds capable of rational thought, they have used them to process data. Such data may come in the form of observed natural phenomena, external physical stimuli, or audiovisual symbols. The senses are constantly gathering data in one form or another and transmitting them to the brain, where they are ingested. Sometimes the data is interpreted and carefully analyzed for the purpose of deriving needed information. Sometimes it is tucked away in the proximate memory for future recall. But most often it passes fleetingly through a person's central processing unit—i.e., the brain—and ends up in remote recesses where it is soon lost and forgotten. Forgetting is also a distinctly human function.

The scenario just described is important in that information is being generated which serves some purpose, useful or otherwise. Once this information is formed, it is usually disgorged through either an action, utterance, written message, gesture, or what have you with the intent of imparting some meaning to an idea, thought, plan, scheme, or feeling. Information so generated has been used or misused from time immemorial to do such diverse things as gather food, seek shelter, navigate the seas, wage war, establish peace, educate children, cure diseases, collect taxes, create inflation, conquer space, and lately, build neutron bombs. Our purpose here, however, is not to make any moral pronouncements on the use or misuse of information, but rather to provide some insight into the fundamental nature of data processing by presenting it in the light of distinctively human qualities.

As a data processing apparatus, the mind is highly intelligent and flexible, but slow, inefficient, and forgetful. Hence, people have throughout the centuries built machines to assist them with their tasks of processing data and generating information. In interfacing with the environment, much of the data that human beings have had to deal with has been quantitative, requiring them to perform calculations with numbers, a task that more often than not has tended to boggle their cerebral circuitry. All data processing machines invented and constructed, from the abacus to ENIAC, were essentially calculating machines for processing numerical data. It was not until the arrival of second-generation electronic computers that computing machines became more than just calculators: they became machines capable of processing alphabetic data as well. Furthermore, they became repositories for storing information. Thus, people have greatly extended their data processing ability with sophisticated electronic machinery that can "think" a lot faster and "remember" a lot longer than they can. Computers, then, are an extension of the mind, and certainly not a replacement for it.

Let us now consider data processing in the more restrictive sense of *information technology,* as it is commonly understood in today's world.

The term *data* refers to an unorganized set of facts or symbols to which meaning must be given. *Information,* on the other hand, is an organized set of facts or symbols conveying some predefined meaning. *Data processing* is the operation of converting data into information through a predetermined sequence of instructions. These definitions notwithstanding, one ought not get too hung up on the technical distinction between the terms *data* and *information,* as they are often used interchangeably. However, it is helpful to think of information as the end result of data processing.

A *data processing system* is an organized method for converting data into information. Data processing systems can be simple or complex, completely manual, partly manual and partly machine driven, or completely machine driven. Data processing systems that incorporate computers are usually referred to as electronic data processing systems and, whether manual or machine driven, employ the same fundamental principle: data are put into the system and processed, and information is put out. (See Figure 1–1.)

The data processing systems discussed in this book will be based on microcomputers. More will be said about this later; let us first finish our brief discussion of general data processing principles.

Some of the more important steps involved in data processing are summarized in the following list:

Capture refers to the gathering of data and its preparation for entry into the system. Often it is done with the aid of a specially designed form called a *source document,* which prompts collection of the essential data elements.

Input denotes the actual entry of data into the system for subsequent processing.

Classifying is the grouping of data according to certain characteristics in order to facilitate analysis.

Sorting is the arrangement of data in a given sequence for the purpose of locating and identifying essential elements.

Computation is the derivation of numerical results through the application of mathematical algorithms.

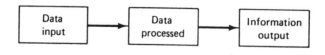

Figure 1–1
The data processing scenario

Formatting is the organization of data according to some predetermined standard for producing readable and intelligible results. It is during formatting that—in the strict sense—data becomes information.

Output refers to the extraction of information (data that has been processed) from the system and its subsequent presentation in a readable form. Output may consist of a printed report or a screen display.

The above list of processing steps is by no means exhaustive, but it is fairly representative of the ways in which data is treated in most systems, be they manual or machine driven. One data processing step that is not listed is *storage;* given its significance in data processing, it is deserving of special attention. *Data storage* refers to the recording of raw or previously processed data on some medium for future use or retrieval. The storage of information is what provides a data processing system with its capacity for recall, or memory if you prefer. Information for which there may be no immediate need is filed away for recall at a later time when it is needed. This capacity for recalling previously generated information is perhaps the most important and useful feature of any data processing system.

To take advantage of a system's capacity for recall, data is organized into structures called *files.* Some files contain information that must be readily available, and hence are stored in a manner permitting relatively quick and easy access. Other files—e.g., Company X's payroll accounts for 1979—do not contain time-critical information, and thus are usually placed in remote storage, rendering them not so easily accessible.

A file is a collection of related data records. A *record* is a body of known or hypothetical facts pertaining to a particular class of objects, e.g., students at a university, employees of Company X, passengers of a national airline, items in a department store's inventory, individual savings or checking accounts, fugitives from the law, and so many other groups of people or things about which it is necessary to have information. In today's world of exploding information, there is a file, built out of records, for just about everything.

In a similar manner, records are constructed from smaller units called fields or data items. A *field* or *data item* is a particular fact pertaining to the class of objects for which a record is being kept. Fields or data items may contain the name of a person, identification number of an inventory item, salary of an individual, blood type of a hospital patient, birth date of an employee, or any other fact, depending on the nature of the record itself.

Finally, fields are composed of characters, which are the fundamental building blocks of records. A *character,* within the context of data processing, is a numeral, 0 through 9; a letter of the alphabet, A through Z; a punctuation mark; or a mathematical symbol. Characters, or character data as they are sometimes called, are classified into three main types: numeric, alphabetic, and special characters. The standard set of characters used in data processing systems is shown in Table 1-1. Note that the blank or space is considered an alphabetic character.

Just as characters are classified by type, fields are classified according to the character data they contain. Fields that consist solely of numeric characters are called *numeric fields*,[1] fields that consist solely of alphabetic characters are called *alphabetic fields,* and fields that are a combination of numeric, alphabetic, and/or special characters are called *alphanumeric fields.* Most fields tend to be either numeric or alphabetic, and it is important to understand the differences between the two types.

Records within a file are usually identified by a specific field. For example, if we are dealing with an employee file, the field that is likely to be used to identify records is the employee identification number. The field used to identify records in a file is called the *file key* or *record key.* Files may have more than one key, in which case we say the file has a *primary* key and one or more *secondary* or *alternate* keys. In the case of our hypothetical employee file, the primary key may be the employee identification number, and the secondary key may be the social security number.

A key concept associated with file records and fields is the *record and field size.* Electronic data processing systems have definite constraints on the space available for storing files; therefore, one has to be conscious of the number of records stored in a file and the size of those records. Record size is measured in terms of the total number of characters that make up the component fields of the record. As indicated previously, fields are made up of groups of characters; hence, the size of a field is defined to be the number of positions set aside for storing character data. Thus, a social security number containing nine digits and two embedded hyphens (represented as *nnn-nn-nnnn*—the *n*'s represent the digits that make up the number) has a constant field size, or length, as it is sometimes called, of eleven. For fields that contain items that vary in length, e.g., names, the size is not so easily determined. The general rule of thumb for determining the size of a field that is to contain character strings of variable length is to allow for the string of maximum length—within reason, of course. Thus,

Table 1-1
Character types and their elements

Character type	Character elements or symbols
Numeric	Numerals 0 through 9
Alphabetic	Letters of the alphabet (A through Z) and the blank (space).
Special characters	/ & , . : - ; + = $ * ( ),etc.

[1] Depending on context, it is sometimes permissible to include decimal points and algebraic signs in numeric fields. More will be said about this in a later chapter.

since few names exceed thirty characters, it is generally safe to reserve thirty character positions for a field that is to contain a name.

The description of the fields that make up a record, together with the specification of the size of those fields, is called a *record layout* or *record format.* In a record layout it is customary to list the fields in the order they appear in the record and to assign them a sequential number, which, by the way, is not part of the field itself. Also given in the layout is the name of the field, its size, its starting position relative to the beginning of the record, and the type of data it contains.

In some ways the ideas concerning files and file construction presented above may seem intuitively obvious. When we get to the core of this book, however, you will find that these ideas are of extreme importance and should be thoroughly understood. To get a clearer picture of them, consider Figure 1–2 (p. 8), which shows the employee file of a hypothetical company, X.

The file diagram and record layout in the figure is computer oriented. The record layout is just one of many possible layouts that could be designed for this type of file. The record length in this case is 200 characters, which is a fairly good-sized record for a computer-based file. We could have economized on space by cutting the name and address fields to, say, 20 characters, by not storing the hyphens in the social security and date fields, and by doing away with expansion space. These cutbacks would save us 55 character positions, which represents a considerable savings of storage space. In computer systems, storage space is an expensive commodity that should be used as economically as possible. By reducing the record length, we can increase the number of records that can be stored in the file. Designing files and constructing record formats involves numerous trade-offs, more of which will be discussed in a later chapter.

MODERN MICROCOMPUTER SYSTEMS

In the previous section we discussed data processing systems from a general point of view. Let us now look at them within the special framework of microcomputers. Microcomputer systems have much the same basic architecture found in larger computer systems. The main differences are those of scale. Like their bigger kin, microcomputers ingest data in coded form, process them according to some set of programmed instructions, and disgorge the resulting information in some readable format. To perform these functions, the systems they are part of employ an array of physical devices built around a small but powerful silicon chip commonly known as the *microprocessor.* This compact electronic wonder is the "cerebrum" of the system. The microprocessor, combined with the internal system memory,

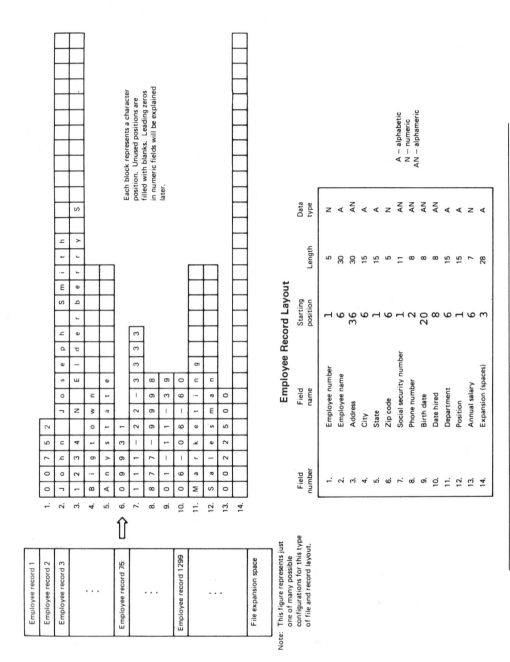

Each block represents a character position. Unused positions are filled with blanks. Leading zeros in numeric fields will be explained later.

Note: This figure represents just one of many possible configurations for this type of file and record layout.

	Employee record 1
	Employee record 2
	Employee record 3
	. . .
	Employee record 75
	. . .
	Employee record 1299
	. . .
	File expansion space

Employee Record Layout

Field number	Field name	Starting position	Length	Data type
1.	Employee number	1	5	N
2.	Employee name	6	30	A
3.	Address	36	30	AN
4.	City	6	15	A
5.	State	1	15	A
6.	Zip code	6	5	N
7.	Social security number	1	11	AN
8.	Phone number	2	8	AN
9.	Birth date	20	8	AN
10.	Date hired	8	8	AN
11.	Department	6	15	A
12.	Position	1	15	A
13.	Annual salary	6	7	N
14.	Expansion (spaces)	3	28	A

A — alphabetic
N — numeric
AN — alphameric

Figure 1-2
Record organization and format

8

makes up the *microprocessing unit.* Supporting the microprocessing unit are a number of electronic and electromechanical devices called *peripheral devices,* which serve as the means for getting data into the system and extracting information from it. Generally speaking, there are four major types of physical devices that make up a microcomputer system.

Input devices accept mechanically or electromagnetically transcribed data in coded form and convert it to electrical impulses that are decipherable to the microprocessing unit. They are the instruments through which data and programs are entered into the system. The principal input device of microcomputer systems is the typewriter keyboard with video display.

The *microprocessing unit* (MPU) is the electronic circuitry that performs all logical and computational operations and controls the flow of data throughout the system's environment. It is sometimes called the central processing unit (CPU). The MPU includes the control unit and the arithmetic and logic unit, which together make up the microprocessor. In addition, there is the all-important memory unit, where data coming into the system is temporarily held for processing.

Output devices receive electrical impulses from the microprocessing unit, convert them to coded characters, and reproduce them in readable form. In other words, they convey and communicate the processed data to the external world. The most common output devices are the video display screen and the line printer.

Mass storage devices are used to record encoded data processed by the MPU on some electromagnetic storage medium, such as a floppy disk or magnetic tape. Informational files that must be kept for present or future use are stored on these media, which are, in effect, an extension of the computer's memory. The principal mass storage devices are the disk drive and the cassette tape recorder.

Storage devices serve a dual function. In addition to storing data, they act as input and output devices since data and information are routinely transferred to and from them as part of the system's file processing operation. Because of this characteristic, storage devices are also called *input/output,* or simply *I/O,* devices. Much of the programming of computer systems involves the transfer of data and information to and from storage media.

As previously mentioned, the center of activity within a microcomputer system is the microprocessing unit. Let us take a closer look at its three principal components.

The *control unit* controls the overall functioning of the system, deciphering program instructions and firing them into action. It governs the activity of the input/output devices, causing them to come into play at the appropriate time. It is the system's "policeman," regulating the flow of computer activities.

The *arithmetic and logic unit* (ALU) contains the accumulators and registers that serve as tracking devices for keeping the system informed of the exact status of each programming step as it occurs. The registers serve as address buffers for storing the addresses of program instructions and data items in the memory unit, and the accumulator serves as a storage point for computational results.

The *memory unit* is a temporary repository for data and program instructions. All data processed by the microcomputer system passes through the memory unit. In addition, program instructions are stored there, as well as intermediate and final computational results produced in the accumulator. Technically speaking, the memory unit is the place where data becomes information. Data brought into it is stored in an input area, processed in a work area, and formatted in an output area, each of which is not a hardwired component of the memory unit. The size and location of these areas can vary depending on the program that is running at the time.

A component of the microcomputer system closely associated with the function of the MPU is the *clock,* which times and synchronizes the sequence of processing events. The interaction among the various components of the microcomputer system is depicted in Figure 1–3.

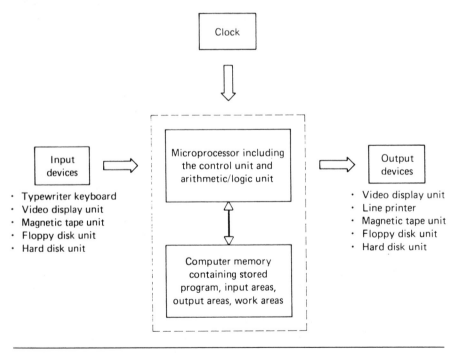

Figure 1–3
The various components of a microcomputer system in
action. The MPU is contained within the dashed lines. Notice that
the storage devices are listed under both input and output devices.

Much of the processing power and many of the capabilities of the microcomputer system depend on the size of the memory unit, i.e., the number of data characters that can be stored inside memory. Memory consists of a number of cells—often referred to as bytes—each of which is capable of storing one character of data. In microcomputers memory size is measured in K's, where one K equals 1024 bytes. Memory units are manufactured in sizes that are integer-powers-of-2 multiples of K, e.g., $2^1 \cdot K = 2K$, $2^2 \cdot K = 4K$, $2^3 \cdot K = 8K$, $2^4 \cdot K = 16K$, etc. An 8K memory unit would contain 8,192 bytes of internal storage, a 16K memory unit would contain 16,384 bytes, and so on. Microcomputers that are available today range in memory size from 4K for smaller machines designed for strictly personal use to 640K for larger machines designed for business use. Throughout this book, our discussion will be aimed at larger machines having 64K of memory and up—in particular, the IBM®[2] Personal Computer (PC).

There are basically two types of memory: *read-only* memory, abbreviated ROM, and *random-access* memory, abbreviated RAM. ROM is memory that contains fixed programs and data that can be input into the computer. It is not erasable and therefore cannot be reused for other purposes, as magnetic recording tape can. ROM is the kind of memory you find in preprogrammed devices such as video games and in computers that have a hard-coded instruction set. In the latter, ROM may often contain instructions for booting the system, a process that loads the operating system (the set of programs that make the computer usable) into the computer's RAM. RAM, on the other hand, is erasable and reusable. Its memory cells can be accessed not only for retrieving programs and data, but also for recording them. Thus, ROM permits a one-directional flow of data, whereas RAM permits a two-directional flow. In this text, we shall be concerned only with RAM.

Finally, the way data is stored in the memory unit is an important feature of microcomputers. Each byte of memory has an address by which it can be referenced, and much of the internal activity of the microprocessing unit is concerned with computing and keeping track of the program instructions and data with which the unit is currently working. The data stored in these memory bytes can be joined together to form contiguous character strings—the fields of the previous section. Each field has an address that corresponds to the address of the first byte in the string. In order to access a field inside memory, the computer must know two facts: the internal address of the first byte in the character string, and the length of the string. In like manner, records are stored as strings of the contiguous fields that make up the record. Here again, the record address is the address of the first byte of the first field of the record, and the record length or displacement is the sum of the lengths of all the fields that make up the record. The location inside memory at which a record is stored is exclusively the com-

[2] IBM is a registered trademark of International Business Machines.

puter's choice. Figure 1–4 shows how the record depicted in Figure 1–2 could be stored in the memory unit. A point to remember is that rarely, if ever, are complete files stored in memory; computers operate on just one record at a time, and there simply is not enough internal memory available for storing entire files, which are normally kept on secondary storage devices.

The internal memory unit is not designed for use as a medium for storing permanent files of any kind. One of the main reasons for this is cost. Memory panels, which comprise the circuitry of the computer's internal memory unit, are about thirty times more expensive per byte of storage than the secondary storage devices. Hence, data files are kept on secondary storage media, where they can be readily accessed and recalled. That is why we say that secondary storage devices are in effect extensions of the computer's memory.

The $5\frac{1}{4}$-in. floppy disk is the standard secondary storage medium for micros. The larger systems can employ hard disk units capable of storing many millions of bytes of data. One of the more common configurations of the IBM PC employs two $5\frac{1}{4}$-in. floppy disks, each of which is capable of storing 320K bytes (with DOS release 1.1) or 366K bytes (with DOS 2.0) of data, which are adequate for most small-business applications. It is this disk configuration around which the methodology in this text has been developed.

PROGRAMMING LANGUAGES

The term *program,* as it relates to computers, is pretty much a part of everyone's vocabulary. Whenever people talk about computers they are almost sure to interject the word *program* at some point in their discussion, even though they may not fully understand what a program is. But everyone does seem to understand that computers and programs are tied together in some more or less obscure way. Programs, they know, somehow make computers work. But what, precisely, is a program, as it relates to computers?

A *program* is a set of specific instructions that tell the computer what to do. It is a means of directing the computer's activity toward the accomplishment of a specified data processing task. A computer program can be simple or complex, depending on the nature of the task to be accomplished. If the task is simple, the program is usually simple; if the task is complex, the program is likely to be complex. When you put together a set of instructions for a computer, you are said to write or code a program.

Instructions, whether directed to person or machine, must be communicated via a mutually understood language. Just as there are standard but

Memory bytes

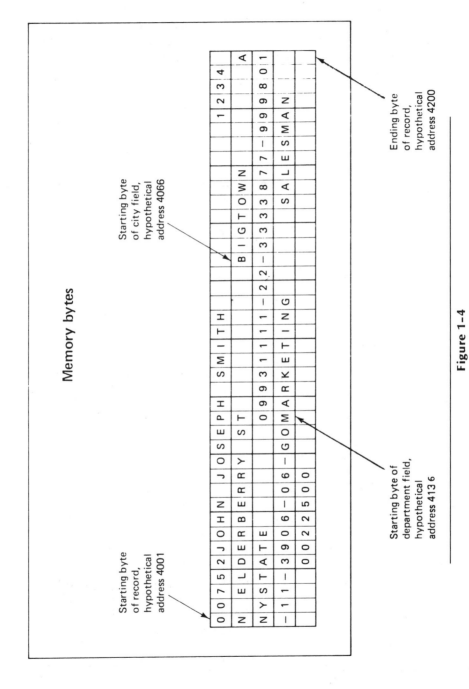

Figure 1-4

Employee Record 752 as it appears inside a computer's memory

13

varied languages for effecting people-to-people communications, there are standard but varied languages for effecting people-to-computer communications. These languages are called *computer languages* or *programming languages,* and like spoken languages, they possess a peculiar syntax and grammar. The syntax and grammar of computer languages are, however, far simpler than the syntax and grammar of spoken languages.

There are three species of computer language: machine language, assembler language, and high-level or procedure-oriented language. *Machine language* is the native tongue of a particular computer and is the only language the computer understands. Machine language, which employs a strictly numeric code structure, varies from one manufacturer to another and is said, therefore, to be machine dependent. Programs in machine language are very difficult to code, which is why they are rarely attempted.

Assembler language is one step above machine language. It employs a symbolic code structure that makes use of mnemonic instructions in place of numeric instructions. These mnemonic instructions are easier to remember than their numeric counterparts, making the task of coding an assembler-language program somewhat simpler. Assembler language is also machine dependent, but it is often used to code programs because it is highly efficient in terms of execution speed. (Execution speed is the speed at which the program can accomplish its task within the computer.) Assembler language must be converted to object code (another name for machine-language code) before the computer can act upon it. This conversion is done by a special manufacturer-supplied program called a *translator* or *assembler.*

High-level or *procedure-oriented languages* are one step above assembler language. They employ an instruction set in which several assembler-language commands are built into a single command called a macro instruction. High-level languages are easier to code than assembler language, allowing the programmer to concentrate more on the data processing problems he is attempting to solve and less on the intricacies of the language syntax. In addition, they are machine independent, meaning that a program coded in a high-level language can, with slight modifications, be run on computers of different makes. They are, however, less efficient than assembler language, and they, too, must be converted to object code before the computer can act on them. The conversion is done by a program called a *compiler.* Some of the more common high-level languages are BASIC (Beginner's All-Purpose Instruction Code), FORTRAN (Formula Translator), PASCAL, and of course, COBOL (Common Business Oriented Language), the subject of this book.

Until recently, BASIC was the only high-level language used for programming microcomputers. Easy to learn and requiring only a moderate amount of memory (4K is usually adequate), it readily lends itself to the needs of the personal computer hobbyist and student. However, it is limited in its ability to process large data files.[3] Thus, for the larger microcomputer systems that are capable of handling more sophisticated applications, other languages such as FORTRAN, PASCAL, and COBOL may be used. Since these languages have greater processing capabilities, they require considerably more memory (64K of memory for the IBM PC).

Just as spoken languages have dialects, so do the high-level programming languages. That is, variations exist among them that preclude their being used interchangeably in computers of different makes. For example, a BASIC program written for an Apple microcomputer will not work on an IBM PC because each manufacturer uses a different dialect. This is not to say that the program written for the Apple cannot be adapted to the IBM PC; it can, but only after it has been extensively modified to incorporate the syntax of the version of BASIC that is specific to the IBM PC. The ease with which a programming language can be adapted to different computers is sometimes referred to as program portability. The versions of BASIC, FORTRAN, and PASCAL that are used in microcomputers are not highly transferable, and this deficiency, together with other limitations, makes them less than desirable language choices for programming business applications.

Of all the high-level languages, ANS–COBOL (American National Standard COBOL) is the one most often used for business applications. Its design has been chiefly in that direction, and it employs a standardized instruction set. Because of this high degree of standardization, COBOL programs (from now on COBOL will mean ANS–COBOL) are the most transferable of all programs. Nearly every major manufacturer of large-scale computers and minicomputers offers a COBOL compiler, and it is not uncommon to see a COBOL program, originally written for one make of computer, run successfully on a machine of some other manufacturer. This kind of transferability, in addition to its file-handling versatility, has made COBOL the leading computer language in the world of professional data processing. As microcomputer systems steadily infiltrate that world, users of these systems will find themselves leaning heavily toward COBOL. Happily, just as COBOL is itself transferable, so are the COBOL programming skills. Thus, once you have learned to use COBOL proficiently, you have acquired a highly useful skill that can be applied in almost any commercial data processing environment.

---

[3] Most microcomputer manufacturers' versions of BASIC that have extended file processing capabilities tend to be nonstandard and are usually also highly machine dependent.

REVIEW QUESTIONS

1. Explain the distinction between data and information. Is the distinction sufficiently important to justify its being made?

2. What is meant by a data processing system? Give some examples of data processing systems that do not involve computers.

3. Identify the principal steps of data processing.

4. Explain the role of data storage in a data processing system. How does a computer augment that role?

5. Define the terms file, record, field, and character. How are these constructs related to one another?

6. When designing a file for a computer system, why should we be concerned about the size of the records and fields?

7. Construct a record layout for a business contact file that contains the following fields:

   Name of contact person
   Company name
   Mailing address
   Telephone number
   Type of business
   Major product lines (10 maximum)

8. Identify and describe the major types of physical devices that make up a microcomputer system.

9. What are the principal functions of storage devices in a computer system? Do these storage devices have analogs in a manual data processing system? If so, name some.

10. Describe the MPU. John Von Neumann, the great mathematician most responsible for developing the theory underpinning electronic computers, tried to establish a parallel relationship between a computer processor and the human brain. Do you think such a relationship exists? If so, why? If not, why not?

11. What is meant by the acronym *ROM*? What is meant by *RAM*? How are these two concepts different?

12. What is a byte? How are bytes accessed and referenced within the computer's memory unit?

13. Define the term *program*. What is a programming or computer

language? Identify and describe the three species of computer languages. How are they similar? How are they different?

14. What are the main advantages of COBOL as a programming language?

15. Define program transferability. Why is COBOL considered one of the most transferable of all computer languages?

2

INTRODUCTION TO COBOL

Programming languages are classically presented to the new student in two ways. The first and most common is to flood the student with an over-abundance of seemingly unrelated details regarding syntax and grammar, leaving it to his wit and wiles to put those details together like so many scattered pieces of a picture puzzle. This approach usually delays the learning process, and it is some time before the student develops a sense of how those details relate to the whole. The second technique is to present a very general overview of the language, followed by a carefully explained example of a simple but complete source program. This approach almost always starts the student off with a definite feel for the language, so that he is better able to piece together the details that are presented later. In other words, the student can begin putting together his picture puzzle with the major pieces already in place. In this text, we have adopted the second approach of presenting COBOL. By the time you finish this chapter, you should have enough feel for COBOL to start fitting in place its many details with some dexterity and confidence.

COBOL: AN OVERVIEW

Of all high-level programming languages in use today, COBOL is perhaps the most structured and tightly organized. It possesses a well-defined syntax and a standard vocabulary consisting of over 250 words, called *reserved words*. These words, which form the symbolic basis of the language code set, or source code, are ordinary English words such as ASSIGN, PICTURE, IF, READ, ADD, COMPUTE, WRITE, STOP, and so many more; a complete list of reserved words is presented in Appendix A.

Each reserved word performs a specific function within the program. For example, READ will cause input data to be transmitted from an input device into RAM memory, and WRITE will cause data to be transferred from the MPU to some specified output device. In addition to the reserved words, the vocabulary of COBOL can include any number of English-language words constructed by the programmer to name files, records, fields, and other program internals, such as processing routines and other paragraphs. These programmer-supplied names can, within certain limits to be specified later, be formed to suit the need or whim of the programmer.

In addition to its vocabulary, the COBOL instruction set includes standard symbols to indicate arithmetic operations and relationships. For example, the plus sign (+) indicates addition, the minus sign (−) subtraction, the slash (/) division, and the asterisk (*) multiplication. Some other special symbols that are used are the less than sign (<), the greater than sign (>), and of course, the equals sign (=). (See Table 1 – 1 for a listing of the COBOL character set.)

As with ordinary English, use of the vocabulary and special symbols in COBOL is governed by grammar. Words are built into clauses and sentences, which in turn are arranged into paragraphs. Punctuation is also used: clauses are separated by a comma, and sentences are terminated with a period. Writing program instructions in COBOL is not at all unlike writing instructions in English. As you might suspect by now, the syntax and grammar of COBOL have been inspired by the syntax and grammar of our mother tongue.

When a COBOL program is being written, the lines of source code are usually recorded on a coding form, which is specially designed to facilitate the coding process. Shown in Figure 2–1, this form is divided into 80 vertical columns and 24 lines for entering source code. The columns contain areas for indicating where various types of source-code instructions begin. Some source instructions, for example, begin in Area A (columns 8 through 11), while others begin in Area B (columns 12 through 71). More will be said about this in subsequent chapters, but for now, it is enough to recognize that a distinction exists.

After the source-code lines have been recorded on the coding form, they are entered into the computer via the keyboard. The way they are formatted on the coding form is the way they are entered into the system and stored in the source-program file. That is, each line of program code is actually a single 80-character record entry in the file that is used to store the source program. Note that it is not necessary to record the source program on a coding form. It is important, however, that each line of source code entered into the system conform with the margin and column requirements indicated on the coding fom. The contents of the various columns are as follows.

Columns 1–6 are used for recording a sequence number. Each line of code has a number that identifies the line.

Column 7 is the continuation column. A hyphen placed in this column indicates the continuation of a literal from the previous line. (A literal is a message text consisting of alphanumeric characters.) An asterisk in column 7 of a given line of code indicates that the line is to be treated as a comment. That is, the line will appear on the source listing of the program, but will be ignored by the compiler. Comment lines are normally used to document or to explain what the program does. They serve the function of footnotes within the program.

Columns 8–11 form Area A, where all COBOL division, section, and paragraph names must begin. (See below for a discussion of these.)

Columns 12–72 form Area B, which contains data clauses and actual program instructions. No Area B entry can go beyond column 72.

Columns 73–80 are used for storing a program identifier supplied by the programmer. These columns may be left blank.

Figure 2–2 (p. 24) shows a simple but complete COBOL source pro-

COBOL CODING FORM

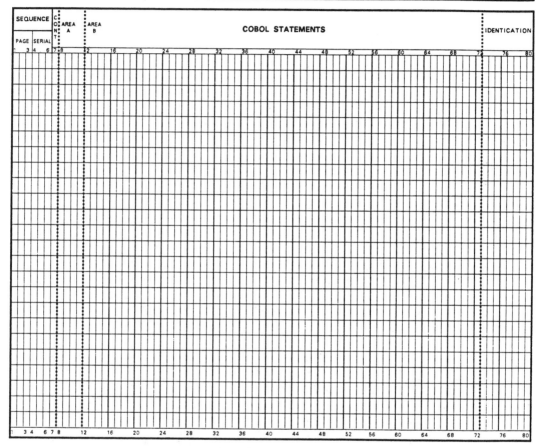

Figure 2-1
COBOL coding form

gram as it might appear on a coding form. Ignoring for now what the program is designed to do, notice that columns 1–6 have been left blank; there is no need to enter sequence numbers in them because the compiler will generate those numbers for us. An asterisk is coded in column 7, introducing spacing between lines of code to facilitate reading the program. Area A

IBM **COBOL Coding Form**

GX28-1464-6 U/M 050*
Printed in U.S.A.

SYSTEM		PUNCHING INSTRUCTIONS	PAGE 1 OF 2
PROGRAM		GRAPHIC	CARD FORM # †
PROGRAMMER	DATE	PUNCH	

```
SEQUENCE   A    B                          COBOL STATEMENT                 IDENTIFICATION
(PAGE)(SERIAL)
       01   IDENTIFICATION DIVISION.
       02   PROGRAM-ID. LISTTEN.
       03  *
       04   ENVIRONMENT DIVISION.
       05   INPUT-OUTPUT SECTION.
       06   FILE-CONTROL.
       07       SELECT LIST-FILE ASSIGN TO PRINTER.
       08  *
       09   DATA DIVISION.
       10   FILE SECTION.
       11   FD  LIST-FILE
       12       LABEL RECORD ARE OMITTED.
       13   01  LIST-LINE                PIC X(132).
       14  *
       15   PROCEDURE DIVISION.
       16  *
       17   MAIN-PROCESSING-ROUTINE.
       18       PERFORM OPEN-FILES.
       19       PERFORM READ-AND-LIST 10 TIMES.
       20       PERFORM CLOSE-FILES.
```

† A standard card form, IBM Electro C61897, is available for punching source statements from this form. Instructions for using this form are given in any IBM COBOL reference manual. Address comments concerning this form to IBM Corporation, P.O. Box 50020, Programming Publishing, San Jose, CA 95150.

*No. of forms per pad may vary slightly

Figure 2-2
COBOL source program on coding form

IBM

GX28-1464-6 U/M 050*
Printed in U.S.A.

SYSTEM			PUNCHING INSTRUCTIONS		PAGE 2 OF 2
PROGRAM			GRAPHIC		CARD FORM #
PROGRAMMER		DATE	PUNCH		

SEQUENCE (PAGE) (SERIAL)	CONT	A	B	COBOL STATEMENT
01			STOP RUN,	
02	*			
03		OPEN-FILES.		
04			OPEN OUTPUT LIST-FILE.	
05	*			
06		READ-AND-LIST.		
07			ACCEPT LIST-LINE.	
08			WRITE LIST-LINE.	
09	*			
10		CLOSE-FILES.		
11			CLOSE LIST-FILE.	
12				
13				
14				
15				
16				
17				
18				
19				
20				

IDENTIFICATION

† A standard card form, IBM Electro C61897, is available for punching source statements from this form. Instructions for using this form are given in any IBM COBOL reference manual. Address comments concerning this form to IBM Corporation, P.O. Box 50020, Programming Publishing, San Jose, CA 95150.

*No. of forms per pad may vary slightly.

Figure 2-2, cont'd

contains the names of the program divisions, sections, and paragraphs mentioned above. All lines starting in column 12 are actual program instructions. Columns 73–80 have been left blank since a program identifier is superfluous here. Finally, notice the periods—most of which are necessary—at the end of nearly every line of code. In COBOL, a period is considered a terminator, which means that the particular clause or sentence immediately preceding it has ended. If the periods are left out, an error condition could result.

THE STRUCTURE OF COBOL

As is evident in Figure 2–2, the word DIVISION appears with some regularity among the Area A entries. The reason for this is that every COBOL program consists of four main divisions, as follows:

```
IDENTIFICATION DIVISION
ENVIRONMENT DIVISION
DATA DIVISION
PROCEDURE DIVISION
```

The divisions, each of which has a predefined function described below, must occur in the program in the order shown.

The IDENTIFICATION DIVISION names the program. In addition, it may contain certain other identifying information about the program, such as the date it was written, the author's name, and remarks concerning what the program does. It is the least complex division in terms of function and coding requirements.

The ENVIRONMENT DIVISION has several functions, the most important of which are to specify the data files used for input and output operations and to associate each file with a particular physical device. This division consists of two main sections: the CONFIGURATION SECTION, which is optional, and the INPUT–OUTPUT SECTION, which is required when there are data files. The CONFIGURATION SECTION is used both to identify the make and model of the computer on which the program is compiled and executed and to specify certain processing features to be employed in the program. The INPUT–OUTPUT section is used to perform the data file specification function.

The DATA DIVISION defines the characteristics of both the data files and records to be processed by the program and all data elements or fields that will in any way be referenced or manipulated within the program. This division consists of four main sections, of which the three most important are the FILE SECTION, the WORKING–STORAGE SECTION, and the SCREEN SECTION. The FILE SECTION defines each data file, together with its associated record format. It is required whenever there are data files to process. The WORKING-STORAGE SECTION is used to specify and define storage areas for special-purpose data elements and intermediate computational results. It is, if you will, the programmer's "scratch pad." While not always required, it is difficult to envision a COBOL program of any substance without a WORKING-STORAGE SECTION. The SCREEN SECTION is used to define the format of the CRT screen when the screen is to function as an input or output video display form. It is required only when the CRT screen is used in this manner. Depending on the application, the DATA DIVISION can be tedious and time consuming to code. Understanding its many intricacies is crucial to the mastery of COBOL programming.

The PROCEDURE DIVISION contains the instructions that do the actual processing of the data. In this division, the data is brought into memory, manipulated and prepared for output, and then transferred to an output or storage device. The instructions are usually grouped into paragraphs, each of which performs a particular input, processing, or output function. The PROCEDURE DIVISION is the most flexible and complex part of the COBOL program, and most of what is covered in this book will have to do with this division.

A SAMPLE PROGRAM

Suppose that the COBOL program coded on the form in Figure 2-2 has been entered into the computer and listed on the line printer. The resulting listing is shown in Figure 2-3 (p. 28). Let's examine the program and try to develop some understanding of it. We shall describe the overall function of the program and then examine its format and contents line by line.

The function of the program is to list ten lines of a message entered through the keyboard on the line printer. As each line of the message is entered, it is transferred directly to the printer and listed. The processing steps are quite simple. First, the list file is opened—that is, the line printer is made ready for action. Next, a line of the message text is received through the keyboard and listed on the line printer. This sequence occurs ten times in succession. Then the list file is closed—in other words, the printer is disengaged and released from its programmed assignment. Finally, the computer is informed that the program is done and execution is terminated.

Several things about the format of the program listing are noteworthy:

1. The numbers in the leftmost column are sequential line numbers generated by the computer. They were not entered as part of the program code.

2. The numbers occupying columns 1 through 5 are optional sequen-

```
 1   00001    IDENTIFICATION DIVISION.
 2   00002    PROGRAM-ID. LISTTEN.
 3   00003  *
 4   00004    ENVIRONMENT DIVISION.
 5   00005    INPUT-OUTPUT SECTION.
 6   00006    FILE-CONTROL.
 7   00007        SELECT LIST-FILE ASSIGN TO PRINTER.
 8   00008  *
 9   00009    DATA DIVISION.
10   00010    FILE SECTION.
11   00011    FD  LIST-FILE
12   00012        LABEL RECORD IS OMITTED.
13   00013    01  LIST-LINE                PIC X(132).
14   00014  *
15   00015    PROCEDURE DIVISION.
16   00016  *
17   00017    MAIN-PROCESSING-ROUTINE.
18   00018        PERFORM OPEN-FILES.
19   00019        PERFORM READ-AND-LIST 10 TIMES.
20   00020        PERFORM CLOSE-FILES.
21   00021        STOP RUN.
22   00022  *
23   00023    OPEN-FILES.
24   00024        OPEN OUTPUT LIST-FILE.
25   00025  *
26   00026    READ-AND-LIST.
27   00027        DISPLAY "ENTER YOUR LINE"
28   00028        ACCEPT LIST-LINE.
29   00029        WRITE LIST-LINE.
30   00030  *
31   00031    CLOSE-FILES.
32   00032        CLOSE LIST-FILE.
```

Figure 2-3
COBOL program listing

tial line numbers assigned and entered by the programmer. They could have been omitted without producing any ill effects.

3. An asterisk is inserted in column 7 to allow for spacing between the lines of code. Such spacing is optional and could be omitted; its function is strictly cosmetic.

4. Area A entries begin in column 8. Generally, all division, section, and paragraph names, together with certain data definitions, must start in Area A. In this text, all Area A items will be specified as they are introduced.

5. Area B entries begin in column 12. Generally, all instructions and most data items must start in column 12 or beyond (but not past column 72). Again, in this text, Area B items will be specified when they are introduced.

6. The shaded words in the sample are programmer-supplied names. The unshaded words are reserved words, which have a predefined program function. Some of the reserved words appearing in the listing as TO and IS on lines 7 and 12, respectively, are optional and could be omitted. Their function is to promote readability of the code. Nonrequired reserved words will be indicated as such as they are introduced.

7. Almost every line of code is terminated with a period; there is no period, however, at the end of line 15. For some entries a period is

mandatory, for some it is optional, and for some it is precluded. The rules governing the use of the period will be explained below.

The program has exactly 25 lines of code, not counting blank lines. We shall now list each line and explain its function. For simplicity's sake, the sequence number is omitted.

IDENTIFICATION DIVISION.

indicates the start of the program and the beginning of the IDENTIFICATION DIVISION.

PROGRAM-ID. LISTTEN.

names the program LISTTEN and identifies it by that name to the operating system.

ENVIRONMENT DIVISION.

signals the start of the ENVIRONMENT DIVISION.

INPUT-OUTPUT SECTION.

indicates the start of the INPUT–OUTPUT SECTION.

FILE-CONTROL.

signals the beginning of the paragraph in which all the files used by the program are identified and assigned to I/O devices.

SELECT LIST-FILE ASSIGN TO PRINTER.

instructs the operating system to assign the output file (LIST–FILE) to the line printer.

DATA DIVISION.

indicates the beginning of the section in which all the files named in the FILE–CONTROL paragraph are defined and described to the system.

FILE SECTION.

marks beginning of the file definitions.

FD LIST-FILE

is the first line of the definition of the file named in the SELECT statement above. A period is not permitted here since the definition of the file is continued on the next line.

LABEL RECORD IS OMITTED.

instructs the system not to look for an identifying label in the file being defined. As we shall see later, there is no need for the line printer to have an identifying file label.

01   LIST-LINE   PICTURE X(132).

describes what each record of the file named LIST-FILE looks like. The record itself has been named LIST-LINE. The clause PICTURE X(132) tells the system that the record will be up to 132 characters in length and will contain character (alphanumeric) data. The 01 at the beginning of the line indicates that we are dealing with a record-level data item.

PROCEDURE DIVISION.

marks the beginning of the PROCEDURE DIVISION, the fourth and final program division.

MAIN-PROCESSING-ROUTINE.

is a programmer-supplied paragraph name. The three sentences that follow it cause the actual processing to occur. The fourth sentence causes the program to terminate. In general, all the AREA B entries, or sentences, that follow a particular paragraph header belong to that paragraph.

PERFORM OPEN-FILES.

is a COBOL command that causes the instructions contained under the paragraph OPEN-FILES to be executed. (All paragraph names are programmer supplied.) In general, the PERFORM command causes all instructions under the paragraph named to be executed, after which program control returns and passes to the next sentence after the PERFORM command. PERFORM is perhaps one of the most powerful and useful COBOL procedural commands.

PERFORM READ-AND-LIST 10 TIMES.

causes all the instructions under the paragraph READ-AND-LIST to be executed ten times in succession. The main program processing takes place in paragraph READ-AND-LIST.

PERFORM CLOSE-FILES.

causes the instructions under the paragraph name CLOSE-FILES to be executed.

STOP RUN.

tells the system that all program processing has been completed and the job is finished. Control is passed back to the operating system.

OPEN-FILES.

signals the start of paragraph OPEN-FILES. (See PERFORM OPEN-FILES., above.)

OPEN OUTPUT LIST-FILE.

enables the system to open the line printer (LIST-FILE) as an output device. To *open* a file means to render it accessible on the device to which it has been assigned. All files must be opened before they can be accessed.

READ-AND-LIST.

signals the start of paragraph READ-AND-LIST. (See PERFORM READ-AND-LIST 10 TIMES., above.)

DISPLAY "ENTER YOUR LINE NOW"

causes messages to be displayed on the video display screen.

ACCEPT LIST-LINE.

enables the user to enter a line of message text through the keyboard, and then, when the return key is struck, transfer the message text to the MPU and place it in memory in the output area named LIST-LINE, which was defined in the FD paragraph of the FILE SECTION.

WRITE LIST-LINE.

causes the contents of the area LIST-LINE (which was initialized with a message text value by the ACCEPT command) to be transferred to and listed on the output file device, here the line printer.

CLOSE-FILES.

signals the start of the paragraph CLOSE-FILES. (See PERFORM CLOSE-FILES., above.)

CLOSE LIST-FILE.

the last line of the program, causes the print file called LIST-FILE to close. To *close* a file means to release a file held captive by a particular program for use by some other program. Any file opened by a program mut be closed before that program is terminated.

Bear in mind that in the above coding the main sequence of processing was specified in the paragraph MAIN–PROCESSING–ROUTINE. First, the principal file was opened. Next, the message text was entered and listed on the print device. Finally, the principal file was closed. This sequence of events—opening files, processing files, and closing files, is what happens in the vast majority of computer programs.

MORE ON THE RULES OF CODING

Earlier, we presented the rules for coding COBOL programs on the coding form. Just enough information was given about them to assist you through the sample program. Let us now return to these rules and discuss them in more detail.

1. Columns 1–6 are used for a six-digit, programmer-supplied sequence number, such that the lines of code are in ascending order. These columns may be left blank.

2. Column 7 is used primarily to indicate comments or a continuation of the previous line of program code. Its special-purpose functions are explained more fully in items 6, 7, and 8.

3. Columns 8–11 are reserved for Area A entries. All division, section, and paragraph names must begin in one of these columns. In addition, level numbers (elements of the DATA DIVISION to be defined in Chapter 4) may appear in Area A. The level numbers 01 and 77 and the file descriptor indicator FD must begin in Area A.

4. Columns 12–72 are used for Area B entries, which include all elements of program code not mentioned in item 3, such as level numbers other than 01 and 77, file characteristics, and procedural instructions.

5. Columns 73–80 are reserved for free-text entries. Most often, these columns are used for recording program identification. They may be left blank.

6. Explanatory comments of any kind may be inserted on any line of the source program by placing an asterisk (*) in column 7. In the program example, an asterisk was used to effect spacing between lines of program code. These comment lines, however, can contain any free text, and they are often used to record explanations concerning a certain line or section of code. Comment lines are ignored by the compiler.

7. Any line of program source code may be continued on the following line. A nonnumeric literal (a quoted message that is not identified by any data name) is continued by placing a hyphen (-) in column 7. The literal must be carried to column 72 before continuing to the next line. Furthermore, it must pick up in column 12 of the continued line with a single quotation mark. Any other line of COBOL code may be continued onto the next line from any point in Area B of the previous line to any point in Area B of the continued line. Intervening spaces are ignored, and Area A is left blank on the continued line.

8. A slash (/) in column 7 is treated as a comment line, except that it will cause the form to advance to the top of the next page.

The rules of coding must be carefully followed. Any violation will be treated as an error by the compiler.

RULES OF PUNCTUATION

As indicated previously, punctuation plays an important part in COBOL syntax. Particularly important is the period, although the set of punctuation marks used in COBOL includes the comma, semicolon, and others. The following is a complete list of punctuation symbols:

Symbol	Meaning
	space
,	comma
;	semicolon
.	period
(	left parenthesis
)	right parenthesis
''	quotation mark

The following general rules of punctuation are used in writing a COBOL source program:

1. Any punctuation mark indicated in this text as being a part of a COBOL format is required. For example, the period is a part of the division name format (cf. IDENTIFICATION DIVISION.).

2. Periods, commas, and semicolons must not be preceded by a space. They must, however, be followed by at least one space.

3. At least one space must be placed between two successive words, parenthetical expressions, and literals. Two or more spaces in a

row are treated as a single space, except within a nonnumeric literal enclosed in quotation marks.

4. A left parenthesis may not be followed by a space, and a right parenthesis may not be preceded by a space. Thus, (base-salary + overtime   ) is incorrect, whereas (base-salary + overtime) is correct.

5. An arithmetic operator and an equals sign must always have at least one space preceding it and at least one space following it.

6. A comma may be used to separate successive operands in a statement, as, for example, in

MOVE ZERO TO AMOUNT-1, AMOUNT-2, AMOUNT-3.

(An *operand* is a data name whose contents are the object of some COBOL command.)

7. A comma or semicolon may be used to separate a series of clauses or statements, as, for example, in

LABEL RECORDS ARE OMITTED, DATA RECORD IS PRINT-REC.
ADD SALES TO GROSS; SUBTRACT EXPENSES FROM GROSS.

The rules of punctuation may not be altogether clear to you now. Practice in COBOL coding is recommended so that you can fully understand them. As with the rules of coding, the rules of punctuation must be followed or errors will occur when the source program is compiled.

FORMATION OF WORDS

All words in COBOL are of two types: reserved words and programmer-supplied names. Reserved words belong to the standard COBOL vocabulary and have a predefined invariant format. Programmer-supplied names are, of course, constructed by the programmer. COBOL words are composed of a combination of not more than 30 contiguous characters from the following set:

0 through 9   (digits)
A through Z   (letters)
            (hyphen)

In constructing programmer-supplied words, the following rules apply:

1. All words must contain at least one letter, except procedure paragraph names, which may consist entirely of digits.

2. A word must not begin or end with a hyphen. It may, however, contain one or more embedded hyphens.

Programmer-supplied names may be used to name files, records, data fields, procedure paragraph names, and various conditions to be explained in a later chapter. Here again, the rules of word formation will become clearer with practice. Any variation from them will cause a compilation error.

FORMAT NOTATION

In presenting the many syntactical elements of COBOL, a formal system of notation is used. This system comprises the general formats of all the various clauses and statements supported by COBOL. The standard notation provides the most effective means of communicating the many intricate details of this most elegant of programming languages. Study carefully the following rules governing its use.

1. All words that are printed entirely in capital letters are reserved words, which belong to the standard vocabulary of COBOL.
2. All underlined reserved words, called *keywords,* are required unless the format containing them is optional. If any keyword is missing or misspelled, the compiler will consider it to be in error. Reserved words that are not underlined, called *optional* words, may be included or omitted at the discretion of the programmer. Optional words are used solely for improving readability of the program.
3. The symbols $<$, $>$, and $+$ are required when present in statement formats, even though they are not underlined.
4. Where shown, punctuation marks and other special characters are required. Additional punctuation can be inserted at the programmer's option, as long as the rules for punctuation are followed.
5. Lowercase letters that occur in formats represent generic terms such as data names, condition names, descriptions, etc., for which a valid programmer-supplied word or entry must be inserted.
6. Any part of a statement or entry enclosed in square brackets ([,]) is optional. Those parts between matching braces ({,}) represent a choice of mutually exclusive options.

To illustrate the format notation just described, and to reinforce the concept of program structure introduced earlier, a skeletal model of a

```
IDENTIFICATION DIVISION.
PROGRAM-ID. program-name.
[AUTHOR. comment entry. . .]
[DATE-WRITTEN. comment entry. . .]
[DATE-COMPILED. comment entry. . .]
[SECURITY. comment entry. . .]
ENVIRONMENT DIVISION.
[CONFIGURATION SECTION.
[SOURCE-COMPUTER. entry]
[OBJECT-COMPUTER. entry]
[SPECIAL-NAMES. entry]]
[INPUT-OUTPUT SECTION.
FILE-CONTROL. entry. . .
[I-O-CONTROL. entry. . .]]
DATA DIVISION.
[FILE SECTION
        file description entry. . .
        record description entry. . .
[WORKING-STORAGE SECTION.
        data-item description entry. . .]
[LINKAGE SECTION.
        data-item description entry. . .]
[SCREEN SECTION.
        screen description entry. .
[PROCEDURE DIVISION [USING identifier-¹. . .].
[DECLARATIVES.
[section-name SECTION. USE sentence.
[paragraph-name. [sentence . . . ] . . . ] . . . ]
END DECLARATIVES.
[[section name SECTION. [segment number]]
```

Figure 2-4
COBOL program skeleton

COBOL program is presented in Figure 2-4. The model will be fleshed out in the remaining chapters of this book.

RUNNING A COBOL PROGRAM ON AN IBM PC

In this section we apply some of the elements of COBOL so far presented to a practical situation: coding, entering, compiling, and executing a program on an IBM PC. The hardware configuration for the IBM PC used throughout this book is as follows:

1. Monochrome monitor
2. 64K of RAM memory
3. Two 320K disk drives
4. IBM Personal Computer Graphics Printer

The software configuration is

1. DOS 1.1 Operating System
2. COBOL Compiler (Updated Version) by Microsoft.

As mentioned in the preface, the text is based on two different COBOL compilers. All of the COBOL syntax is common to both compilers, but the compilation process is slightly different between the two. Any relevant differences we run across will be noted below.

Getting Your COBOL Compiler Package Ready to Use

Upon opening your COBOL package, you will find that the updated version contains two diskettes and an update package to the manual. The most significant addition to the manual is Appendix K, which discusses the rebuilding of an indexed file. If your manual does not contain Appendix K, take it back to the place of purchase for an exchange, update, or refund. If you have the original release of the package, inquire with your dealer as to how you may receive the update.

One of the first things any purchased software package will tell you to do is to back up or copy their software onto another diskette. This is an excellent habit to acquire because you never know when someone will destroy a diskette.

The COBOL package comes with two diskettes called COBOL and LIBRARY, respectively. COBOL contains the main program required to compile a COBOL program. Its files are:

```
COBOL
COBOL1.OVR
COBOL2.OVR
COBOL3.OVR
COBOL4.OVR
REBUILD.EXE
RUNED.BAT
RUNEC.BAT
```

The compilation process for COBOL requires that two passes be made on your source code. Pass one determines whether you have met the rules of syntax for COBOL; if you have, pass two then creates an object file (machine-executable code), establishes file-control blocks for your program, and checks for certain errors.

The LIBRARY diskette contains the files

```
COBOL1.LIB
COBOL2.LIB
COBRUN.EXE
LINK.EXE
```

LIBRARY is used to perform the final step in your compilation process before running your program: LINKing the program. The LINKer program will perform the following steps to enable your program to run properly:

1. Combine separately produced object modules.
2. Search all library files for definitions of unresolved external references.
3. Resolve external cross-references.
4. Produce a printable listing called a link map that shows all resolved external references together with error messages.
5. Produce a relocatable load module.

Each overlay and link step will be explained as it is performed, so that you will not be prevented from running your first COBOL program.

Before starting, it is recommended that you copy your COBOL and LIBRARY diskettes on blank diskettes as described in the manual. You might copy both diskettes onto one blank diskette and call it COBOL AND LIBRARY. After copying all files on both diskettes using the DOS COPY command as described in your DOS manual, you must also copy the DOS file called COMMAND.COM from your DOS diskette. If you forget to do so, you will receive a message to insert your DOS diskette in drive A. You might place all COBOL and LIBRARY files and the COMMAND.COM file on one diskette, which would reduce the amount of diskette handling. If you are not comfortable with one diskette, however, feel free to use two. In either situation, please do not forget to attach the write-protect tabs to the diskettes onto which you copied COBOL and LIBRARY.

Entering Your COBOL Program

It is recommended that, before entering your COBOL source code into a file, you begin with a blank diskette. Use a "work" diskette for program development, and once the program is complete, copy the source files onto an archive diskette. The object-code file should be copied to whichever diskette you determine is necessary to run your program. Always remember to protect or save your source code.

In order to compile a COBOL program, you must produce a source file containing the statements that are necessary to accomplish the required data processing step. To simplify this procedure, we shall input the sample program shown in Chapter 2, by using the program EDLIN from your DOS diskette. We shall not review each of the EDLIN commands here because the manual does a splendid job of explaining them. You can begin the session by booting your system with DOS and entering the current date and time. (Refer to your DOS manual for starting your system.)

After booting, load the EDLIN program into your system by typing EDLIN filename.filespec. (Filename is the name of your source-program file; filespec is the specification name you must call the file.) For illustrative purposes, we shall use the filename LISTTEN for our program, and the filespec .COB, although this filespec is not a requirement of the COBOL package. It is suggested that you call your files exactly what they are to eliminate the guesswork later in searching for a particular file. Now type

    EDLIN LISTTEN.COB

and hit the return key. EDLIN will respond with the *__, which is the prompt character. Next, type I, which enables you to insert lines in your file. Then enter the statements for the LISTTEN program in Chapter 2. Be sure to follow the rules for COBOL statements and variable names when you input your source-program statements. At the end of your EDLIN session, use CNTL–BREAK to get out of the insertion mode, and E to actually end the EDLIN session. Your COBOL source statements are now ready for compilation.

Compiling Your Program

Basically, a *compilation* is a translation or conversion of the human-understandable statements that comprise COBOL source code into machine-understandable statements. With the current version of COBOL, compilation is a two-pass procedure. To begin, do the following:

1. Change your system default drive from drive A to drive B by typing B: and hit the *enter* key.
2. Insert the diskette containing COBOL in drive A. Insert the diskette with your COBOL source statements in drive B.
3. Type A:COBOL and press *enter* to compile your program. (A: is the drive identifier; COBOL is the compiler program you wish to run.)

Once the COBOL compiler begins to execute, the prompt

    SOURCE filename [.COB]:__

is displayed. Respond with the program name you entered in the EDLIN edit session, viz.,

    LISTTEN

Your display will now say

    SOURCE filename [.COB]:LISTTEN

The COBOL compiler will now inquire whether the object-file name displayed is appropriate for the program you are compiling. The compiler will use the filename you supplied in response to the SOURCE prompt. If the name is not appropriate, enter a new name; if it is appropriate, just hit the *enter* key. In either case, your display will then say

OBJECT filename [LISTTEN.OBJ] __

and the last prompt will be

SOURCE listing [NUL.LST] __

If this is the first time in compiling a COBOL program you can elect to hit the return key and the system assumes you do not want or need the compiled listing. If you would like to have the compiled list saved on diskette, type in the filename of your source file. It is suggested, however, that you give the file the same name as the program for consistency in the event that the listing needs to be printed. The reason for naming the listing is to have it available for printing when necessary. It never seems to fail that when no listing is created, errors cannot be found and you have to compile the program again. If you do not supply a name for a listing, the compilation will not produce a listing. Accordingly, respond to the above prompt by entering LISTTEN. Your screen should now say

Source filename [.COB]:LISTTEN
Object filename [LISTTEN.OBJ]:
Source listing [NUL.LST]:LISTTEN

The compiler will now begin translating your program from the COBOL source statements into machine-language equivalents. If there are no errors in your source code, the screen will say

No Errors or Warnings

If your source program contains errors, the compiler will display

XX Errors or Warnings

where XX is the total number of errors and warnings. Note the difference between an error and a warning. A warning is just that—the compiler is telling you that there is something that is not quite correct, so review it and change it to eliminate the warning message. Granted that this is sometimes not as easy as it sounds, but it is wise to take the time to correct the warnings so that they do not hide a real error in your code. An error is a serious violation of the COBOL syntactical rules, so that the compiler will not translate the source code to its machine-language equivalent. All errors must be corrected in order for you to get a machine-language program that can perform the function for which it has been written.

Assuming that your program contains no errors, you may go on to link it for subsequent execution. If the program has errors, you must return to EDLIN, change the statements containing the errors, and repeat the compilation process again.

Linking a COBOL Program for Execution

Linking a computer program is the process of converting the program from machine-understandable code to executable (able-to-run) code. If you understand the linkage process, you will not have to perform the link each time you run the program. If your COBOL compiler and LIBRARY programs are on one disk, you do not have to remove the compiler diskette from drive A:. If, on the other hand, your compiler and LIBRARY are on separate diskettes, remove the compiler diskette and replace it with the LIBRARY diskette in drive A:. Then type

    A:LINK

Make sure that you have the correct copy of the LIBRARY diskette in your drive, because if you do not the link will fail.

The first prompt the linkage program presents as it begins to work is

    Object Modules [.OBJ]:__

This prompt is asking for the file you would like to link. Recall that the compiler supplied you with a default name for this file on the basis of what you responded for the source file. To be consistent with our earlier recommendations, respond to the prompt with

    LISTTEN

The next prompt you will receive will ask you for the name of the run-time module. You will use this name to process your program at any point in time without referencing any diskettes. When the name is supplied, the system will create a stand-alone executable file that will perform the intended function. The linkage program will supply the name for the run-time file from the name you typed previously. Thus, the prompt should read:

    Run File [LISTTEN.EXE]:__

If this name is satisfactory, depress the *enter* key.

The next prompt is for the linkage map, which is a listing of all the modules loaded into your COBOL run-time file to provide the correct results for the problem. The screen will say:

```
List File [NUL.MAP]:__
```

Since you do not really need to produce this listing, depress the return key for this prompt.

The last prompt is

```
Libraries [.LIB]:__
```

for a set of libraries, two of which are required to perform the link, and one of which is for when the program runs. The files that comprise these libraries contain the run-time modules to make your program work. Hit the *enter* key, the only valid response to this prompt.

If the linkage program needs more memory space, it will create a temporary file called VM.TMP, which is a work file for the link. You must not remove the default diskette while this work file is being created. At the end of the link the work file is erased. The linkage program also erases all files whose names have been supplied in the prompts above, thereby adding to linkage time. The process does not take long, however, and when it is complete we are ready to execute our COBOL program. To do so, just type in the name, LISTTEN, of the run-time module. If you then type in the statements shown on p. 43, the output will appear on your line printer.

The COBRUN module is located either on your default drive or on the library drive. It must be found in order for your program to work.

If you would like to have your COBOL program on a diskette all by itself, you must copy several files before you can use the program. First, copy COBRUN.EXE from your LIBRARY diskette. This file contains all your run-time modules that are called by any COBOL program. Next, copy the COMMAND.COM file from your DOS diskette. Experience has shown that when you execute a COBOL program, it is best to have the diskette containing the program, COBRUN.EXE, and COMMAND.COM in drive A, which should be the default drive. If it is not, then when your program finishes or is terminated by a CNTL–BREAK, the COBRUN.EXE file asks you to place the DOS diskette in drive A. [Refer to your COBOL manual for information concerning COBRUN.EXE if you are developing software for sale; you must obtain permission from the vendor (IBM) concerning this module.]

There is a shorthand notation for doing a compilation or a link without responding to the prompts one at a time. You should, however, learn the full prompts before proceeding with the abbreviated versions. The short-hand prompt for compiling the source-code file LISTTEN is

    A:COBOL LISTTEN,,;

This command performs the entire compilation in one line, producing the same results as shown before. Refer to your COBOL manual for further variations.

The structure for performing a link is similar to that for compiling. For the file LISTTEN, the command is

    A:LINK LISTTEN;

This command is all that is required to avoid having to respond to the prompts one at a time.

A new release of DOS (version 2.0) was developed for the new IBM PC called the XT (for extended). So far, experience shows that there is no difference in performance between the old and the new versions. As with the former, the new version requires that the COMMAND.COM file be on the same diskette as the COBRUN.EXE file. One bug that the new release has is that the COBOL compiler returns with the memory full error and cannot load phase zero of the compilation program. However, this problem is overcome by adding more memory (128K minimum) to the PC. Any other bugs or differences between the new and old versions of DOS that affect the performance of COBOL will be considered as they arise in the text.

This data could be entered to process the program we have discussed.

```
HELLO COBOL PROGRAMMERS
THE PURPOSE OF THIS PROGRAM
IS TO ACCEPT TEN LINES
OF MESSAGE TEXT
FROM THE KEYBOARD
AND TO LIST THEM
DIRECTLY ON THE LINE PRINTER
AS EACH LINE IS ENTERED,
IT IS LISTED ON THE PRINTER.
THE PROGRAM IS NOW COMPLETE.
```

REVIEW QUESTIONS

1. What is a COBOL reserved word? Give some examples.
2. What features does COBOL have in common with spoken languages in general? What does it have in common with our particular tongue?

3. The COBOL coding form comprises two principal areas denoted Area A and Area B. What are the columnar boundaries of each area? How is each area used?

4. Identify the four divisions of the COBOL program. Describe the functions of each.

5. What is the primary role of the WORKING–STORAGE SECTION? The SCREEN SECTION?

6. Must anything be coded in column 1 through 6 of a COBOL program? What is the purpose of column 7? Are any entries required in columns 73 through 80?

7. How does punctuation in the COBOL program compare with punctuation in written English?

8. From the list of names shown below, indicate those which are invalid, giving the reason:

ANY–NAME	ANNUAL–INTEREST–$
123–PRINT–AREA	SALARY+COMMISSION
NAME&ADDRESS	–DEDUCTIONS
GRAND--TOTALS	CLOSE
A–VERY–LONG–DESCRIPTION	B

3

THE IDENTIFICATION AND ENVIRONMENT DIVISIONS

THE IDENTIFICATION DIVISION

All COBOL programs start with the header IDENTIFICATION DIVISION. This division names the program and may contain other identifying information such as the date the program was written, the author's name, and remarks concerning what the program does.

The IDENTIFICATION DIVISION is the simplest division of a COBOL program and has the following structure:

```
IDENTIFICATION  DIVISION.
PROGRAM-ID.     program-name.
[AUTHOR.     [comment entry]. . . ]
[INSTALLATION.     [comment entry]. . . ]
[DATE-WRITTEN.     [comment entry]. . . ]
[DATE-COMPILED.     [comment entry]. . . ]
[SECURITY.     [comment entry]. . . ]
```

Of the above entries, only the division header and the PROGRAM-ID paragraph are required.

Each paragraph name identifies the type of information that the paragraph contains. The PROGRAM-ID paragraph must be the first paragraph listed. The program-name, which identifies the object program, may consist of any alphanumeric string of characters, the first of which must be a letter of the alphabet. Program-name may contain fewer than six characters, but if it has more than six, only the first six characters are used. Some examples of valid program-names are:

```
LISTIT.
AB005.
BILLJONES.
ORDERENTRY.
```

The possibilities are endless, and you can choose whatever name best appeals to you, as long as you follow the rules. Don't forget the period at the end of the name.

The contents of the other paragraphs, if included, consist of free text. These paragraphs are treated solely as documentation and have no meaning to the compiler. Example 3-1 shows a fully coded IDENTIFICATION DIVISION.

Example 3-1   The IDENTIFICATION DIVISION

```
IDENTIFICATION  DIVISION.
PROGRAM-ID.  LISTTEN.
AUTHOR.  BILL ATKINSON.
INSTALLATION.  COMMUNITY COLLEGE COMPUTER CENTER.
DATE-WRITTEN.  JULY 2, 1982.
DATE-COMPILED.  JULY 3, 1982.
SECURITY.  NONE REQUIRED.
```

Remember, only the first two entries in the example are required. Good programming style, however, favors the inclusion of the rest of them.

THE ENVIRONMENT DIVISION

The ENVIRONMENT DIVISION has several functions, chief of which are that it specifies the data files required for input and output operations and associates each of them with a particular physical device; and that it identifies the type of hardware constituting the computer system and indicates other auxiliary input and output functions. To appreciate fully the functions of the ENVIRONMENT DIVISION, it is important to understand the relationship between data files and the physical files that support them.

In any program that references or produces data files, it is necessary to establish a link between those files and the actual physical devices upon which they are stored or upon which they will be recorded. In other words, you must name each file that is to be accessed and instruct or "tell" the program, via a symbolic name, which physical input or output unit each file has been assigned. For example, suppose you would like to print the contents of a certain data file that is stored on a floppy disk. Two physical input/output units are involved: the floppy disk unit that contains the input file, and the line printer that will produce the printed output file. These two units essentially form the environment necessary for the accomplishment of this particular data processing task. What you, the programmer, must do is give the data file on the floppy disk a name and assign that file by its name to the floppy disk unit, which is specified by a symbolic reserved name. In addition, you must give the output file a name and assign it by its given name to the line printer, which is specified by another symbolic reserved name. The program then knows which internally defined file goes with which physical device. This concept of assigning internal files to external physical devices is fundamental to all programming languages, and we will return to it later in this chapter. Meanwhile, an examination of Figure 3–1 will help clarify the idea.

The general format of the ENVIRONMENT DIVISION is given below. The elements are listed in the order of their appearance in the program.

```
ENVIRONMENT DIVISION.

[CONFIGURATION SECTION.

SOURCE–COMPUTER.    Computer-name [WITH DEBUGGING MODE].

OBJECT–COMPUTER.    Computer-name
[MEMORY SIZE integer WORDS/CHARACTERS/MODULES]
[PROGRAM COLLATING SEQUENCE IS ASCII].
```

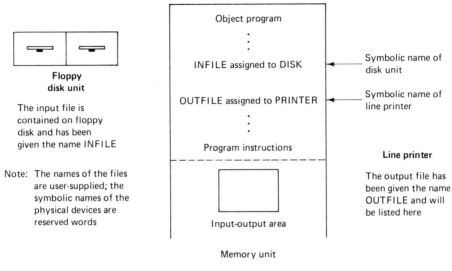

Figure 3-1
The link between data files and physical devices within a program

```
[SPECIAL-NAMES.    [PRINTER IS mnemonic-name]
   [ASCII IS STANDARD-1]
   [CURRENCY SIGN IS literal]
   [DECIMAL-POINT IS COMMA].]

[INPUT-OUTPUT SECTION.
   FILE-CONTROL.    [file-control entry]. . .
[I-O-CONTROL.

   [SAME [RECORD    AREA FOR file-name. . . ]. . .]
      [SORT
      [SORT-MERGE].]
```

The entire CONFIGURATION SECTION, consisting of three paragraphs—SOURCE-COMPUTER, OBJECT-COMPUTER, and SPECIAL-NAMES—is optional. The SOURCE-COMPUTER and OBJECT-COMPUTER paragraphs, together with any comments contained in them (except for the clause WITH DEBUGGING MODE, if it is present) are treated as documentation and are ignored by the compiler. WITH DEBUGGING MODE is used to invoke certain compiler features for tracking errors in a program.

The SPECIAL-NAMES paragraph is used to relate certain device names to user-supplied names, and to change default editing characters. The PRINTER IS phrase allows you to define a name to be used in the DISPLAY UPON statement, which occurs in the PROCEDURE DIVISION.

The CURRENCY SIGN IS clause will substitute a single, nonnumeric literal for the currency symbol ($) if the latter is not desired on an output format for one reason or another. The designated character must be neither a quotation mark, nor any characters defined for the PICTURE clause (see Chapter 4), nor any of the digits 0 through 9. The DECIMAL-POINT IS COMMA clause will substitute a comma for the decimal point in formatted numeric output. These two rarely used clauses are mentioned here for the sake of completeness.

The entry ASCII IS STANDARD-1 (or, alternatively, ASCII IS NATIVE) means simply that the data representation used internally adheres to the American Standard Code for Information Interchange. This convention is assumed by the compiler even if the ASCII entry is not present. The terms NATIVE and STANDARD-1 are identical. Like the two previous clauses, the ASCII entry is superfluous but is mentioned for the sake of completeness.

The INPUT-OUTPUT SECTION, which is mandatory unless there are no data files, consists of two principal paragraphs: FILE-CONTROL and I-O-CONTROL. The FILE-CONTROL paragraph specifies the files to be used by the program and associates them with their respective physical devices. We shall discuss the code needed to implement file control shortly. The I-O-CONTROL paragraph provides a means for conserving memory space through the use of the SAME AREA entry, whose general format is

```
              RECORD
    SAME      SORT            AREA  FOR filename-1,
              SORT-MERGE      filename-2, filename-3, . . .
```

All the files named in the SAME RECORD AREA clause share the same record-storage area, though they do not necessarily have the same organization or access. No file may be listed in more than one SAME AREA clause. Note that not all COBOL compilers support the SORT or SORT-MERGE options. Hence, it may not be possible to use them on your system. Check your system literature before attempting to use either of these options.

Each file of a COBOL program is identified in the FILE-CONTROL paragraph of the INPUT-OUTPUT section by a separate SELECT statement having the general format

```
    SELECT file-name ASSIGN  TO  DISK/PRINTER

    [FILE  STATUS  IS data-name-1]
    [ACCESS  MODE  IS SEQUENTIAL]
    [ORGANIZATION  IS  [LINE] SEQUENTIAL]].
```

The SELECT entry must begin in Area B, as must all the optional clauses that go with it. This clause tells the system that a particular file called filename will be assigned to or associated with a certain physical input-output device, i.e., either a disk unit (DISK) or the line printer (PRINTER). SELECT . . . ASSIGN, then, establishes the vital link between the file and the device that supports it.

The optional clauses following the SELECT clause can be listed in any order. For example, the ORGANIZATION clause may precede the ACCESS clause, which, in turn, may precede the FILE STATUS clause. The ACCESS and ORGANIZATION clauses are not needed for ordinary sequential input-output processing; we shall examine them later, when we discuss indexed and relative record files.

A *sequential file* is a file whose records are arranged and accessed in the same order in which they been entered in the file. Such files are sometimes called *entry-sequenced files.* Records in a sequential file must be processed in the order in which they occur on the physical storage device. They cannot be accessed or processed in random order, as can be done with indexed or relative record files.

A *line sequential file* is a special variety of sequential file. Like an ordinary sequential file, it has variable-length records; that is, the length in bytes of its constituent records can vary. However, the system must have some means of knowing the exact boundaries of each record.

The records in a sequential file contain a two-byte prefix in which a numeric value is stored that denotes the number of bytes that compose the record. (See Figure 3–2.) The records in a line sequential file have a one-byte suffix that contains a line delimiter that indicates the end of a record. (See Figure 3–3.) In either case the system is able to discern the complete record body regardless of any variations in length.

Both types of sequential file are accessed sequentially, and the ACCESS clause need not be specified for them. However, the ORGANIZATION clause must be specified for line sequential files.

The FILE STATUS clause of the SELECT statement enables you both to monitor all input and output operations involving disk files and to identify and trace error conditions arising from faults that could be present during file accessing, e.g., a damaged disk. Although the FILE STATUS clause is not mandatory, it is prudent to use it with indexed or relative record files

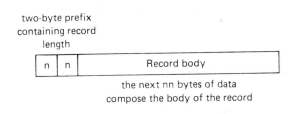

Figure 3-2
Sequential file organization

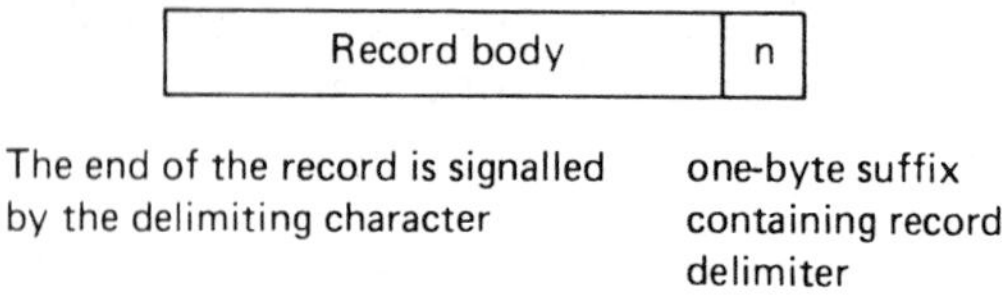

```
┌─────────────────────────────┬───┐
│        Record body          │ n │
└─────────────────────────────┴───┘
```

The end of the record is signalled   one-byte suffix
by the delimiting character   containing record
                                             delimiter

Figure 3-3
Line sequential file organization

since it provides a mechanism for exercising default options when a record that is requested is not found.

The FILE STATUS clause is referenced by a user-supplied name defined in the WORKING–STORAGE or LINKAGE SECTIONS of the DATA DIVISION. The item data-name-1 is set up as a two-byte alphanumeric field. Each of the two bytes is actually a status field into which the system moves a value each time an input or output request is made for the file associated with the particular FILE STATUS clause. The left-hand byte of data-name-1 can have any one of the following values:

Value	Meaning
0	Successful completion of I/O operation
1	End-of-file encountered during an input operation
2	Invalid key (used only for indexed and relative record files)
3	A nonrecoverable I/O error has occurred.

The right-hand byte of data-name-1 contains additional information concerning the particular I/O operation. The two bytes are used in conjunction to pinpoint a number of conditions associated with file I/O operations. The file monitoring process will be discussed further in subsequent chapters.

The following example of a fully coded ENVIRONMENT DIVISION is illustrative of the principles discussed in this chapter. The code references two line sequential disk files, which are to be monitored, and one print file.

Example 3-2   The ENVIRONMENT DIVISION

```
ENVIRONMENT DIVISION.
CONFIGURATION SECTION.
SOURCE–COMPUTER. IBM–PC.
OBJECT–COMPUTER. IBM–PC.
INPUT–OUTPUT SECTION.
FILE–CONTROL.
   SELECT PAY–FILE ASSIGN TO DISK
      ORGANIZATION IS LINE SEQUENTIAL
      FILE STATUS IS PAY–STATUS.
```

```
SELECT TAX-FILE ASSIGN TO DISK
   ORGANIZATION IS LINE SEQUENTIAL
   FILE STATUS IS TAX-STATUS.
SELECT LINEOUT ASSIGN TO PRINTER.
I-O-CONTROL.
   SAME RECORD AREA FOR PAY-FILE, TAX-FILE.
```

REVIEW QUESTIONS

1. What is the primary use of the IDENTIFICATION DIVISION? Could it have been done without?

2. (T or F) The ENVIRONMENT DIVISION serves as the link between the program and the physical input/output devices that are employed by the program.

3. (T or F) The CONFIGURATION SECTION is a required entry.

4. Describe the function of the INPUT–OUTPUT SECTION. Is this section always required?

5. What is the function of the FILE STATUS clause? What does a value of 0 in the first byte of the file status field indicate? What does a value of 3 indicate? Would a value of 1 or 2 in this field indicate an error condition? Explain.

PROBLEMS

1. Create the IDENTIFICATION DIVISION and the ENVIRONMENT DIVISION for a program that will read an employee data file and print only selected fields concerning the employee.

2. Instead of using an employee data file and producing an employee roster, write a program which will read a stock owner file, and print a location report of all certificates. (Create the IDENTIFICATION and ENVIRONMENT DIVISIONS.)

4

THE
DATA
DIVISION

DATA DESCRIPTIONS
AND THE PICTURE CLAUSE

The DATA DIVISION is the most difficult of the four COBOL program divisions to understand and learn. Its importance to effective and efficient COBOL programming makes it worth learning, however. In the DATA DIVISION, all data elements are defined to the program and the type of data that characterizes these elements is specified. For example, data elements consisting entirely of numbers are identified as numeric items, and elements consisting of mixed symbols, i.e., letters and numbers, are identified as alphanumeric items. Data elements may be grouped in any number of ways depending on the needs of the program application or problem to be solved.

The central feature of the DATA DIVISION is an element of COBOL syntax called the PICTURE clause. This most important clause enables the programmer to specify the data type and length of each data element referenced within the program. Much of this and the next chapter will be aimed at explaining many of the uses and variations of the PICTURE clause. Let us begin, however, with a related topic.

DATA ITEMS

Data items fall into two main classes: *structural* data items, which specify how data elements are related in terms of groupings; and *form* data items, which specify the type of data represented by a particular data element. Table 4-1 gives a breakdown of the different species of structural and form data items there are; note how the numeric items are further broken down into several subspecies.

Table 4-1
Structural and form data items

Structural data items	Form data items
1. Group items	1. Numeric items
2. Elementary items	a. External decimal items
	b. Internal decimal items
	c. Binary items
	d. Index-data items
	2. Alphanumeric items
	3. Report items

Structural Data Items

As Table 4-1 shows, the structural data items are broken down into group items and elementary items. A *group item* is a data item that is divided into smaller group items or into elementary items. An *elementary item* is one that is not subdivided into subordinate data items. Note that a group item can consist of other group items called subordinate group items, which, in turn, consist of elementary items.

Group items are distinguished by numeric identifiers called *level numbers*. For group items containing subordinate group items, the lower the level number, the higher is the group item in relative ranking within the overall data structure. Equal level numbers indicate an equal rank within the hierarchy. To gain a clearer idea of the grouping hierarchy within a data structure, let us consider some specific examples.

Example 4-1 Consider the employee record layout shown earlier in Figure 1-4. Here we have a data structure with a fairly simple hierarchy: one group item at the record level, and all other items elementary items of equal rank.

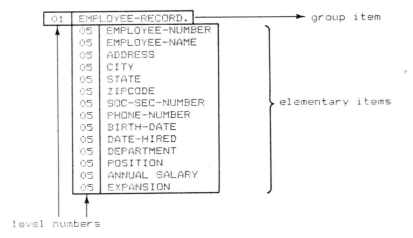

Notice that the elementary items all have the same level number, and that the group item has a level number that is higher. This is exactly as it should be to reflect the structural relationship between them. Also, the level number 01 must always be used to identify the highest group item or record in a data structure. However, the level numbers for subordinate group items and elementary items may be chosen arbitrarily from within the range 02 through 49, but must be ordered according to the hierarchy of the data structure. Thus, we could have chosen 02 or 20, for instance, instead of 05 to identify the relationships among the items in the example.

Example 4-2   Sometimes it is useful or convenient to subdivide elementary items into subordinate items, effectively converting the elementary items to group items. This is particularly true of data items containing calendar dates. For example, the BIRTH–DATE and DATE–HIRED fields of Example 4–1 can be subdivided into fields containing the month, day, and year, thus creating subordinate group items within the same data structure. Notice how the hierarchy and level numbers would change in such a case:

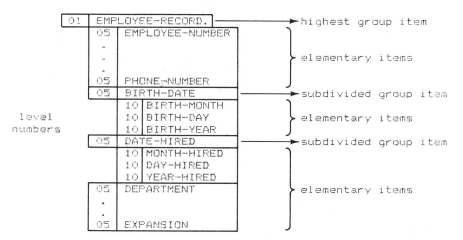

The new data structure formed has the following features: (1) There are now two subordinate group items within the structure. (2) Some of the elementary items have the same level numbers as the subordinate group items, indicating their equal rank within the data hierarchy. (3) The elementary items within the subordinate group items have lower level numbers than the latter, indicating their lower rank. Later we shall see more complicated data structures employing three or more grouping levels.

Form Data Items

Numeric items   Numeric items contain numeric data only and comprise four species. An *external decimal item* is a data item such that each digit in it is represented by the particular numeric character that denotes that digit. That is, an external decimal item (sometimes referred to as a zoned-decimal item) is stored in its ordinary numeric form, where each digit occupies a single byte of storage. Thus, the number 21,975, when represented as an external decimal item, would occupy contiguous bytes of storage as shown in Figure 4–1.

An *internal decimal item* is stored in a mode called *packed decimal* format. This method of storing numeric items is often used as a means of

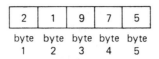

Figure 4-1
External decimal item

conserving storage. Think, for a moment, of a byte as consisting of two equal but separate half-bytes. Each half-byte is capable of storing a single digit of numeric data, so that one byte is capable of storing two digits of numeric data. When numbers are stored in packed decimal format, two digits are placed in each byte, except for the rightmost byte, which contains the last digit of the number in the first half-byte and the algebraic sign of the number in the second half-byte. Thus, suppose that we wanted to pack the number 21,975, which in the external decimal format required five bytes. In packed format, the same number can be stored in three bytes as shown in Figure 4-2.

Remember, packed decimal format always carries an algebraic sign (positive or negative, as the case may be) in the last half of the rightmost byte. This important fact must be taken into account when determining the number of bytes needed for storing packed numeric data. In general, a number that contains n digits requires $n/2 + 1$ bytes when packed. (If n is odd, the quotient $n/2$ is truncated. For example, for $n = 3$, $n/2 = 1$; and for $n = 7$, $n/2 = 3$.) Table 4-2 shows the relationship between the number of digits in a number and the number of bytes required for packing the number.

A *binary item* is a numeric item that is stored as a base-two number. Binary storage is the most efficient way of storing numeric data, although data stored in this form cannot be easily interpreted on an output medium. A binary item treats each bit[1] within a byte as a binary digit. For example, a two-byte binary item contains sixteen bits and can store a number from −32,767 thru +32,767. The leftmost bit is used to store the sign, and the remaining fifteen bits are used to store the number in binary form.

```
+---+---+---+---+---+---+
| 2 | 1 | 9 | 7 | 5 | S |
+---+---+---+---+---+---+
  byte      byte    byte    algebraic sign
   1         2       3      positive or negative
```

Figure 4-2
Packed decimal format

[1] The term *bit* is an acronym for binary digit; each byte contains eight bits.

Table 4-2
Packing numeric data

Number n of digits in a number	Number of bytes required for packing the number
1	1
2	2
3	2
4	3
5	3
6	4
7	4
8	5
9	5
10	6
11	6

If a bit is on, it denotes the binary digit 1. If a bit is off, it denotes the binary digit 0. Therefore, a sixteen-bit configuration can represent any base-two number between + −1 +32,767 to − −1 −32,767, where one bit is reserved for the sign of the number. Figure 4-3 shows how the number +32,001 would be stored in binary form.

The efficiency of binary representation becomes apparent when you consider that the largest external decimal item that fits into two bytes is +99 and the largest packed decimal item that fits into two bytes is +999. Binary items are particularly useful for subscripting arrays. (See Chapter 10.)

An *index-data item* is a special binary item used in table handling. More will be said about it in Chapter 12, where tables and table searching will be covered.

Alphanumeric items An *alphanumeric item* consists of any combination of letters, numerals, special characters, and blanks. Data fields that hold names, addresses, special messages, codes, and other such elements constitute alphanumeric items. Alphanumeric items normally

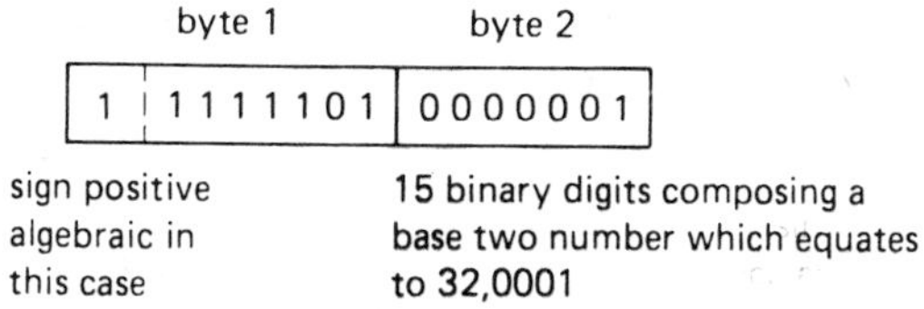

```
        byte 1          byte 2
    ┌───────────────┬───────────┐
    │ 1 │ 1 1 1 1 1 0 1 │ 0 0 0 0 0 0 1 │
    └───────────────┴───────────┘
  sign positive        15 binary digits composing a
  algebraic in         base two number which equates
  this case            to 32,0001
```

Figure 4-3
A two-byte binary item

Figure 4-4
Alphanumeric character string (street address) stored in 15 contiguous bytes

consist of character strings in which each character in the string is assigned one byte of storage. A typical item of this type is a street address. (See Figure 4–4.)

Notice that the field in the figure contains numerals, letters, special characters (the periods), and blanks. As is plain, alphanumeric items are used for expressing freely formatted data.

Report items A *report item* reports numeric data in a form consistent with the nature of the data. Depending on context, numeric data can be presented on an output report in many different ways. For example, a monetary field usually contains decimal points, dollar signs, and commas. On a financial report the amount 6822 dollars and 67 cents would normally be formatted as

$6,822.67

In other words, the report item enables you to format numeric data in such a way that its meaning is intelligible and recognizable. A report item is stored internally in the form of an alphanumeric item or character string. (See Figure 4–5.)

DESCRIBING DATA ENTRIES

Each data-field item in a COBOL program must be described by a separate entry consisting of a level number, a data-name, a data-item definition, and other clauses specifying additional characteristics. These data entries are used to describe input records, output formats, and other data elements referenced within the program. The general format of the data entry is

```
            level-number  {data-name}     REDEFINES clause *
  {FILLER      }
            (PICTURE clause)       (VALUE clause)
            (USAGE clause)*        (JUSTIFIED clause)
            (OCCURS clause)*       (BLANK clause)
            (SIGN clause)*
```

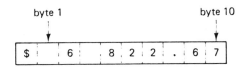

Figure 4-5
Report item stored internally as a 10-byte character string

This format appears formidable, but fortunately, not all the clauses are needed for every data item; in most cases, only two or three are needed. For all data items, you must use a level-number and a data-name or FILLER specifier. For group items, only those clauses marked by an asterisk may be used. For elementary items, all the clauses may be used. In most cases, a level-number and data-name suffice to describe a group item. In addition to the level-number and data-name or FILLER specifier, most elementary items require only a PICTURE clause, which the rest of this chapter will deal with.

THE PICTURE CLAUSE

The PICTURE clause is used to describe the exact specifications of elementary data items. PICTURE, which may be abbreviated PIC, is a reserved word. The general format of the PICTURE or PIC clause is

$$\left\{ \begin{array}{l} \text{PICTURE} \\ \text{PIC} \end{array} \right\} \quad \text{IS} \quad \left\{ \begin{array}{l} \text{Numeric form} \\ \text{Alphanumeric form} \\ \text{Report form} \end{array} \right\}$$

As shown, the three forms for PICTUREs are numeric, alphanumeric, and report. The numeric form is used for numeric data items. A numeric item in the PICTURE clause is symbolized by the numeral 9, with each repetition indicating a separate position for a digit (digit position). For example, a numeric item composed of five digit positions would contain five 9's.

Example 4-3 Suppose we need an external decimal item for storing a number having up to three digits. The PICTURE clause would then have the form

PICTURE 999.

or, in abbreviated fashion,

PIC 999.

A numeric item can contain up to 18 digits. COBOL provides an abbreviated notation for indicating the number of digit positions in the PICTURE clause. This notation has the general form

PICTURE 9(n)

or

PIC 9(n)

where n, which can have any value from 1 to 18, is a repetitive factor specifying the number of digits. This abbreviated notation is particularly useful when dealing with numbers that have many digits, as shown in Example 4-4.

Example 4-4 A PICTURE clause for an external decimal item containing 10 digits has the form

PICTURE 9(10)

or

PIC 9(10)

The notation 9(10) is clearly preferable to 9999999999.

Earlier, we saw that numeric data can be represented in several different ways, chief of which are external decimal, packed decimal, and binary. So far, we have only shown the description for external decimal items (sometimes referred to as display items). Now let us look at the PICTURE clauses for packed decimal and binary items.

In processing numeric data it is often necessary to keep track of a number's algebraic sign. Some computer languages do this automatically, but COBOL must be told when it is working with signed numeric data. This is done by including the letter S in the picture clause, as follows:

PICTURE S9(n)

or

PIC S9(n)

S will always appear as the first element in the digit specifier. This notation means that if the number assumes a value greater than zero, the item will carry a positive sign; if the number should assume a value less than zero, then the item will carry a negative sign. If S is not included in the digit specifier, then the item will carry no sign, and COBOL will assume that its value is always positive. Note that S does not take up a character position in the field.

Another important aspect of numeric data is the number of decimal places a number is to be carried to. In ordinary arithmetic usage, if the location of the decimal point is not specified, then the decimal point is assumed to be to the right of the number, indicating that it is a whole number and has no fractional part. The same convention holds in COBOL: the letter V is used to indicate the location of the decimal point in the PICTURE clause of a numeric data item and is referred to as an assumed decimal point. As with S, V does not actually take up a character position in the numeric data field; it merely indicates to the COBOL program where the decimal point should be. The general form of the PICTURE clause of a numeric item using an assumed decimal point is

PICTURE 9(n)V9(r)

or

PIC 9(n)V9(r)

where n represents the number of digits to the left of the assumed decimal point and r represents the number of digits to the right.

The sign specifier S is often used in conjunction with the assumed decimal point in the PICTURE clause.

Example 4-5 A signed external decimal item having 10 digits with two decimal places would have the PICTURE clause

PIC   S9(8)V99

Example 4-6 A signed external decimal item having five digits with five decimal places would have the PICTURE clause

PIC SV9(5)

Recall that a packed decimal item stores two digits in each byte, so that such an item consisting, for example, of five digits would occupy three bytes. The PICTURE clause for this item would be the same as that for a display item, but with the specifier COMP–3 appended to it as shown in Example 4–7.

Example 4–7 A signed packed decimal item consisting of nine digits with two decimal places has the PICTURE clause

    PIC S9(7)V99   COMP–3

and occupies five bytes of storage.

The PICTURE clause for a binary item, while similar in form to that of a packed decimal item, has a somewhat different meaning. For display and packed items, each occurrence of the numeral 9 specifies an occurrence of a digit. For binary items, however, each 9 specifies a byte of storage. The number of 9's in the PICTURE indicates the number of contiguous bytes contributing to the formation of the binary number in storage. Usually, a binary item has no assumed decimal (actually, binary) point. It can, however, have a sign. A binary item is distinguished by the specifier COMP appended to it.

Example 4–8 A signed binary item consisting of two contiguous bytes for storing a 15-bit base-two number would have the PICTURE clause

    PIC   S99   COMP

We shall see later that COMP and COMP–3 can be components of the USAGE clause as well as stand alone in a PICTURE clause. That is, the PICTURE clauses in Examples 4–7 and 4–8 could have been written

    PIC S9(8)V99 USAGE IS COMP–3
    PIC S99 USAGE IS COMP

(USAGE IS falls inside that wide range of COBOL reserved words that are optional and need not be explicitly stated. Critics of COBOL frequently contend that the language is somewhat wordy and hence cumbersome to code. One way to compress source code and facilitate the coding process is to omit optional reserved words. This approach is generally adhered to by most professional programmers, and in the interest of conciseness and efficiency, will be followed here as well.)

The alphanumeric form of the PICTURE clause is used for character data such as that shown in Figure 4–4. The PICTURE clause for this type of data is denoted by the letter X, with each repetition indicating another character position. An alphanumeric item requiring 20 character positions, for example, would contain 20 X's. The abbreviated notation shown for numeric items also works for alphanumeric items. The general form is

    PICTURE X(n)

or

    PIC X(n)

where n is the repetition factor.

Example 4-9   A PICTURE clause for an alphanumeric item containing 30 characters has the form

    PICTURE X(30)

or

    PIC X(30)

If an alphanumeric item consists solely of alphabetic characters, its PICTURE clause may use the letter A in place of the letter X to indicate the character positions. The general form of a strictly alphabetic item is

    PICTURE A(n)

or

    PIC A(n)

where, again, n is the repetition factor.

Example 4-10   A PICTURE clause for a strictly alphabetic item containing 25 characters has the form

    PICTURE A(25)

or

    PIC A(25)

Let us now apply the principles of data description thus far presented to code a record layout for the data structure of Example 4-2.

Example 4-11   The data structure of Example 4-2 is a presentation of the record layout depicted in Figure 1-4. In that layout the name, data type, and length of each data field are specified. With the information shown, the record would have the following description:

```
01  EMPLOYEE-RECORD.
    05  EMPLOYEE-NUMBER                 PIC  9(5).
    05  EMPLOYEE-NAME                   PIC  X(30).
    05  ADDRESS                         PIC  X(30).
    05  CITY                            PIC  X(15).
```

05	STATE	PIC X(15).
05	ZIP–CODE	PIC 9(5).
05	SOC–SEC–NUMBER	PIC X(11).
05	PHONE–NUMBER	PIC X(8).
05	BIRTH–DATE.	
	10 BIRTH–MONTH	PIC 99.
	10 FILLER	PIC X.
	10 BIRTH–DAY	PIC 99.
	10 FILLER	PIC X.
	10 BIRTH–YEAR	PIC 99.
05	DATE–HIRED.	
	10 MONTH–HIRED	PIC 99.
	10 FILLER	PIC X.
	10 DAY–HIRED	PIC 99.
	10 FILLER	PIC X.
	10 YEAR–HIRED	PIC 99.
05	DEPARTMENT	PIC X(15).
05	POSITION	PIC X(15).
05	ANNUAL–SALARY	PIC 9(7).
05	FILLER	PIC X(28).

Observe the following features in the example:

1. The group items contain simply a level number and a data-name, which are sufficient descriptors for most group items.

2. The elementary items consist of a level number, data-name, and PICTURE clause, which, again, are sufficient descriptors for most elementary items.

3. For the alphabetic fields, such as EMPLOYEE–NAME, we used the more general data type specifier X instead of A. This practice is standard for most COBOL authors, who seldom use the A data-type specifier.

4. The data items having the name FILLER will not be referenced in the program; FILLER items are employed mainly to account for un-used or unreferenced positions in a data structure.

5. Each entry in the record, and the record reference itself (01 EMPLOYEE–RECORD), is terminated by a period, which is man-datory.

At the beginning of this chapter we saw that numeric data can be represented in COBOL chiefly in three ways: as external decimal, packed decimal, and binary. These representations, however, are of how numeric data items are stored *within memory* or *on some file storage medium,* such as floppy disk. If an attempt were made to print these items on the *video display* or the *line printer,* only the external decimal (DISPLAY) item would produce a readable image since it is stored in character format. (See Figure 4–6.) The packed decimal (COMP–3) and the binary (COMP) items would not be printed in readable form. All you would see of them would be a scramble of symbols having no apparent meaning.

```
┌─────────────────────────────┐
│ 0 │ 2 │ 1 │ 7 │ 6 │ 4 │ 7 │ 9 │ 3 │ 5 │
└─────────────────────────────┘
```

External decimal item in
memory described by
PIC 9 (8) V99

0 2 1 7 6 4 7 9 3 5

Printed output
using the same
PICTURE clause

Figure 4-6
Printed output of an external decimal item with two assumed decimal places

Nonetheless, even printing numeric data in external decimal form is rarely desirable. The reader of such data would not want to see the leading zeros, but would probably like to see the number segmented by commas, which is the standard practice in showing numeric data. If the numeric item was a money field, he or she might also like to see a dollar sign and perhaps a decimal point. Since much of the meaning of numeric information is inherent in its printed format, COBOL provides, through the report form of the PICTURE clause, a means of presenting that information in standard punctuated form. Fields thus presented are often called *edited fields.*

Suppose that the data item in Figure 4–7 represents a money amount. In that case, we would want it to look something like

$ 1,234.56

Now let us see how printed results of this kind can be attained.

In the report form of the PICTURE clause, the following special characters may be used for edited fields:

Z , . $ + − CR DB * / B

The characters Z , . and $ are the most commonly used editing characters for business applications. Hence, our discussion will focus on these four

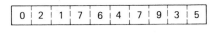

External decimal item in
memory described by
PIC 9 (8) V99

$b2, 176, 479.35

Printed output using
PIC $ZZ, ZZZ, ZZZ.99

Figure 4-7
Printed output of an edited decimal item using the character Z

characters. Once they are understood, the meanings of the others will also be clear.

The Z in the PICTURE clause represents a position for a digit in the edited output field. It has the same meaning as the numeral 9, except that it suppresses leading zeros. The period (.) is used to indicate where in the printed output field the decimal point is to appear. The comma (,) is used to indicate where commas should appear, and the dollar sign ($) indicates where the dollar sign should appear in the printed output of money fields. (As you will see shortly, $ can also be used to represent positions for digits.) These characters can be used in combination to produce the desired results. Keep in mind that all editing symbols are used to describe printed numeric output only, not numeric data stored in main memory or on file media.

Figure 4-7 shows the printed output of an edited decimal item. Notice the following features:

1. There are two PICTURE clauses, one for describing the internally stored data and another for representing the printed output.
2. The leading zero in the printed output has been suppressed.
3. Each position in the printed output is represented by an edit symbol in the associated PICTURE clause. In other words, the printed output is an *image* of its PICTURE clause.
4. There are two 9's to the right of the decimal point in the output PICTURE clause. The reason for this is that Z's to the right of a decimal point are not recognized.
5. The assumed decimal point in the input PICTURE clause is aligned with the explicit decimal point in the output PICTURE clause.

The dollar sign may be used in the fashion of the Z to represent positions of digits in printed numeric output. There is a difference, however: $ is "floated" across the field and printed in the first position to the left of the number where a nonsignificant digit would occur. (See Figure 4-8.)

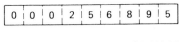

External decimal item in memory described by PIC 9 (7) V99

$2, 568.95

Printed output using PIC $, $$$, $$$.99

Figure 4-8
Printed output of an edited external
decimal item using the floating dollar sign

Table 4-3
Using the Z, $ and . in edit patterns for numeric data

Value of internal numeric item	Internal PICTURE clause	Output PICTURE clause (edit pattern)	Printed image
00749	PIC 9(5)	PIC 9(5)	00749
00749	PIC 9(5)	PIC Z(5)	bb749
12867	PIC 9(5)	PIC Z,ZZZ	2,867
147823	PIC 9(4)V99	PIC Z(5).9	b1487.2
147823	PIC 9(4)V99	PIC Z(4).99	1478.23
147823	PIC 9(4)V99	PIC ZZ,ZZZ.99	b1,478.23
00042	PIC 9(3)V99	PIC $,$$$.99	bbbb$.42
39842	PIC 9(3)V99	PIC $,$$$.99	b$398.42
04768	PIC V9(5)	PIC .9(5)	.04768
04768	PIC 9(3)V99	PIC $$$.99	$47.68

Note: The b's in the last column represent blanks or spaces.

Formatting printed output with the edit characters in the PICTURE clause is not a self-evident task. It requires some thought and practice. Table 4-3 should help clarify some of the ideas involved. Observe from the table that:

1. A print position is reserved for every character in the output PICTURE clause. If the number to be printed is shorter than its PICTURE, the image is padded with blanks on the left.

2. If the number is longer than the output PICTURE, the image is truncated. (See third entry in table.)

3. If the assumed decimal point and the explicit decimal point are not correctly aligned, inaccurate results may be printed. (See fourth entry in table.)

4. Enough positions must be reserved in the output PICTURE clause to accommodate the largest possible number that can be stored in the field to be printed.

COBOL provides a means of representing signed numbers on printed output through the use of four edit characters in the output PICTURE clause: +, −, CR, and DB. The plus sign (+) and the minus sign (−) are used in the same way the dollar sign is used: each occurrence represents a digit position, and the sign is "floated" in the same manner. If + is used in the PICTURE clause, a plus sign will appear in front of the printed number if its sign is positive, a minus sign if its sign is negative. If − is used, a minus sign will appear if the printed number is negative; otherwise no sign will be printed. The PICTURE clause associated with the internally stored number must use the sign specifier S.

The edit characters CR (credit) and DB (debit) are normally used in conjunction with money fields. If the sign of the field is positive, CR will be printed to the right of the number; if the sign is negative, DB will be printed there. These specifiers are the last entry in the PICTURE clause. Table 4–4 shows how signed numeric values are handled.

An asterisk (*) may be used in the output PICTURE clause in exactly the same manner as the Z specifier, except that leading asterisks occur instead of zeros. Used in the same manner, a slash (/) will appear on the printed output in the same positions. B will print a blank in the positions corresponding to where it occurs in the PICTURE clause. Table 4–5 shows how these edit characters are used.

In all of the tables showing the usage of edit signs, we used the external decimal format in the internal PICTURE clause. This was done strictly as a matter of convenience. Had we used the packed decimal or binary formats instead, the end results would have been the same.

As you may have inferred from the tables, there are many ways to format the printed output for numeric data items. The particular format to use will depend on the nature of the application and the imagination of the programmer. The next chapter shows how the PICTURE clause fits into the general context of a COBOL program.

Table 4–4
Using the +, −, CR and DB in edit patterns for numeric data

Value of internal numeric item	Internal PICTURE clause	Output PICTURE clause (edit pattern)	Printed image
+00750	PIC S9(5)	PIC + + + + +	b+750
−00750	PIC S9(5)	PIC − − − − −	b−750
+135976	PIC S9(4)V99	PIC + +,+ + +.99	+1359.76
−135976	PIC S9(4)V99	PIC − −,− − −.99	−1359.76
+135976	PIC S9(4)V99	PIC − −,− − −.99	b1359.76
+005495	PIC S9(4)V99	PIC Z(4).99CR	bb54.95CR
−005495	PIC S9(4)V99	PIC Z(4).99DB	bb54.95DB
+0176450	PIC S9(5)V99	PIC $$,$$$.99CR	$1,764.50CR
−0176450	PIC S9(5)V99	PIC $$,$$$.99DB	$1,764.50DB

Note: +, −, CR, and DB are mutually exclusive; that is, no more than one of them may appear in any PICTURE clause.

Table 4-5
Using the *, /, and blank in edit patterns for numeric data

Value of internal numeric item	Internal PICTURE clause	Output PICTURE clause (edit pattern)	Printed image
00176428	PIC 9(6)V99	PIC ***,***.99	**1,764.28
+00176428	PIC S9(6)V99	PIC ***,***.99CR	**1,764.28CR
111376	PIC 9(6)	PIC ZZ/ZZ/ZZ	11/13/76
111376	PIC 9(6)	PIC ZZBZZBZZ	11b13b76

SUMMARY: THE PICTURE CLAUSE

The PICTURE clause is important enough in COBOL to warrant a summarization of its properties and uses in addition to the extended treatment it has received in the previous section. It is simple to use, but the rules governing its use must be followed. Remember:

1. A PICTURE clause can be used only at the elementary level.
2. An integer in parentheses following any of the characters X, A, 9, $, Z, *, B, −, and + indicates the number of consecutive repetitions of the PICTURE character.
3. The characters S and V are not counted in the space allocated for internally stored numeric data items.
4. The characters CR and DB account for two character positions in the printed output.
5. A PICTURE for an edited data item must contain at least two consecutive appearances of the +, −, or $ character.
6. The characters S, V, CR, DB, and . can appear only once in a PICTURE clause.
7. The PICTURE clause using the X or A specifier may contain a maximum of 30 characters—for example, PIC X(30) contains 5 character positions.
8. The sign-control characters +, −, CR, and DB cannot be mixed. Only one type is permitted in a PICTURE clause.
9. In the PICTURE clause of an edited numeric data item, each character counts toward a print position.

Table 4-6 presents a summary of the symbols used in the PICTURE clause and their meanings.

Table 4-6
The symbols used in the PICTURE clause and their meanings

Symbol	Meaning
A	Alphabetic character or space.
B	Space-insertion character.
S	Operational sign (not counted in size of data item).
V	Assumed decimal (not counted in size of data item).
X	Alphanumeric character.
Z	Zero-suppression character.
9	Numeric character.
,	Comma-insertion character.
.	Explicit decimal point.
+	Floating plus sign.
−	Floating minus sign.
CR	Credit editing control characters.
DB	Debit editing control characters.
*	Check-protect insertion character.
$	Floating dollar sign.

Table 4–6 is not exhaustive. Some versions of COBOL allow additional PICTURE clause symbols, but the ones shown in the table are common to all versions, and they suffice for the overwhelming majority of business applications.

REVIEW QUESTIONS

1. Identify the two main classes of data items and distinguish between them.

2. Distinguish between an internal and an external decimal item.

3. What is the purpose of level numbers? Show how level numbers are used to decompose a data field into subordinate elements. Give an example or two.

4. Explain the packed decimal format, giving its advantages. How many bytes are required to contain a seven-digit packed numeric item? An eleven-digit packed item?

5. What is the largest numeric value that can be stored in a four-byte binary item? What is the smallest value?

6. Explain the role of the PICTURE or PIC clause. Write PIC clauses for the following data items:

Item name	Data type	Length	Format
STUDENT-NAME	alpha	25	character
RECORD-COUNT	numeric	5 digits	external decimal
BALANCE-DUE	signed numeric	11 digits	packed decimal, two assumed decimal places
INDEX-A	numeric	2 bytes	binary
PART-NUMBER	alphanumeric	10	character

7. Write a COBOL data structure for the record layout containing the following elements:

Field	Length	Data type[1]
1. Salesman Name	25	AN
2. Home Address	30	AN
3. Department	15	AN
4. Date Hired.		
a. Month	2	N
b. Day	2	N
c. Year	2	N
5. Salary[2]	4	P
6. Rate of Commission[3]	3	N
7. Gross Sales[2]	5	P

[1] AN = alphanumeric, N = numeric, P = packed decimal.

[2] Fields 5 and 7 are to contain two assumed decimal places.

[3] Field 6 is to contain three assumed decimal places.

8. Write the printed image for each of the following output PICTURE clauses given the associated values and internal PICTURE clauses:

Value of internal numeric item	Internal PICTURE clause	Output PICTURE clause	Printed image
000546	PIC 9(6)	PIC 9(6)	
000546	PIC 9(6)	PIC Z(6)	
134389	PIC 9(6)	PIC Z,ZZ9	
356780	PIC 9(4)V99	PIC Z(4).99	
008723	PIC V9(6)	PIC 99.9999	
003452	PIC 9(4)V99	PIC $$$$.99	
−345602	PIC S9(4)V99	PIC − −,− − −.99	
345602	PIC S9(4)V99	PIC − −,− − −.99	
−075645	PIC S9(4)V99	PIC $$,$$$.99CR	
+129875	PIC S9(4)V99	PIC $$,$$$.99DB	

PROBLEMS

1. Using the program you began in problem 1, Chapter 3, create all necessary DATA DIVISION entries to describe the input and output files, then code the correct PROCEDURE DIVISION statements to perform the function required.

Input layout

Position	Field name
1–20	NAME
25	SEX
26–30	JOB SKILL
50–51	DEPARTMENT

Output layout

Position	Field name
5–24	NAME
28–29	DEPARTMENT
34	SEX
38–42	JOB SKILL
46–50	ID NUMBER

Consisting of
First initial
First letter of last name
Last 3 digits of JOB SKILL

2. From problem 3–2, complete the DATA DIVISION and PROCEDURE DIVISION entries to produce the Vault Location Report.

Input layout

Position	Field name
1–20	ACCOUNT NAME
21–24	# OF SHARES
28–34	CERTIFICATE #
42–49	NAME OF STOCK

Output layout

Position	Field name
20–27	NAME OF STOCK
36–42	CERTIFICATE #
48–51	# OF SHARES
56–59	VAULT LOCATION

Consisting of
First letter of last name
First 3 digits of CERTIFICATE #

5

THE FILE SECTION AND THE WORKING-STORAGE SECTION

In Chapter 2 we introduced the three most important sections of the DATA DIVISION, viz., the FILE SECTION, the WORKING-STORAGE SECTION, and the SCREEN SECTION, and we briefly explained the function of each.

In this chapter, we shall consider the FILE SECTION and WORKING-STORAGE SECTION in more detail, and introduce the LINKAGE SECTION. We shall leave the SCREEN SECTION for later, as it employs advanced syntactical and functional features not found in the other sections.

The FILE SECTION is used to describe all files and records accessed by the program. It shows such information as the name of the file, the record name, and the number of bytes the record contains. Any COBOL program that accesses files in any way will use the FILE SECTION.

The WORKING-STORAGE SECTION is the program's "scratch pad," where formatted data for printing, fields used in computations, tables, and other data items needed by the program are stored. Though a COBOL program without a WORKING-STORAGE SECTION is not impossible, it is difficult to envision one of any substance that lacks this section.

The LINKAGE SECTION is used for passing data between different programs. Essentially, it enables two or more programs to communicate with one another; that is, it links a program functionally with subordinate programs called subprograms—ergo its name. Syntactically, the LINKAGE SECTION is very much like the WORKING-STORAGE SECTION, but functionally it is quite different. We shall discuss the structure and function of the LINKAGE SECTION in Chapter 12.

Figure 5-1 (p. 80) shows how the various sections are arranged within the DATA DIVISION. The FILE SECTION occurs first, followed by the LINKAGE SECTION, WORKING-STORAGE SECTION, and the SCREEN SECTION. Also shown is how these sections interact with other divisions of the same program, and other external subprograms and system devices. Specifically, the figure shows how various components of the system are linked to the main program (Program A) by data links. A *data link* is a file, record, or data item that is shared or referenced by different divisions within the same program, by a program and a subprogram, or by a program and peripheral devices.

As an example, a data item defined in the FILE SECTION of Program A may be referenced in the PROCEDURE DIVISION, and moved to the WORKING-STORAGE SECTION for producing a computed result, or to the LINKAGE SECTION for communicating with Subprograms B and C. Similarly, a data item entered through the video display terminal would be defined in the SCREEN SECTION and then might be passed to the FILE SECTION through the PROCEDURE DIVISION for entry into a file. The sections of the DATA DIVISION play an important role not only in defining data, but also in linking various programs and system components together.

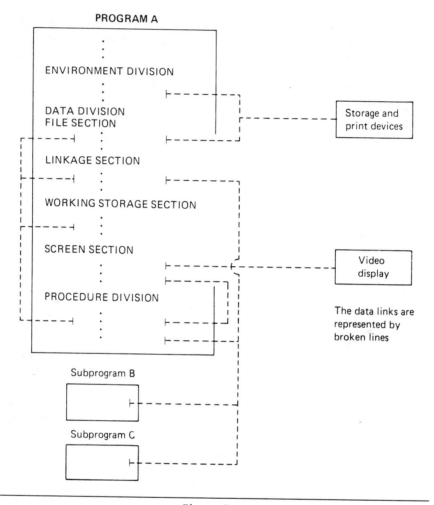

Figure 5-1
Data links between the DATA DIVISION
and other internal and external system components

DEFINING FILES IN THE FILE SECTION

Every file that is specified by a SELECT statement in the ENVIRON-MENT DIVISION must be defined in the FILE SECTION. This file definition is done by means of the FD entry, which contains a number of clauses describing various characteristics of the file, such as the file name, blocking factor, and data record name. The general format of the FD entry is:

```
FD   file-name
     LABEL clause
     [VALUE-OF clause]
     [BLOCK clause]
     [RECORD clause]
     [DATA RECORD(S) clause]
     [CODE-SET clause]
     [LINAGE clause]
```

The clauses following FD file-name can be listed in any order. The only required clause is the LABEL clause, though the VALUE OF clause is needed in the case of disk files. Some of the optional clauses, such as the BLOCK clause and the DATA RECORD(S) clause, serve no actual function within microcomputer COBOL except as documentation. In what follows, we shall focus attention on the more commonly used LABEL, RECORD, and DATA RECORD(S) clauses.

The LABEL clause, though required, is only a formality, performing no essential function. It simply indicates whether or not the particular file has a system label associated with it. As a general rule, this label, which is totally transparent to the program, is not present for any file assigned to a printer and is always present for any file assigned to a disk. The general format of the LABEL clause is

$$\text{LABEL} \quad \begin{Bmatrix} \text{RECORD} \\ \text{RECORDS} \end{Bmatrix} \quad \begin{bmatrix} \text{IS} \\ \text{ARE} \end{bmatrix} \quad \begin{Bmatrix} \underline{\text{OMITTED}} \\ \underline{\text{STANDARD}} \end{Bmatrix}$$

The OMITTED option, which specifies that no label exists for the file, must always be used for files assigned to a printer. The STANDARD option, which specifies that a label does exist for the file, must always be used for files assigned to a disk. The VALUE OF clause is required in the FD entry of any file assigned to a disk. This clause relates the logical file named in the FD entry to the physical file on the disk.[1] The general format is

VALUE OF FILE-ID IS file-name

The file-name is the name of the physical file on the disk and must be enclosed in quotation marks. In addition, it must be spelled exactly as it appears in the disk directory, and the file extension name must be included.

[1] Generally, there are two ways of characterizing a computer file in terms of how it is referenced: *logical* file and *physical* file. The term *logical* refers to the conceptual structure of the file, and the term *physical* refers to the actual file as it is or will be stored on the disk. The COBOL application program recognizes only the logical file, whereas the operating system, which performs file input and output functions, recognizes only the physical file. It is necessary, therefore, to link the two files together within the application program, and this linking is done in the FD entry.

The RECORD clause specifies the size of the associated record or, more precisely, the number of bytes that the record contains. Actually, the size of the record is set in the data descriptions of the items that follow the completed FD entry and that constitute the 01-level record description. The general format of the RECORD clause is

RECORD CONTAINS [integer-1 TO] integer-2 CHARACTERS

If the record is fixed length, then just integer-2, which states the record size in bytes, is specified. If the record is variable length, then integer-1, which states the record size in bytes of the smallest record, must also be specified.

Although the RECORD clause is considered to be documentation, its usage pays off when you compile your program. If the 01 or subordinate levels PICTURE values are different from what has been stated in this clause, the compiler will generate a warning message. The warning is extremely helpful when you are debugging a program.

The DATA RECORD(S) clause specifies the name of the record in the file. This clause is strictly documentary, as the name of the record is the same as the name used in the 01 record description. The general format of the DATA RECORD(S) clause is

DATA   {RECORD   IS } data-name 1
       {RECORDS   ARE}   [data-name 2 . . .]

If more than one data name is used, more than one type of data record is contained in the file. Two or more data records defined in this manner use the same storage area in memory. The order of the data names does not matter.

As a general observation, it is worth mentioning that following every FD entry, there must be an 01-level item describing the record associated with the file. This item may be either a single entry with a PICTURE clause or a group item subdivided into elementary items.

Example 5-1   Suppose we have a file on disk to which we have given the name STUDENT-FILE in the SELECT statement of the ENVIRONMENT DIVISION. Suppose that the name of the physical file on disk is STUDENTS.MST and that the record associated with this file, which we have named STUDENT-REC, contains 80 characters. Then the following is what the FD entry for STUDENT-FILE might look like:

```
FD  STUDENT-FILE
    LABEL RECORDS ARE STANDARD
    VALUE OF FILE-ID IS "B:STUDENTS.MST"
    RECORD CONTAINS 80 CHARACTERS
    DATA RECORD IS STUDENT-REC.
```

```
01  STUDENT-REC.
    05  STUDENT-NAME        PIC  X(20).
    05  STUDENT-ADDRESS     PIC  X(30).
    05  STUDENT-SSN         PIC  9(9).
    05  ADMISSION-DATE.
        10  MONTH           PIC  99.
        10  DAY             PIC  99.
        10  YEAR            PIC  99.
    05  CURRICULUM          PIC  X(10).
    05  FILLER              PIC  X(5).
```

The FD could also have the format

```
FD  STUDENT-FILE
    LABEL  STANDARD
    VALUE  OF  FILE-ID  IS  "B:STUDENTS.MST".
01  STUDENT-REC            PIC  X(80).
```

Example 5–1 shows two ways of writing an FD for the same file. Actually, there are many ways to do so, and the method you choose will depend largely on the application and programming style you eventually develop. The first FD entry is more detailed in that it uses the RECORD and DATA RECORD(S) clauses and gives a field-by-field description of the data record. The second entry gives no information about the record except its size. Sometimes this is all the program needs to know about the file in an application. At other times, it is necessary to define the fields explicitly, particularly if they are to be referenced in the PROCEDURE DIVISION.

Example 5-2   Suppose we intend to set up a file so that we may generate a report on the printer. Suppose further that in the SELECT statement the file associated with the printer is named PRINT-FILE, and that we are using a device capable of printing 132 columns. Then the FD entry for the file might look like the following:

```
FD  PRINT-FILE
    LABEL  RECORDS  ARE  OMITTED
    RECORD  CONTAINS  132  CHARACTERS
    DATA  RECORD  IS  PRINT-REC.
01  PRINT-REC             PIC  X(132).
```

It could also look like

```
FD  PRINT-FILE
    LABEL  OMITTED.
01  PRINT-REC             PIC  X(132).
```

In both FD entries of Example 5–2 we have used a single 01-level entry to describe the print record. The fields constituting the desired printed output line have not been explicitly defined. Usually, these fields are defined in the WORKING–STORAGE SECTION, where the print record is formatted for output. The reasons for this will become clear a little later.

Example 5-3 shows a program incorporating the techniques that have been introduced so far.

Example 5-3 Code the FILE SECTION of a program that accesses a disk file and produces output on the printer. Assume that the disk and print files are the same as described in Examples 5-1 and 5-2.

One possible solution is the following:

```
IDENTIFICATION DIVISION.
PROGRAM-ID. STUDENTS.
ENVIRONMENT DIVISION.
INPUT-OUTPUT SECTION.
FILE-CONTROL.
    SELECT STUDENT-FILE ASSIGN TO DISK
    ACCESS MODE IS SEQUENTIAL
    ORGANIZATION IS SEQUENTIAL.
    SELECT PRINT-FILE ASSIGN TO PRINTER.
DATA DIVISION.
FILE SECTION.
FD STUDENT-FILE
    LABEL RECORDS ARE STANDARD
    VALUE OF FILE-ID IS "B:STUDENTS.MST"
    RECORD CONTAINS 80 CHARACTERS
    DATA RECORD IS STUDENT-REC.
01  STUDENT-REC.
    05  STUDENT-NAME        PIC X(20).
    05  STUDENT-ADDRESS     PIC X(30).
    05  STUDENT-SSN         PIC 9(9).
    05  ADMISSION-DATE.
        10  MONTH           PIC 99.
        10  DAY             PIC 99.
        10  YEAR            PIC 99.
    05  CURRICULUM          PIC X(10).
    05  FILLER              PIC X(5).
FD  PRINT-FILE
    LABEL RECORDS ARE OMITTED
    RECORD CONTAINS 132 CHARACTERS
    DATA RECORD IS PRINT-REC.
01  PRINT-REC               PIC X(132).
```

Notice that in the FD entry for STUDENT-FILE the record STUDENT-REC is explicitly defined in terms of its constituent fields. It has been so defined because each field is referenced in the PROCEDURE DIVISION, where the printed output will be prepared. Like many other examples in this text, Example 5-3 illustrates the technical dependencies among the various components of the COBOL language.

To continue the discussion of the FILE SECTION, the BLOCK clause is used to specify either the number of characters or the number of logical records that constitute a record on the physical file. The general format of this clause is

$$\text{BLOCK CONTAINS integer-1} \quad \begin{Bmatrix} \text{CHARACTERS} \\ \text{RECORDS} \end{Bmatrix}$$

No BLOCK clause may occur in the FD entry for files that are assigned to the printer. If a BLOCK clause does occur in the FD entry for a disk file, it is of no consequence and is treated as a comment. It is, however, examined for correct syntax. The BLOCK clause is normally associated with tape files.

The size of a physical block may be expressed in characters or in records. If the records are variable length, then the size must be expressed in characters. If the BLOCK clause is omitted, the compiler assumes that there is only one record per block. Although superfluous in microcomputer programming, the BLOCK clause is useful in COBOL programs for larger computers.

The CODE-SET clause has the format

CODE-SET IS ASCII

It simply states that both internal and external files are represented in the ASCII code. Here again, this clause is treated as documentation by the compiler. The CODE-SET clause should be specified only for files that are not on disk.

The LINAGE clause, which may be used only for files assigned to the printer, provides a means of framing printed pages and controlling the number of lines of print per page. In other words, it provides a means of setting margins on the page body of printed reports. The general format of the LINAGE clause is:

```
LINAGE IS        { data-name-1 }    LINES
                 { integer-1    }

                     [WITH FOOTING AT {data-name-2} ]
                     [              {integer-2    } ]

      [LINES AT TOP    {data-name-3} ]
                       {integer-3    } ]

      [LINES AT BOTTOM {data-name-4} ]
                       {integer-4    } ]
```

All data names must be set up as unsigned numeric integer data items. All integers must be positive, and integer-2 must not be greater than integer-1. Associated with the LINAGE clause is a numeric data item called LINAGE-COUNTER which is defined internally by the compiler and is incremented automatically in the PROCEDURE DIVISION. The LINAGE clause is used in conjunction with the WRITE and ADVANCING statements, which have not yet been introduced. We shall return to it when we discuss page formatting and overflow conditions in Chapter 6.

DATA FORMATTING AND DATA MANIPULATION IN THE WORKING-STORAGE SECTION

The WORKING-STORAGE SECTION is a much used portion of the COBOL program. It is a dynamic place where many interesting things happen, e.g.,

1. Data records are built and formatted.
2. Report headings are constructed.
3. Data tables are stored and accessed.
4. Intermediate and final computational results are stored.
5. Printed output is formatted.

The WORKING-STORAGE SECTION is the program's internal "scratch pad," and understanding how to use it properly is a key to effective COBOL programming.

The WORKING-STORAGE SECTION is organized in a manner similar to that of the FILE SECTION. For example, it contains data descriptions and employs level numbers and the PICTURE clause to define the various data elements that are stored in it. On the other hand, it does not make use of FD entries, which belong exclusively to the FILE SECTION. One clause, however, that the WORKING-STORAGE SECTION makes use of and the FILE SECTION does not, even though it is associated with the PICTURE clause, is the VALUE clause, which enables the programmer to initialize certain data items with specific values. The general format of the VALUE clause is

VALUE IS literal

The literal may be an explicit numeral or an alphanumeric configuration. The VALUE clause may not be used in the FILE SECTION or the LINKAGE SECTION, except in level-88 condition descriptions, which will be described later. Nor may it be used in a data description entry that contains an OCCURS or REDEFINES clause. Examples 5-4 through 5-9 illustrate the various uses of the VALUE clause.

Example 5-4 Suppose we have a packed decimal numeric data item that we would like to initialize with a value of zero. The item might be, for example, an accumulator for storing a count of records processed. Then one possible definition could be

```
05 RECORD-COUNTER PIC 9(5) COMP-3 VALUE 0.
```

Example 5-5   An alphanumeric data item for storing the message "PROCESSING TERMINATED" might be defined as

```
05 MESSAGE-OUT PIC X(21)
          VALUE "PROCESSING TERMINATED".
```

Note from the above examples that

1. The VALUE clause is used in conjunction with the PICTURE clause of elementary items only. It may not be used with group items.
2. For numeric items (Example 5–4), the value is an explicit numeral that is the desired initialization value. It may be a whole number or a decimal number.
3. For alphanumeric items (Example 5–5), the value of the literal is enclosed in quotation marks, which are required.
4. Each entry must be terminated with a period.

The VALUE clause in the PICTURE of a data item should not be confused with the VALUE OF clause in the FD entry. The two have entirely different functions.

Example 5-6   A packed data item called TAX-RATE that is initialized with a value of + .04253 would be coded as follows:

```
05 TAX RATE PIC S9(5)  COMP-3
          VALUE +.04253.
```

Example 5-7   An unreferenced alphanumeric field that is initialized with blanks would have the form

```
10 FILLER PIC X(20)  VALUE SPACES.
```

The word SPACES in Example 5–7 is one of several COBOL reserved words called figurative constants. A *figurative constant* is a word that denotes a particular constant value. Figurative constants may be used in the VALUE clause or in the PROCEDURE DIVISION in place of the values they denote. They are concise symbols for representing character strings consisting of repetitions of the same character. Had we used the explicit blank character instead of SPACES in Example 5–7, the data item would have been coded as

```
10 FILLER PIC X(20) VALUE "                    ".
        (20 blanks between quotation marks)
```

Note that it is necessary to insert exactly 20 blanks between the quotation marks in the VALUE clause. The use of the figurative constant results in simpler code. A complete list of figurative constants is given in Table 5-1.

As the table shows, all the figurative constants have a singular and plural form. Both forms have exactly the same meaning and can be used interchangeably. Column three shows the kinds of data items that are ordinarily initialized with the particular figurative constant. For example, ZERO would be used to initialize a numeric field with the value 0 or an alphanumeric field with a string of 0's in the form "0000...". LOW-VALUE is the lowest value in the ASCII collating sequence. It is the character represented by a byte having all bits turned off. HIGH-VALUE is the highest value in the ASCII collating sequence. It is the character represented by a byte having all bits turned on. The roles of LOW-VALUE and HIGH-VALUE will become apparent in due course. In Chapter 6 we shall show how figurative constants are used to initialize group data items.

Example 5-8   The data item of Example 5-4 might alternatively be coded as

```
05 RECORD-COUNTER      PIC 9(5) COMP-3 VALUE ZERO.
```

Example 5-9   An alphanumeric item called PRINT-ZEROS containing a string of 15 zeros could be coded as either

```
10 PRINT-ZEROS       PIC X(15) VALUE ZEROS.
```

or

```
10 PRINT-ZEROS       PIC X(15) VALUE "000000000000000".
```

Table 5-1
The figurative constants

Figurative constant	Value	Type of data item
SPACE or SPACES	blank	Alphabetic or Alphanumeric
ZERO, ZEROS, or ZEROES	the number 0 or character "0"	Numeric or Alphanumeric
LOW-VALUE or LOW-VALUES	the lowest ASCII value—all bits off	Alphanumeric
HIGH-VALUE or HIGH-VALUES	the highest ASCII value—all bits on	Alphanumeric

In Example 5-3 we presented a partially coded COBOL program that defines a disk file containing student information and a print file for producing output. Let us now add a WORKING-STORAGE SECTION to that program. Suppose the program is to access the student file on disk and generate a printed report from it with all the fields for each record shown on a single line of print. The report will have appropriate report and column headings, and each page will be numbered. There will be 50 student records per page, and a count of all the records printed will be shown at the end of the report. A layout of the desired report is shown in Figure 5-2 (p. 90).

Notice the two headings in the report layout. The first heading consists of constant data and variable data. The variable data, shown underscored, uses the appropriate editing symbols discussed in Chapter 4. The date is to appear in standard MM/DD/YY format, with suppression of leading zeros. The page number will also have leading zeros suppressed. The second heading consists totally of constants. The detail line consists of variable data, except for the slashes in the DATE-ADMITTED column. In this line, the appropriate PICTURE clause symbols have been used to denote the type of data to be printed. For example, the social security number, SSN, is to be printed as a zoned (external) decimal numeric item, and DATE-ADMITTED is to be printed in the MM/DD/YY format with zeros suppressed. The remaining data elements in the detail line are ordinary alphanumeric items—ergo the X's to depict their format. Finally, the total line consists of a literal (constant) followed by an edited numeric field of four positions punctuated in the standard manner.

One more item must be introduced before we can code the WORKING-STORAGE SECTION of the report program. Many times it is necessary to define data items in the WORKING-STORAGE SECTION that will stand alone, or be independent. These items, which are not part of any record or other data structure, are usually assigned the level number 77 and always have a PICTURE, and sometimes a VALUE, clause associated with them. As level-77 items, they cannot be subdivided into subordinate items, and they can only be used in the WORKING-STORAGE SECTION. When they are thus used, they must be the first entries in the section. Generally, they are reserved for defining counters and constants. The general format of a level-77 item is

```
77  data-name     PIC descriptor  ⎡COMP  ⎤   ⎡VALUE⎤
                                   ⎣COMP-3⎦
```

Example 5-10   A stand-alone decimal item for counting page numbers may be defined by

```
77  PAGE-NUMBER    PIC 9(3) COMP-3 VALUE ZERO.
```

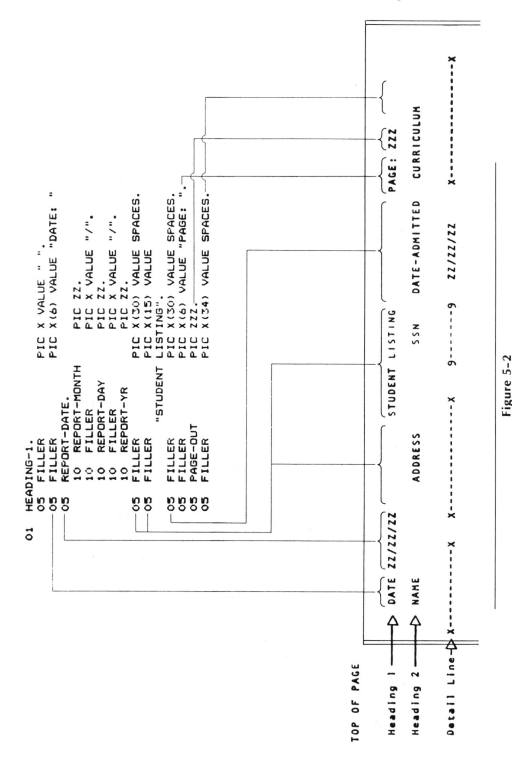

Figure 5-2

A group heading item and its corresponding printed image

Example 5-11   A stand-alone alphanumeric item for storing a message text is

```
77 MESSAGE-1      PIC X(10) VALUE "DATA ERROR".
```

Many programmers do not use level-77 entries. Instead, they define all stand-alone items either as level-01 elementary items or as lower-level elementary items within a level-01 group item. The method used is largely a matter of personal preference, as there is no hard and fast rule for defining such items. Thus, the data items in Examples 5–10 and 5–11 could just as well have been defined as

```
01  PAGE-NUMBER      PIC 9(3) COMP-3 VALUE ZERO.
```

and

```
01  MESSAGE-1        PIC X(10) VALUE "DATA ERROR".
```

respectively.

We are now ready to write the WORKING–STORAGE SECTION of the report program. Example 5–12 shows the code.

Example 5-12

```
WORKING-STORAGE SECTION.
77  PAGE-NUMBER              PIC 9(3) COMP-3 VALUE ZERO.
77  STUDENT-COUNTER          PIC 9(5) COMP-3 VALUE ZERO.
01  HEADING-1.
    05 FILLER                PIC X VALUE " ".
    05 FILLER                PIC X(6) VALUE "DATE: "
    05 REPORT-DATE.
       10 REPORT-MON         PIC ZZ.
       10 FILLER             PIC X VALUE "/".
       10 REPORT-DAY         PIC ZZ.
       10 FILLER             PIC X VALUE "/".
       10 REPORT-YR          PIC ZZ.
    05 FILLER                PIC X(30) VALUE SPACES.
    05 FILLER                PIC X(15) VALUE
                    "STUDENT LISTING".
    05 FILLER                PIC X(30) VALUE SPACES.
    05 FILLER                PIC X(6) VALUE "PAGES: ".
    05 PAGE-OUT              PIC ZZZ.
    05 FILLER                PIC X(34) VALUE SPACES.

01  HEADING-2.
    05 FILLER                PIC X VALUE " ".
    05 FILLER                PIC X(4) VALUE "NAME"
    05 FILLER                PIC X(30) VALUE SPACES.
    05 FILLER                PIC X(7) VALUE "ADDRESS".
    05 FILLER                PIC X(30) VALUE SPACES.
    05 FILLER                PIC X(3) VALUE "SSN".
```

```
        05 FILLER                    PIC X(10) VALUE SPACES.
        05 FILLER                    PIC X(13) VALUE
                      "DATE-ADMITTED".
        05 FILLER                    PIC X(3) VALUE SPACES.
        05 FILLER                    PIC X(10) VALUE
                      "CURRICULUM".
        05 FILLER                    PIC X(22) VALUE SPACES.

    01  DETAIL-LINE.
        05 FILLER                    PIC X VALUE " ".
        05 NAME-OUT                  PIC X(20).
        05 FILLER                    PIC X(14) VALUE SPACES.
        05 ADDRESS-OUT               PIC X(30).
        05 FILLER                    PIC X(7) VALUE SPACES.
        05 SSN-OUT                   PIC 9(9).
        05 FILLER                    PIC X(6) VALUE SPACES.
        05 ADMIT-DATE-OUT.
           10 ADMIT-MON-OUT             PIC ZZ.
           10 FILLER                    PIC X VALUE "/".
           10 ADMIT-DAY-OUT             PIC ZZ.
           10 FILLER                    PIC X VALUE "/".
           10 ADMIT-YR-OUT              PIC ZZ.
        05 FILLER                    PIC X(6) VALUE SPACES.
        05 CURRICULUM-OUT            PIC X(10).
        05 FILLER                    PIC X(22) VALUE SPACES.

    01  TOTAL-LINE.
        05 FILLER                    PIC X VALUE " ".
        05 FILLER                    PIC X(20) VALUE
                   "NUMBER OF STUDENTS".
        05 STUDENTS-OUT              PIC Z,ZZ9.
        05 FILLER                    PIC X(30) VALUE SPACES.
        05 FILLER                    PIC X(30) VALUE SPACES.
        05 FILLER                    PIC X(30) VALUE SPACES.
        05 FILLER                    PIC X(17) VALUE SPACES.
```

Let us examine Example 5-12 to get a better feel for what is happening in the WORKING-STORAGE SECTION of the report program. Recall that the report specifications (see Figure 5-2) require that two counts be maintained, one for the page number and one for the total number of students. To this end, two packed decimal items, PAGE-NUMBER and STUDENT-COUNTER, have been defined and initialized with zeros. Both are stand-alone level-77 entries.

The report also requires four separate print lines: two headings, the detail line, and the total line. Corresponding to these lines are level-01 group items: HEADING-1, HEADING-2, DETAIL-LINE, and TOTAL-LINE, respectively. The group items are arranged in the same order as their corresponding lines of print are to appear on the output report. (They need not be arranged that way, but logically they should be.) Each group item is subdivided into elementary items corresponding to the fields as they are to be printed on each line. Let us now consider each group item in turn.

HEADING-1 corresponds to the first line at the top of the report. The first entry is a FILLER defined as an alphanumeric character with a length of one which is initialized with a space. This entry, which is the same for all four group items, is used for form and line-feed control, and does not take up a print position. Following it are several other 05-level entries, most of which are FILLERs initialized with either constant values or spaces. The FILLERs containing constant values correspond to printed literals on the first line of the report. The FILLERs containing spaces correspond to the gaps separating those printed literals. The named data items (REPORT-MON, REPORT-DAY, REPORT-YR, and PAGE-OUT) correspond to the variable data appearing on the first line. Their values will be filled in by the program during processing. Only those data items that will be referenced within the PROCEDURE DIVISION—i.e., the variable data items—have been assigned data names. The constants and spaces are labelled FILLER. Finally, the sum of the lengths of all data items is 133, which is equal to the allowable length of the print line (132 characters) plus the initial line-feed character.

HEADING-2 corresponds to the second line from the top of the report and consists entirely of FILLERs since the print line it represents contains nothing but constant data that will not be referenced in the PROCEDURE DIVISION. Here again, the sum total of all items in the line is 133. HEADING-1 and HEADING-2 will be printed at the top of each page of the report.

DETAIL-LINE is the most complex of the four group items, consisting of variable data items interspersed with spaces. The length of each variable item represents the number of print positions reserved for that item on the output report. For example, NAME-OUT will permit a student name of up to 20 characters in length to be printed and ADDRESS-OUT will permit a student address of up to 30 characters to be printed. The variable items are not initialized with data. Rather, they will be filled with appropriate values from the input record, a process that will be explained when the PROCEDURE DIVISION is discussed. (See Chapter 6.) The same detail line will be printed over and over; only the values of the variable data items will change.

TOTAL-LINE simply consists of one nonreferenced constant and one variable, viz., STUDENTS-OUT. The rest of the elementary items are comprised of spaces. This line will be printed just once, at the end of the report. The value of STUDENTS-OUT will be obtained from the value accumulated in the 77-level entry, STUDENT-COUNTER.

We close this chapter with Example 5-13, which presents all the code for all the sections of the report program that we have written so far.

Example 5-13

```
IDENTIFICATION DIVISION.
PROGRAM-ID. STUDENTS.

ENVIRONMENT DIVISION.
INPUT-OUTPUT SECTION.
FILE-CONTROL.
```

```
        SELECT STUDENT-FILE ASSIGN TO DISK
            ORGANIZATION IS SEQUENTIAL
            FILE STATUS IS STUDENT-STATUS.

        SELECT PRINT-FILE ASSIGN TO PRINTER.

    DATA DIVISION.
    FILE SECTION.
    FD STUDENT-FILE
        LABEL RECORDS ARE STANDARD
        VALUE OF FILE-ID IS "B:STUDENTS.MST"
        RECORD CONTAINS 80 CHARACTERS
        DATA RECORD IS STUDENT-REC.
    01 STUDENT-REC.
        05 STUDENT-NAME             PIC X(20).
        05 STUDENT-ADDRESS          PIC X(30).
        05 STUDENT-SSN              PIC 9(9).
        05 ADMISSION-DATE.
            10 MONTH                PIC 99.
            10 DAY                  PIC 99.
            10 YEAR                 PIC 99.
        05 CURRICULUM               PIC X(10).
        05 FILLER                   PIC X(5).

    FD PRINT-FILE
        LABEL RECORDS ARE OMITTED
        RECORD CONTAINS 132 CHARACTERS
        DATA RECORD IS PRINT-REC.
    01 PRINT-REC                    PIC X(132).

    WORKING-STORAGE SECTION.
    77 PAGE-NUMBER                  PIC 9(3) COMP-3 VALUE ZERO.
    77 STUDENT-COUNTER              PIC 9(5) COMP-3 VALUE ZERO.
    77 STUDENT-STATUS               PIC 99 VALUE ZERO.

    01 HEADING-1.
        05 FILLER                   PIC X VALUE " ".
        05 FILLER                   PIC X(6) VALUE "DATE: "
        05 REPORT-DATE.
            10 REPORT-MON           PIC ZZ.
            10 FILLER               PIC X VALUE "/".
            10 REPORT-DAY           PIC ZZ.
            10 FILLER               PIC X VALUE "/".
            10 REPORT-YR            PIC ZZ.
        05 FILLER                   PIC X(30) VALUE SPACES.
        05 FILLER                   PIC X(15) VALUE
                    "STUDENT LISTING".
        05 FILLER                   PIC X(30) VALUE SPACES.
        05 FILLER                   PIC X(6) VALUE "PAGE: ".
        05 PAGE-OUT                 PIC ZZZ.
        05 FILLER                   PIC X(34) VALUE SPACES.

    01 HEADING-2.
        05 FILLER                   PIC X VALUE " ".
        05 FILLER                   PIC X(4) VALUE "NAME"
        05 FILLER                   PIC X(30) VALUE SPACES.
        05 FILLER                   PIC X(7) VALUE "ADDRESS".
        05 FILLER                   PIC X(30) VALUE SPACES.
        05 FILLER                   PIC X(3) VALUE "SSN".
```

```
        05 FILLER                  PIC X(10) VALUE SPACES.
        05 FILLER                  PIC X(13) VALUE
              "DATE-ADMITTED".
        05 FILLER                  PIC X(3) VALUE SPACES.
        05 FILLER                  PIC X(10) VALUE
              "CURRICULUM".
        05 FILLER                  PIC X(22) VALUE SPACES.

   01  DETAIL-LINE.
        05 FILLER                  PIC X VALUE " ".
        05 NAME-OUT                PIC X(20).
        05 FILLER                  PIC X(14) VALUE SPACES.
        05 ADDRESS-OUT             PIC X(30).
        05 FILLER                  PIC X(7) VALUE SPACES.
        05 SSN-OUT                 PIC 9(9).
        05 FILLER                  PIC X(6) VALUE SPACES.
        05 ADMIT-DATE-OUT.
           10 ADMIT-MON-OUT           PIC ZZ.
           10 FILLER                  PIC X VALUE "/".
           10 ADMIT-DAY-OUT           PIC ZZ.
           10 FILLER                  PIC X VALUE "/".
           10 ADMIT-YR-OUT            PIC ZZ.
        05 FILLER                  PIC X(6) VALUE SPACES.
        05 CURRICULUM-OUT          PIC X(10).
        05 FILLER                  PIC X(22) VALUE SPACES.

   01  TOTAL-LINE.
        05 FILLER                  PIC X VALUE " ".
        05 FILLER                  PIC X(20) VALUE
              "NUMBER OF STUDENTS".
        05 STUDENTS-OUT            PIC Z,ZZ9.
        05 FILLER                  PIC X(107) VALUE SPACES.
```

REVIEW QUESTIONS

1. How is the SELECT statement of the ENVIRONMENT DIVISION related to the FILE SECTION?

2. Write an FD entry for an indexed disk file having the name B:NAME.MAST. The records contain 120 characters.

3. Distinguish between a logical file and a physical file. How are they tied together in a COBOL program?

4. Code through the FILE SECTION a program that will access a sequential disk file and produce output on the printer. Use the record layout developed in Review Question 7, Chapter 4.

5. Describe the function of the LINAGE clause. How is it used to control the number of lines on each of the printed pages of the output report?

6. Explain the role of the WORKING-STORAGE SECTION, enumerating its specific uses. How is it different from the FILE SECTION?

7. What is the purpose of the VALUE IS clause? Give some examples of its use.

8. What is a figurative constant? Name some of the more important ones.

9. What is a 77-level data item? Are these items really required? What can be used in its place?

10. Identify the errors in the following code:

```
FILE SECTION
FD PRINT-FILE.
    LABEL RECORDS ARE STANDARD
    RECORD CONTAINS 132 CHARACTERS
    DATA RECORD IS PRINT-REC.

01 PRINT-REC              PIC X(132)      VALUE SPACES.

WORKING STORAGE-SECTION.
77 HOLD-ITEM.
    05 PART-NUMBER        PIC X(10).
    05 PRICE              PIC 9(5).99.
    05 QUANTITY           PIC 999
    05 FILLER             PIC X(10)       VALUE SPACES.

01 HEADING-1.
    05 FILLER             PIC X(30)       VALUE SPACE.
    05 FILLER             PIC X(09)       VALUE A COMPANY.
    05 FILLER             PIC X(20)       VALUE SPACES.
    05 PAGE-NUMB          PIC ZZX.
    05 FILLER             PIC X(30)       VALUE SPACES.
```

PROBLEMS

1. Add to the program you have developed in problem 1, Chapter 4, the WORKING-STORAGE entries necessary for the heading lines depicted on p. 97. Code the changes necessary in the PROCEDURE DIVISION to produce the same listing with the additional heading lines.

2. Create the heading lines shown on p. 98 for the program from problem 2, Chapter 4, and implement the changes in the PROCEDURE DIVISION. Be sure to include the necessary code for a page number.

LINE NO.	WORD NO. / PRINT POSITION		LINE NO.	REMARKS

```
                    STOCK          CERTIFICATE          VAULT
                     NAME            NUMBER     SHARES   LOC.        PAGE XXX

                    XXXXXXX         XXXXXXX      XXXX    XXXX
```

6

THE
PROCEDURE
DIVISION

The PROCEDURE DIVISION is that part of the COBOL program "where the action takes place"—where the programming logic is implemented and where the files, records, and data defined in the previous program divisions are manipulated to produce the desired results. No single chapter, or even book, could convey all there is to know about the PROCEDURE DIVISION. It will be enough here to explain its function and introduce sufficient syntax to enable us to complete the report program begun in Chapter 5. From this point on, we shall adopt a functional approach to COBOL, allowing our discussion to be guided by the data processing applications under consideration. Thus, in this chapter we shall be concerned with structuring logic, opening and closing files, reading records, formatting printed output, and finally, printing reports. By the time you have completed this chapter, you should be able to write simple COBOL programs. In fact, you should not continue beyond the chapter until you have successfully coded, compiled, and run at least one of the programs dealt with in the exercises.

PROCESSING LOGIC
AND PROCEDURE DIVISION STRUCTURE

Processing logic may be broadly defined as the set of instructions that accomplish a program's data processing task. In COBOL, processing logic is contained in the PROCEDURE DIVISION of the program. There are no hard and fast rules for setting up the processing logic, and the form that it ultimately takes is more often than not a reflection of the logical workings of the mind of the programmer. If the programmer does not have a firm understanding of the processing task and the rules of the programming language he or she is working in, or if the programming task is very complex, the processing logic can become convoluted to the point that it is very difficult, if not impossible, to follow. Eventually, the program may function correctly, but if it is ever necessary to modify it, no one—not even the programmer—may be able to determine where changes in the processing logic must be made.

While there are no definitive rules for setting up processing logic within a COBOL program, there are general guidelines for structuring the PROCEDURE DIVISION to prevent the program from degenerating into an unintelligible morass. One highly useful method involves the concept of top-down modular design. Specifically, this means that program tasks are broken down into discrete modules by function, and these modules are assembled into an orderly structure within the PROCEDURE DIVISION. This approach has the following advantages:

1. Modular program code is usually more compact, so that the tendency to write redundant code is virtually eliminated. Hence, the program is shorter and runs more efficiently.
2. Modular code is easier to comprehend, making the job of modifying the program at some later time simpler.
3. Modules of code can easily be extracted from one program and inserted in another, thereby reducing the time required to develop additional programs having similar functions.

The grammar of COBOL lends itself nicely to modular design. It enables the careful programmer to structure processing logic within the PROCEDURE DIVISION so that it is compact, intelligible, and efficient. To see how this is accomplished, it is necessary to look at the syntactical organization of the PROCEDURE DIVISION.

All high-level programming languages employ some means of labelling instructions to accomplish logical branching. We can move control from one point in a program to another simply by using a branch instruction—usually a GO TO—followed by the label of the first instruction in the chain of instructions to be executed. In BASIC and FORTRAN, each instruction is numbered, and these numbers serve as the identifying labels. In COBOL it is not necessary to label each instruction. Instead, we organize instructions into functional sets called *paragraphs* and assign labels to the paragraphs.

Paragraph labels or names follow the usual naming convention of COBOL and must begin in AREA A and terminate with a period. In Figure 6-1, the PROCEDURE DIVISION is divided into functional paragraphs, each of which has a label assigned to it. Each paragraph may be thought of as a logical module of code designed to perform a specific task. READ-FILE, for example, contains all the instructions associated with the process of bringing a logical record into memory from which to extract data. PRINT-LINE contains the instructions necessary for formatting and printing the output line. PRINT-LINE ends with an unconditional branch to READ-FILE so that the next logical record can be processed. The first instruction in READ-FILE is the READ statement for fetching the next record. The program will keep looping back to that instruction until all records from the input file have been read. When the end of the file is reached, control branches to the CLOSE-FILES paragraph, where the final processing steps occur. (This last branch, by the way, is a conditional branch.) The program is terminated by the STOP RUN command, which, though located at the physical end of the program in this instance, need not always be located there.

Even though the paragraphs in Figure 6-1 might represent distinct functional modules, the description of the structure of the PROCEDURE DIVISION is not yet complete: there is still the matter of what the proponents of structured COBOL call top-down design. *Top-down design*

Procedure Division

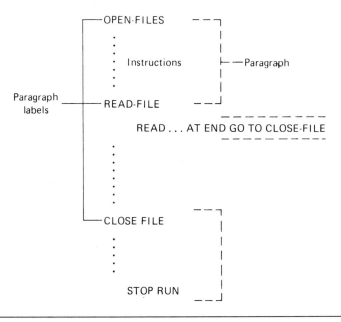

Figure 6-1
Structure of the PROCEDURE DIVISION

simply means that all functional modules are invoked at the beginning of the PROCEDURE DIVISION in the order needed to accomplish the processing task. In other words, the beginning paragraph embodies all the logic necessary to call the functional modules into play. This approach avoids the use of complex logical branching that may be difficult to follow. To implement top-down design, the following steps should be observed:

1. Break each processing function into a self-contained module of code.
2. Arrange the modules in the order that they are to be used.
3. Prefix each paragraph name with a sequential number. The numbers can be arbitrarily chosen, but they should be arranged in ascending order.
4. Use the PERFORM command to invoke the processing modules in their proper order.

The PERFORM command, which was discussed briefly in Chapter 2, is complicated in both syntax and usage, but we need not go into its more esoteric uses here. Two simple formats of the PERFORM command are

PERFORM   paragraph name.

and

PERFORM   paragraph name-1 THRU paragraph name-2.

In the first format, paragraph name is the module to be executed. All instructions listed under paragraph name are executed until another paragraph name is encountered, or, if there is no other paragraph name, until the last instruction in the program is executed. In the second format, paragraph name-1 is the first module to be executed, and paragraph name-2 is the last module to be executed. All instructions in all modules beginning with paragraph name-1 through and including paragraph name-2 are executed. With either format, after the PERFORM command is completed program control passes to the next instruction.

Figures 6–2 and 6–3 illustrate the above two formats of the PERFORM command.

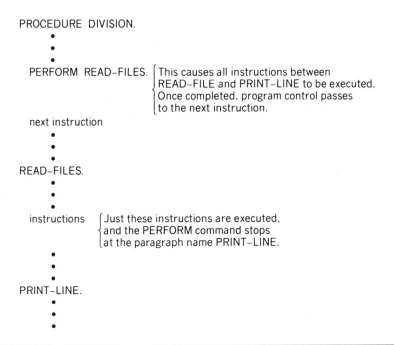

Figure 6–2
Simple PERFORM statement

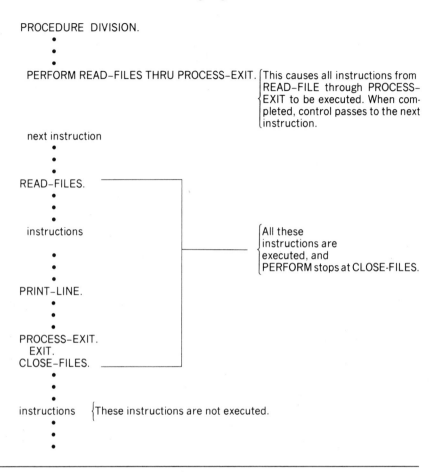

Figure 6-3
Simple PERFORM . . . THRU statement

Notice in Figure 6-3 the statement EXIT in the module called PRO-
CESS-EXIT. EXIT is normally used to conclude the PERFORM . . . THRU
scenario. However, it also provides the ability to escape from such a routine
at any point in the process. In either case, EXIT must be the only statement
in the named module or paragraph. Figure 6-4 brings together the ideas
we have discussed concerning top-down modular design.

Notice in the figure that each paragraph name begins with a three-
digit number, and the paragraphs are arranged in ascending sequence according to that number. We could have used four- or five-digit numbers had
we so desired, but for this simple illustration, three will suffice. The
numbers, so arranged, act much like addresses pointing a person reading

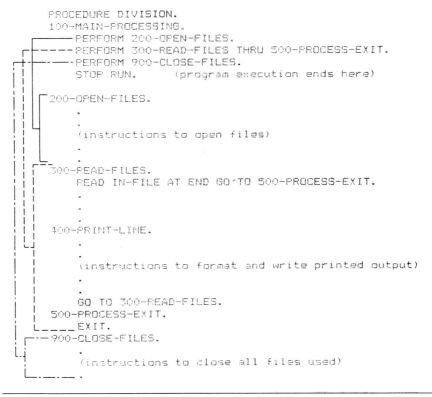

```
PROCEDURE DIVISION.
  100-MAIN-PROCESSING.
      PERFORM 200-OPEN-FILES.
      PERFORM 300-READ-FILES THRU 500-PROCESS-EXIT.
      PERFORM 900-CLOSE-FILES.
      STOP RUN.      (program execution ends here)

  200-OPEN-FILES.
      .
      .
      (instructions to open files)
      .
      .
  300-READ-FILES.
      READ IN-FILE AT END GO TO 500-PROCESS-EXIT.
      .
      .
      .
  400-PRINT-LINE.
      .
      .
      (instructions to format and write printed output)
      .
      .
      GO TO 300-READ-FILES.
  500-PROCESS-EXIT.
      EXIT.
  900-CLOSE-FILES.
      .
      (instructions to close all files used)
      .
```

Figure 6-4
Structured programming logic using top-down modular design

the program to the relative location of each processing module. The first paragraph, 100-MAIN-PROCESSING, contains the nucleus of the programming logic. A trained person reading through this paragraph can quickly discern the scope and extent of the processing logic and form a rough and ready index of the functional modules. The first PERFORM statement, whose scope is indicated by the solid line in the figure, opens the various files. The second PERFORM statement (scope given by dashed line) reads the input file and prints the output. This alternate reading and printing is repeated until the end of the input file is reached. Control is then passed to the EXIT statement, and the third PERFORM statement (scope given by dotted line) invokes the module to close the files. Control then passes to the next statement, STOP RUN, which terminates the program. The top-down module approach may seem a bit redundant in that even if the first paragraph (100-MAIN-PROCESSING) were eliminated, the program would still perform its designated task. Nonetheless, it does impose a discipline on the programmer that is definitely conducive to the formulation of tighter and more efficient program code.

This concludes our discussion of the structure of the PROCEDURE DIVISION. We next look at some COBOL commands, or verbs, that deal with file manipulation.

OPENING AND CLOSING FILES

Before a file may be accessed by a program, it must be opened. To *open* a file simply means to render it accessible to a computer process. The COBOL command for opening a file is, not surprisingly, the verb OPEN, and its general format is

OPEN $\left\{ \begin{matrix} \text{INPUT} \\ \text{I--O} \\ \text{OUTPUT} \\ \text{EXTEND} \end{matrix} \right\}$ file name . . .

The file name is the same name used in the SELECT and FD statements.

INPUT is used for opening disk files for reading only. Records cannot be written to a file that has been opened in INPUT mode. More than one IN-PUT file can be opened in the same OPEN statement.

Example 6-1   The following command opens two files named DSKFILE1 and DSKFILE2 for input.

```
OPEN INPUT DSKFILE1, DSKFILE2.
```

OUTPUT is used to open files for writing only. Disk files, printer files, and communication files can be opened for output. Records on a file opened in OUTPUT mode cannot be read. Here again, multiple files can be named in the same OPEN statement.

Example 6-2

```
OPEN OUTPUT DSKFILE, PRNTFILE.
```

opens a disk file named DSKFILE and a printer file named PRNTFILE for output.

I–O is used for opening random-access disk files for either reading or writing. In I–O mode, records can be read from the file, written to the file, or deleted from it. I–O cannot, however, be used to create new disk files: these must be opened in OUTPUT mode. Use of I-O is somewhat complicated, and we shall not need it until Chapter 11, on file organization.

EXTEND is used for opening a file to which records are to be appended. It is similar in function to OUTPUT, except that the records are written at the end of the existing file. Here, a word of caution regarding OUTPUT is in order. When used in conjunction with disk files, OUTPUT will create *new files only*. If an existing disk file is opened in OUTPUT mode, it will be destroyed. To add or write new records to an existing disk file, either I-O or EXTEND must be used, depending on the organization of the file. The distinction between I-O and EXTEND will be made clear in Chapter 11.

Just as we can name multiple files in the same OPEN statement, we can also specify multiple modes in the same statement.

Example 6-3 The following code opens one disk file named DSKFILE1 for input, another disk file named DSKFILE2 for output, and a print file named PRNTFILE, also for output, using a single OPEN statement:

```
OPEN INPUT DSKFILE1, OUTPUT DSKFILE2, PRNTFILE.
```

Every file opened in a COBOL program should be closed before the program is terminated. Closing a file simply means that the file is no longer in use and hence can be accessed by another program. If you fail to close the files of your program, the operating system will close them for you after the program terminates. The COBOL command for closing a file is, again not surprisingly, the verb CLOSE, and its general format is

```
CLOSE {file name [WITH LOCK] } . . . .
```

If the file is closed with the LOCK phrase, it cannot be opened again in the same program. It can, however, be opened by other programs later. If the LOCK phrase is not used, as is usual, the closed file can be reopened in the same program. As with the OPEN statement, multiple files can be named in the same CLOSE statement.

Example 6-4 The code

```
CLOSE DSKFILE1, DSKFILE2, PRNTFILE.
```

closes the files mentioned in Example 6-3.

FILE INPUT OPERATIONS

Once a file is opened, either data from that file can be brought into the program, or data from the program can be exported and written to that file, depending on the mode of conveyance specified in the OPEN statement.

These functions are together referred to as *file input and output operations*. Bringing data from a file into the program is called *reading,* and exporting data from a program to a file is called *writing.* In COBOL, the convention is to read files and to write records. For reading files we use the READ statement, and for writing records to files we use the WRITE statement, as expected.

The READ statement has several different formats, depending on the organization of the file being read. For now, we shall deal only with sequential disk files; the general format of the READ statement for such files is

```
READ  filename [INTO  dataname]
      [AT END  imperative statement].
```

where file name is the same as the name used in the SELECT and FD statements. In order to understand the optional features shown in brackets, let us examine how the READ statement works for sequential files in COBOL.

Sequential files are files whose records are stored in the order in which they have been entered. Each time a READ instruction is issued, the next record in sequence in the file is brought into memory. The process usually continues until all the records have been read and the end of the file is reached. There are two things to consider: what happens to a record that is read into memory, and what happens when the end of the file is reached.

A record read into memory is deposited in the record input area in the FILE SECTION of the program specified by the 01 label entry following the FD statement of the file being read. It may be useful, however, to have that record brought into an alternative area within the WORKING–STORAGE SECTION of the DATA DIVISION. To bring it in there, the INTO phrase of the READ statement is employed, and the data name following INTO designates the area to be used in the WORKING–STORAGE SECTION. Figure 6–5 illustrates the operation (p. 110).

If the file is read until the end of file is reached, the program logic must indicate some action. This action is specified by the imperative statement following the AT END phrase. The imperative statement is usually a command, such as a GO TO, that causes the program to exit from the READ loop. The idea is illustrated in Figure 6–4, where the imperative statement following the AT END phrase of the READ command directs program control to the EXIT statement. The AT END phrase should always be used when reading a sequential file.

FORMATTING DATA FOR OUTPUT

The principal product of any computer program is data that is output. The data can be a number of displays on a video screen, a disk file, or, most frequently, a printed report. In any event, it must be formatted in a manner

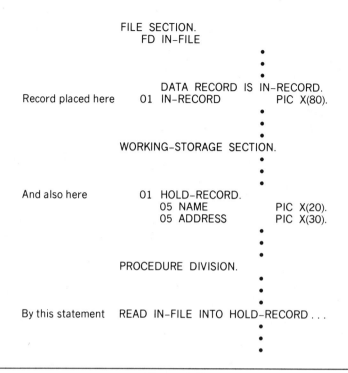

Figure 6-5
The READ . . . INTO statement

suitable for reproduction on the particular output medium. To accomplish the formatting task, COBOL employs a combination of techniques, notably the PICTURE clause explained earlier and the MOVE statement, which we will now introduce.

Data formatting is done in a simple manner in the PROCEDURE DIVISION. The data is ingested by the program into main storage and deposited in an input area. The data fields are then moved either one at a time or en masse to an output area during which the desired formatting takes place. The resultant product is then transferred to the output medium.

The details of data formatting start with individual fields. Often, it is necessary to move data from one field to another in main storage. These fields are sometimes called *operands*. The *source field* is the field from which the data is being moved, and the *target field* is the field to which the data is being moved. The source field may be an elementary item, a literal, or a figurative constant. The target field is an elementary item that has a PICTURE clause suitably defined to reflect the desired format of the data received. When data is moved from one elementary item to another, the source and target fields may have identical PICTURE clauses. More often, the PICTURE clause of the target field is an edited item containing appropriate edit symbols. To accomplish the movement of data, COBOL uses the MOVE statement, whose general format is

MOVE operand-1 TO operand-2 [operand-3 . . .]

Operand-1 is the name of the source field, if the latter is a defined data item; a constant value, if it is a literal; or one of the figurative constants. Operand-2, operand-3, etc. are the names of the receiving or target fields. Notice that we can have multiple receiving fields in a single MOVE statement. After the move is completed, the target operands will contain the contents of the source operand, and the contents of the source or sending operand remain the same.

In general, there are two types of moves: numeric and alphanumeric. In a numeric move, the source field is a numeric item or numeric constant, and the receiving field is a numeric or edited item. In an alphanumeric move, the source field is an alphanumeric item or nonnumeric literal, and the target field is an alphanumeric item. The two types of moves should seldom be mixed (with an exception—see below). Table 6-1 shows the permissible moves for data fields.

Example 6-5 Let source and target fields be as follows.

Source field: 05   QUANTITY-IN   PIC 9(5).
Target field: 05   QUANTITY-OUT   PIC 9(5).

Table 6-1
Examples of moving data from a sending field to a receiving field

| Sending field | | Receiving field | |
PIC	Contents	PIC	Contents
9(5)	12345	9(5)	12345
9(5)	12345	9(3)	345
9(5)	12345	9(7)	0012345
9(5)V99	12345ᴧ67	9(3)V9	345ᴧ6
9(5)V99	12345ᴧ67	9(7)V999	0012345ᴧ670
X(5)	'12345'	X(5)	'12345'
X(5)	' '	X(3)	'123'
X(5)	' '	X(7)	'12345bb'
9(5)	12345	X(5)	12345
9(5)		X(3)	123
9(5)		X(7)	12345bb
X(5)	12345	9(5)	illegal move

Then

      MOVE QUANTITY-IN TO QUANTITY-OUT.

will move numeric data from the source field to the target field.

Example 6-6   Let the target field be given by

      05 REC-COUNTER   PIC 9(5) COMP-3.

where REC-COUNTER is a record-counter field. Then

      MOVE 0 TO REC-COUNTER.

or

      MOVE ZEROS TO REC-COUNTER.

will initialize REC-COUNTER with zeros using a constant value and a figurative constant, respectively.

Example 6-7   Let source and target fields be as follows.

Source field: 10 NAME-IN   PIC X(20).
Target field: 10 NAME-OUT   PIC X(20).

Then

      MOVE NAME-IN TO NAME-OUT.

will move alphanumeric data from the source field to the target field.

Example 6-8   Let the target field be given by

      15 MESSAGE-OUT   PIC X(17).

Then

      MOVE "THIS IS A MESSAGE" TO MESSAGE-OUT.

will move the literal in quotes to the alphanumeric field, MESSAGE-OUT.

Example 6-9   Let

      05 MESSAGE-1   PIC X(10).
      05 MESSAGE-2   PIC X(15).
      05 MESSAGE-3   PIC X(20).

be target fields. Then

      MOVE SPACES TO MESSAGE-1, MESSAGE-2, MESSAGE-3.

will initialize the above alphanumeric fields with blanks.

     In Examples 6-5 through 6-9, the source fields are the same length as the target fields. What happens when they are of different lengths? The

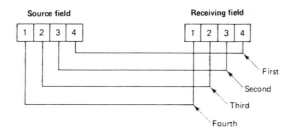

Figure 6-6
Right justification of numeric data
in moving from the source field to the receiving field

answer depends on the type of fields involved. First, consider the case of numeric fields.

Whenever numeric data is moved from one field to another, the digits are moved from the right, one at a time. First, the rightmost digit of the source field is placed into the rightmost digit of the receiving field. Then the next rightmost digit of the target field is placed into the next rightmost digit of the target field. The process continues until all the digits of the source field have been moved to the target field. The digits are then said to be *right justified*. (See Figure 6-6.)

Notice in Figure 6-6 that both fields are the same length, and there are no problems. If the receiving field were shorter than the sending field, then the leftmost digits of the sending field would be truncated, and the wrong number would be stored there. The situation is shown in Example 6-7.

Example 6-10   Let the sending and receiving fields be as follows.

Sending field: FIELDA
Receiving field: FIELDB

Then

    MOVE FIELDA TO FIELDB.

will move numeric data from FIELDA to FIELDB, and the contents of the two fields before and after the move are as follows.

	Sending field	Receiving field
Before move:	92341	0000
After move:	92341	2341

If the sending field is shorter than the receiving field, then the remaining leftmost digits of the receiving field are padded with zeros, and the correct number is stored in the receiving field.

Example 6-11   Let the sending and receiving fields be as follows.

Sending field: FIELDA
Receiving field: FIELDB

Then

    MOVE FIELDA TO FIELDB.

will move numeric data from FIELDA to FIELDB, and the contents of the two fields before and after the move will be as follows.

	Sending field	Receiving field
Before move:	7613	960120
After move:	7613	007613

Notice in Example 6-10 that the leftmost digit of the sending field is truncated, and in Example 6-11 that the two leftmost digits of the receiving field are filled with zeros, following the move. When moving numeric data, it is always a good practice to make sure that the source and target fields are the same length in terms of the number of decimal digits they are specified to contain.

When alphanumeric data is moved from one field to another, the characters are moved from the left, one byte at a time. This is called left justification. First, the leftmost character of the sending field is placed into the leftmost byte of the receiving field. Then the second leftmost character of the sending field is placed into the second leftmost byte of the target field. The process continues until all the characters of the source field have been moved to the target field. The characters are then said to be *left justified*. (See Figure 6-7.)

As with numeric data, truncation or padding occurs when the fields are of different lengths. If the sending field is longer than the receiving field, then the rightmost characters of the sending field are truncated (see Example 6-12); and if the receiving field is longer than the sending field, then the rightmost characters of the receiving field are padded with blanks. (See Example 6-13.)

Example 6-12   Let the sending and receiving fields be as follows.

Sending field: FIELDA
Receiving field: FIELDB

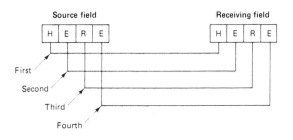

Figure 6-7
Left justification of alphanumeric data
in moving from the source field to the receiving field

Then

MOVE FIELDA TO FIELDB.

will move alphanumeric data from FIELDA to FIELDB, and the contents of the two fields before and after the move are as follows.

	Sending field	Receiving field
Before move:	TROUBLE	XYZZb
After move:	TROUBLE	TROUB

Example 6-13   Let the sending and receiving fields be as follows.

Sending field: FIELDA
Receiving field: FIELDB

Then

MOVE FIELDA TO FIELDB.

will move alphanumeric data from FIELDA to FIELDB, and the contents of the two fields before and after the move are as follows.

	Sending field	Receiving field
Before move:	GOOD	ZZ6+9K
After move:	GOOD	GOODbb

Notice in Example 6-12 that the rightmost characters of the sending field are truncated, and in Example 6-10 that the two rightmost characters of the receiving field are filled with blanks, following the move. Here again, when moving alphanumeric data, it is a good practice to make sure that the source and target fields are the same length in bytes.

In alphanumeric moves in which the sending field is a figurative constant, the number of characters moved is governed by the length of the receiving field. That is, the character represented by the figurative constant is replicated across the entire length of the receiving field.

Example 6-14   Let the sending and receiving fields be as follows.

Receiving field: FIELDB

Then

        MOVE SPACES TO FIELDB.

will move the figurative constant SPACES to FIELDB, and the contents of the field before and after the move will be as follows.

	Sending field	Receiving field
Before move:	b	XYZ2S+
After move:	b	bbbbbb

Example 6-15   Let the sending and receiving fields be as follows.

Receiving field: FIELDB

Then

        MOVE ZEROS TO FIELDB.

will move the figurative constant ZEROS to FIELDB, and the contents of the field before and after the move are as follows.

	Sending field	Receiving field
Before move:	0	23 X 7A
After move:	0	00000

Before doing arithmetic computations involving external decimal (display) numeric items, it is often desirable to convert these items to packed decimal form. The packing process can be accomplished by the MOVE statement as shown in Example 6-16.

Example 6-16   Let the source and target fields be as follows.

```
Source field:   10 QUANTITY-IN     PIC 9(7).
Target field:   10 QUANTITY-OUT    PIC S9(4) COMP-3.
```

Then

    MOVE QUANTITY-IN TO QUANTITY-OUT.

will pack a seven-digit numeric display item from the source field into a seven-digit signed packed decimal field (the target field). The contents of the two fields before and after the move are as follows.

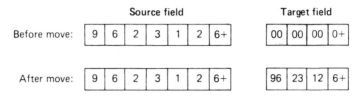

Conversely, it is often desirable to convert a packed decimal item to the display form. This unpacking process can also be accomplished by the MOVE statement.

Example 6-17   Let the source and target fields be as follows.

Source field: 10 QUANTITY-WORK   PIC S9(4) COMP-3.
Target field: 10 QUANTITY-OUT   PIC 9(7).

Then

    MOVE QUANTITY-WORK TO QUANTITY-OUT.

will unpack a seven-digit, numeric signed packed decimal item from the source field into a seven-digit numeric display item in the target field. The contents of the two fields before and after the move are as follows.

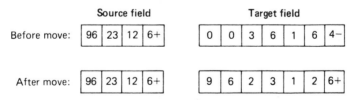

The MOVE statement is necessary for formatting numeric fields from printed output. Numeric items are moved to report items that are part of the group item defining the output print format. In Chapter 4 we explained what report items are and how they are used to represent properly punctuated numeric information. Now all you need to know is how to get the appropriate numeric values into those fields.

Example 6-18   Let the source and target fields be as follows.

Source field: 10 PAYMENT-IN   PIC S9(5)V99.
Target field: 10 PAYMENT-OUT   PIC $$$,$$$.99.

Then

        MOVE PAYMENT-IN TO PAYMENT-OUT.

will move a signed packed numeric item in the source field to a report item in the target field. The contents of the two fields before and after the move, together with the printed output, are as follows.

	Source field	Target field
Before move:	02 | 46 | 15 | 9+	Y | b | X | b | 2 | 1 | 7 | 4 | 0 | b
After move:	02 | 46 | 15 | 9+	b | 0 | 2 | , | 4 | 6 | 1 | . | 5 | 9

Finally, we shall consider moving group items. Any one group may be moved to any other; however, when such a move is made, a straight character transfer is effected, and no changes are made to the data regardless of the PICTURE clauses of the elementary items that compose the receiving group item. If, for example, the receiving group items contain report items, they will not reflect the edit changes characterized by their PICTURE clauses. This is not to say that moves from group items to group items should not be done—just that they are not advantageous unless (1) the sending item is a figurative constant (e.g., SPACES, ZEROS, LOW-VALUES, HIGH-VALUES) and the receiving items consist of all alphanumeric fields having X's in their PICTURE clauses; (2) the group items have identical formats; or (3) the sending item is a group item and the receiving item is an elementary alphanumeric field.

Knowing how to do group moves is important for building data records. Examples 6-16 through 6-19 show some permissible group moves.

Example 6-19   Let the target group items be given by

        01 PRINT-LINE
            05 NAME   PIC X(30).
            05 FILLER   PIC X(10).
            05 ADDRESS   PIC X(30).
            05 FILLER   PIC X(10).
            05 ID-NUMBER PIC 9(5).

Then

        MOVE SPACES TO PRINT-LINE.

will blank out the output record PRINT-LINE.

Example 6-20   Let the source group items be given by

```
01  IN-REC.
    05  NAME       PIC  X(30).
    05  ADDRESS    PIC  X(30).
    05  CITY       PIC  X(10).
    05  STATE      PIC  XX.
    05  ZIP-CODE   PIC  9(5).
    05  PHONE      PIC  X(12).
```

and the target group item be

```
01  OUT-REC        PIC  X(89)
```

Then

```
MOVE  IN-REC  TO  OUT-REC.
```

will move the contents of IN-REC from a given disk file to OUT-REC on another disk file.

Example 6-21   Let the source group items be given by

```
01  PRINT-LINE.
    05  FILLER     PIC  X(5)  VALUE  SPACES.
    05  NAME-OUT   PIC  X(30).
    05  FILLER     PIC  X(5)  VALUE  SPACES.
    05  ADDR-OUT   PIC  X(30).
    05  FILLER     PIC  X(5)  VALUE  SPACES.
    05  CITY-OUT   PIC  X(10).
    05  FILLER     PIC  XX  VALUE  ", ".
    05  STATE-OUT  PIC  XX.
    05  ZIP-OUT    PIC  Z(6).
    05  FILLER     PIC  X(5)  VALUE  SPACES.
    05  PHONE-OUT  PIC  X(12).
```

and the target group item be

```
01  PRINT-REC      PIC  X(133).
```

Then

```
MOVE  PRINT-LINE  TO  PRINT-REC.
```

will move the formatted print line PRINT-LINE to PRINT-REC.

Example 6-21 showed how a formatted print line is moved to the record output area. Example 6-22 shows how the print line itself is built.

Example 6-22   Suppose that we wish to print, from a disk, a name and address record having the format depicted by IN-REC in Example 6-20. We desire the printed output to have the format shown in Example 6-21. Then the print image, PRINT-LINE, is built simply by moving the data elements from IN-REC to PRINT-LINE as follows:

```
MOVE NAME      TO NAME-OUT.
MOVE ADDRESS   TO ADDR-OUT.
MOVE CITY      TO CITY-OUT.
MOVE STATE     TO STATE-OUT.
MOVE ZIP-CODE  TO ZIP-OUT.
MOVE PHONE     TO PHONE-OUT.
```

If IN-REC contained the record

```
DESANCTIS, PAUL
6577 SHERWOOD RD
PHILADELPHIA
PA
19151
215-867-9999
```

Then, based on the format of PRINT-LINE, the output record would appear as follows on the printed report:

DESANCTIS, PAUL 6577 SHERWOOD RD PHILADELPHIA PA 19151 215-867-9999

FILE OUTPUT OPERATIONS

After a record is formatted for output, it is usually sent to the output device. To output records to a disk or print file, the WRITE command is used. The general format of the WRITE command is

```
WRITE record name [FROM data name]
[ｌAFTER  ｌ ADVANCING ｌoperand LINE (S)ｌ]
[ｌBEFOREｌ ADVANCING ｌPAGEｌ]

      [AT ｌEND-OF-PAGEｌ imperative statement]
          ｌEOP           ｌ
```

Only the first line of the format is needed for writing records to storage media. The remaining phrases are used for writing lines of output on a printer. Accordingly, we shall first consider writing records to storage media, particularly disk files.

Unlike the READ command, the WRITE command uses the same format for all file organizations. The record name is the name of the 01-level record item following the FD statement of the output file.

Before it is written to a file, a record must be *constructed*—that is, all of its fields must be filled with appropriate data. This is usually accomplished by building the output record in the WORKING-STORAGE SECTION of the program and then moving it to the output area in the FILE SECTION, i.e., the 01-level record item following the FD statement. The actual move is accomplished by the FROM phrase of the WRITE statement, as shown in Figure 6-8.

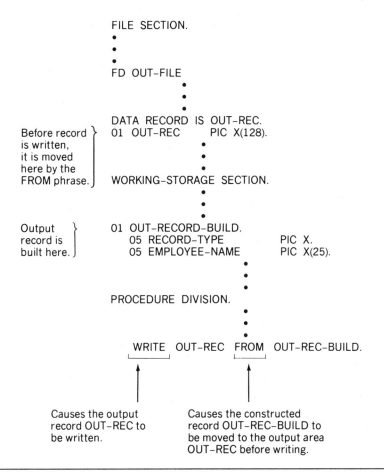

Figure 6-8
The WRITE statement, with FROM phrase

WRITE . . . FROM has the effect of MOVE followed by WRITE. For example, the WRITE statement in Figure 6-8 could have been replaced with

```
MOVE OUT-REC-BUILD TO OUT-REC,
WRITE OUT-REC.
```

and the end result would have been the same.

Now let us see how all the features of the WRITE command are employed to write lines of output on a printer. In general, there are three main tasks involved in printing a report, particularly one consisting of numerous records:

1. Printing the report headings.
2. Printing the records.
3. Skipping to a new page when the current page is filled.

The report often consists of many pages, each with the same general format. At the beginning of the printing process, the report headings, if there are any, are placed at the top. Records are then fed to the printer, one at a time, and printed until the first page is full. When the first page is full, a form feed instruction is issued, causing the printer to advance to the top of the next page, at which time the headings are again printed and the entire process is repeated until all the detail records have been printed.

Figure 6-9 shows the general page format of a report. Each page consists of a top margin; the page body, which is the printable portion of the page; and a bottom margin. The page body is in turn comprised of a heading, a detail area, and a footing, and usually includes left and right vertical margins. The detail area normally consists of printed records, or detail lines, which may be single, double, or triple spaced according to the requirements of the report or the whim of the programmer. The page format of a computer report is not unlike the format of a typewritten page, and COBOL provides the tools for setting margins, spacing detail lines, etc. Just keep in mind that none of these page-formatting tasks are done automatically; they must be programmed.

Vertical margins on the page are set by placing blank FILLERs of appropriate size at either end of the internally defined print-line format. Top and bottom margins, and footing, if used, are set by specifying values in the corresponding entries of the LINAGE clause of the WRITE statement. The number of lines constituting the page body is also specified in this clause.

Causing the printer to advance one or more lines during the printing process is called *line feed.* Causing the printer to advance to the top of a new page is called *form feed.* Line feed is accomplished by using the ADVANCING option in the WRITE statement, and form feed is accomplished by using the END-OF-PAGE option in conjunction with the LINAGE clause of the FD entry for the print file. Example 6-23 shows how the FD statement is set up for a printed report.

Example 6-23 Suppose that you want to print a report with a page body consisting of 56 lines, no footing, and top and bottom margins of 5 lines each. The FD statement would then have the form

```
FD  PRINT-FILE
    LABEL RECORDS ARE OMITTED
    RECORD CONTAINS 132 CHARACTERS
    DATA RECORD IS PRINT-REC
    LINAGE 56 TOP 5 BOTTOM 5.
01  PRINT-REC               PIC X(132).
```

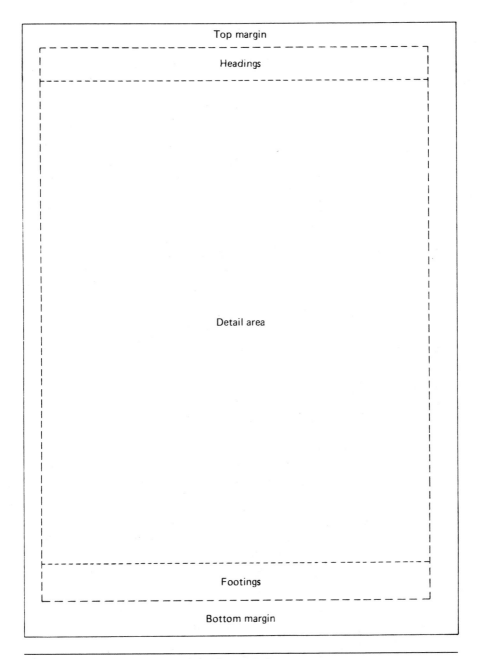

Figure 6-9
General page format of a computer report

The LINAGE clause specifies the general format of each page of the report. All that remains is to print the records, provide for spacing between lines, and skip to a new page when the current page is full. Example 6–24 addresses this task.

Example 6–24   Suppose that you desire to print each detail line of Example 6–21, leaving a blank line between records. (That is, the report is to be double spaced.) The WRITE statement would then have the form

```
WRITE PRINT-REC FROM PRINT-LINE
   AFTER ADVANCING 2 LINES,
   AT EOP PERFORM HEADING-ROUTINE.
```

Note that the detail lines are printed *after* the skipping occurs. That is, the carriage advances the page two horizontal positions before the line is printed. The imperative statement following the keyword EOP is a PER-FORM command that executes a paragraph, HEADING-ROUTINE, that contains logic for issuing a form feed and printing the report heading.

When generating a continuous report, we usually want to print the heading on each new page. This is normally accomplished by executing a stand-alone paragraph containing the WRITE statement necessary to produce the desired heading.

Example 6–25   The code

```
HEADING-ROUTINE.
   WRITE PRINT-REC FROM HEADING-1
   AFTER ADVANCING PAGE.
WRITE PRINT-REC FROM HEADING-2
   AFTER ADVANCING 2 LINES.
```

will print a two-line report heading following a form-feed instruction. Notice that

1. The first WRITE statement occurs AFTER ADVANCING PAGE, which means that the printer is positioned to a new physical page before the first heading is printed.

2. The second heading, which is generated by the second WRITE statement, is double spaced as the result of the ADVANCING 2 LINES specification.

3. The EOP option is not used since it is obviously not needed at the top of a new page.

The following summary brings together the numerous details we have presented regarding the steps necessary to produce printed output.

1. To set up the page format, it is necessary to use the LINAGE clause in the FD statement of printer files for the purpose of defining margins, page length, and footing area.

2. The logic for issuing a form-feed instruction and printing the report heading should be included as a separate routine that can be performed on condition that the current page is full.

3. All data formats destined for printing, such as heading and detail lines, must be moved to the output area first. The move is accomplished by using the WRITE . . . FROM option.

4. Spacing between printed lines is accomplished by using the AD-VANCING option of the WRITE statement.

5. Page overflow (skipping to a new physical page when the current one is full) is done by using the EOP or END-OF-PAGE option of the WRITE statement. Remember, however, that this option cannot be used unless a LINAGE clause has been specified in the printer's FD statement.

Example 6-26 presents the code for the report program of Chapter 5 in its entirety.

Example 6-26

```
IDENTIFICATION DIVISION.
PROGRAM-ID. STUDENTS.

ENVIRONMENT DIVISION.
INPUT-OUTPUT SECTION.
FILE-CONTROL.
     SELECT STUDENT-FILE ASSIGN TO DISK
        ORGANIZATION IS SEQUENTIAL
        FILE STATUS IS STUDENT-STATUS.

     SELECT PRINT-FILE ASSIGN TO PRINTER.

DATA DIVISION.
FILE SECTION.
FD   STUDENT-FILE
        LABEL RECORDS ARE STANDARD
        VALUE OF FILE-ID IS "B:STUDENTS.MST"
        RECORD CONTAINS 80 CHARACTERS
        DATA RECORD IS STUDENT-REC.
01   STUDENT-REC.
        05   STUDENT-NAME          PIC X(20).
        05   STUDENT-ADDRESS       PIC X(30).
        05   STUDENT-SSN           PIC 9(9).
        05   ADMISSION-DATE.
             10   ADMIT-MONTH      PIC 99.
             10   ADMIT-DAY        PIC 99.
             10   ADMIT-YEAR       PIC 99.
        05   CURRICULUM            PIC X(10).
        05   FILLER                PIC X(5).

FD   PRINT-FILE
        LABEL RECORDS ARE OMITTED
        RECORD CONTAINS 132 CHARACTERS
        LINAGE IS 56 TOP 5 BOTTOM 5
        DATA RECORD IS PRINT-REC.
01   PRINT-REC                     PIC X(132).
```

```
WORKING-STORAGE SECTION.
77  PAGE-NUMBER              PIC 9(3) COMP-3 VALUE ZERO.
77  STUDENT-COUNTER          PIC 9(5) COMP-3 VALUE ZERO.
77  STUDENT-STATUS           PIC 99 VALUE ZERO.

01  HEADING-1.
    05  FILLER               PIC X VALUE " ".
    05  FILLER               PIC X(6) VALUE "DATE: "
    05  REPORT-DATE.
        10  REPORT-MON           PIC ZZ.
        10  FILLER               PIC X VALUE "/".
        10  REPORT-DAY           PIC ZZ.
        10  FILLER               PIC X VALUE "/".
        10  REPORT-YR            PIC ZZ.
    05  FILLER               PIC X(30) VALUE SPACES.
    05  FILLER               PIC X(15) VALUE
            "STUDENT LISTING".
    05  FILLER               PIC X(30) VALUE SPACES.
    05  FILLER               PIC X(6) VALUE "PAGE: ".
    05  PAGE-OUT             PIC ZZZ.
    05  FILLER               PIC X(34) VALUE SPACES.

01  HEADING-2.
    05  FILLER               PIC X VALUE " ".
    05  FILLER               PIC X(4) VALUE "NAME"
    05  FILLER               PIC X(30) VALUE SPACES.
    05  FILLER               PIC X(7) VALUE "ADDRESS".
    05  FILLER               PIC X(30) VALUE SPACES.
    05  FILLER               PIC X(3) VALUE "SSN".
    05  FILLER               PIC X(10) VALUE SPACES.
    05  FILLER               PIC X(13) VALUE
            "DATE-ADMITTED".
    05  FILLER               PIC X(3) VALUE SPACES.
    05  FILLER               PIC X(10) VALUE
            "CURRICULUM".
    05  FILLER               PIC X(22) VALUE SPACES.

01  DETAIL-LINE.
    05  FILLER               PIC X VALUE " ".
    05  NAME-OUT             PIC X(20).
    05  FILLER               PIC X(14) VALUE SPACES.
    05  ADDRESS-OUT          PIC X(30).
    05  FILLER               PIC X(7) VALUE SPACES.
    05  SSN-OUT              PIC 9(9).
    05  FILLER               PIC X(6) VALUE SPACES.
    05  ADMIT-DATE-OUT.
        10  ADMIT-MON-OUT        PIC ZZ.
        10  FILLER               PIC X VALUE "/".
        10  ADMIT-DAY-OUT        PIC ZZ.
        10  FILLER               PIC X VALUE "/".
        10  ADMIT-YR-OUT         PIC ZZ.
    05  FILLER               PIC X(6) VALUE SPACES.
    05  CURRICULUM-OUT       PIC X(10).
    05  FILLER               PIC X(22) VALUE SPACES.

01  TOTAL-LINE.
    05  FILLER               PIC X VALUE " ".
    05  FILLER               PIC X(20) VALUE
            "NUMBER OF STUDENTS".
```

```
05  STUDENTS-OUT              PIC  Z,ZZ9.
05  FILLER                    PIC  X(30) VALUE  SPACES.
05  FILLER                    PIC  X(30) VALUE  SPACES.
05  FILLER                    PIC  X(30) VALUE  SPACES.
05  FILLER                    PIC  X(17) VALUE  SPACES.

PROCEDURE DIVISION.

100-MAIN-PROCESSING.
    PERFORM 200-OPEN-FILES.
    PERFORM 300-HEADING-RTN.
    PERFORM 400-READ-FILE THRU 400-PROCESS-EXIT.
    PERFORM 500-TOTAL-LINE.
    PERFORM 600-CLOSE-FILES.
    STOP RUN.

200-OPEN-FILES.
    OPEN INPUT STUDENT-FILE OUTPUT PRINT-FILE.

300-HEADING-RTN.
    ADD 1 TO PAGE-NUMBER GIVING PAGE-OUT.
    WRITE PRINT-REC FROM HEADING-1 AFTER ADVANCING PAGE.
    WRITE PRINT-REC FROM HEADING-2
        AFTER ADVANCING 2 LINES.

400-READ-FILE.
    READ STUDENT FILE AT END
        GO TO 400-PROCESS-EXIT.
    MOVE STUDENT-NAME TO NAME-OUT.
    MOVE STUDENT-ADDRESS TO ADDRESS-OUT.
    MOVE STUDENT-SSN TO SSN-OUT.
    MOVE ADMIT-MONTH TO ADMIT-MON-OUT.
    MOVE ADMIT-DAY TO ADMIT-DAY-OUT.
    MOVE ADMIT-YEAR TO ADMIT-YR-OUT.
    MOVE CURRICULUM TO CURRICULUM-OUT.
    ADD 1 TO STUDENT-COUNTER.
400-PRINT-LINE.
    WRITE PRINT-REC FROM DETAIL-LINE
        AFTER ADVANCING 2 LINES
        AT EOP PERFORM 300-HEADING-RTN.
    GO TO 400-READ-FILE.

400-PROCESS-EXIT.
    EXIT.

500-TOTAL-LINE.
    MOVE STUDENT-COUNTER TO STUDENTS-OUT.
    WRITE PRINT-REC FROM TOTAL-LINE AFTER
        ADVANCING 3 LINES.

600-CLOSE-FILES.
    CLOSE STUDENT-FILE, PRINT-FILE.
```

The above code has three commands that have not been discussed. Their functions are almost intuitively obvious, so we shall discuss them only cursorily here. The ADD statement increments the two counters in the program by one. The GO TO statement merely transfers control back to the start of the record-processing section at 400–READ–FILE. The STOP RUN command terminates the program and returns control to the operating system. It is the last executable statement in any COBOL program.

It is recommended that you set up a test file of data and code, compile, and run the above program on your computer. By comparing the program code with the printed results and tracing each result to the source code that produced it, you will, in a manner more direct than any purely theoretical discussion can impart, greatly improve your understanding of COBOL.

CREATING A DISK FILE TO ACCESS DATA FILES

The previous section suggested that you code, compile, and run the program of Example 6–23. In order for that program to function properly, a student data file that has several data elements for each student must be available. The program shown here will enable the reader to create such a data file and halt processing at any time. You can either create the input data to this program or use the sample data file from Appendix C. The program will display what you must enter for each student, and accept whatever is typed. It is suggested that you use the sample data file rather than create input data so that you may compare the results you obtain with those presented in Appendix C.

Before beginning the program, you should understand the syntax and function of the COBOL COPY verb. The COPY verb allows the programmer to place any COBOL source code in a diskette file that is separate from the actual source code of the running program. This diskette file will be retrieved from your default disk at compilation time and inserted in your source program in the appropriate place. The advantage of this approach is that it eliminates the need to retype source code that is the same from program to program. Once it has been entered and tested, you know that there will be no problems with the code per se. This use of the COPY statement refutes the argument that any COBOL program uses a lot of overhead in coding the same code over and over again. Unfortunately, most critics of COBOL are not well versed in its capabilities.

The format of the COPY statement is

```
COPY  filename.fileext
```

The statement must begin in AREA B and may be placed anywhere in your COBOL source code. Remember that the file must be on your default diskette and must meet all the rules of COBOL for spacing, variable names, etc.

Now boot your system and enter the data descriptions for the data record required for this program and the program on pp. 126–127 using

EDLIN or any other text processor. Listed below are the data descriptions from p. 125.

```
01  STUDENT-REC.
    05  STUDENT-NAME         PIC  X(20).
    05  STUDENT-ADDRESS      PIC  X(30).
    05  STUDENT-SSN          PIC  9(9)
    05  ADMISSION-DATE.
        10  ADMIT-MONTH      PIC  99.
        10  ADMIT-DAY        PIC  99.
        10  ADMIT-YEAR       PIC  99.
    05  CURRICULUM           PIC  X(10).
    05  FILLER               PIC  X(5).
```

Be sure to give the name .COB as the file extension when you create the source-copy file. One possibility for the entire file name is STDREC.COB, for *student record COBOL.*

The following is the program to enter the data into a file. It will enable you to enter all data from Appendix D into the data file. You may copy the program as is or change it to enhance its performance.

```
IDENTIFICATION DIVISION.
PROGRAM-ID. CREATE.

ENVIRONMENT DIVISION.
INPUT-OUTPUT SECTION.
FILE-CONTROL.
    SELECT STUDENT-FILE ASSIGN TO DISK
        ORGANIZATION IS SEQUENTIAL
        FILE STATUS IS STUDENT-STATUS.
DATA DIVISION.
FILE SECTION.
FD  STUDENT-FILE
    LABEL RECORDS ARE STANDARD
    VALUE OF FILE-ID IS "B:STUDENTS.MST"
    RECORD CONTAINS 80 CHARACTERS
    DATA RECORD IS STUDENT-REC.

    COPY STDREC.COB

WORKING-STORAGE SECTION

01  WORK-AREA.
    05  REPLY                   PIC X VALUE " ".

PROCEDURE DIVISION.
BEGINNING-OF-PROGRAM.
    DISPLAY "IS THIS A RESTART? ENTER Y OR N"
    ACCEPT REPLY.
    IF REPLY = "Y" PERFORM RESTART-OPEN, ELSE
    PERFORM FIRST-OPEN.
MAIN-LOOP-PROCESSING.
    DISPLAY "IN ORDER TO STOP THIS PROGRAM ENTER QUIT"
    DISPLAY "FOR STUDENT NAME"
```

```
        DISPLAY "ENTER STUDENT NAME"
        ACCEPT STUDENT-NAME.
        IF STUDENT-NAME = "QUIT" GO TO CLOSE-FILE.
        DISPLAY "ENTER STUDENT ADDRESS"
        ACCEPT STUDENT-ADDRESS.
        DISPLAY "ENTER STUDENT SOCIAL SECURITY NUMBER"
        ACCEPT STUDENT-SSN.
        DISPLAY "ENTER ADMISSION DATE IN MMDDYY FORMAT"
        ACCEPT ADMISSION-DATE.
        DISPLAY "ENTER CURRICULUM"
        ACCEPT CURRICULUM.
        WRITE STUDENT-RECORD.
        GO TO MAIN-LOOP-PROCESSING.
    MAIN-LOOP-EXIT. EXIT.
    FIRST-OPEN.
        OPEN OUTPUT STUDENT-FILE.
    FIRST-EXIT. EXIT.
    RESTART-OPEN.
        OPEN EXTEND STUDENT-FILE.
    RESTART-EXIT. EXIT.
    CLOSE-FILE.
        CLOSE STUDENT-FILE.
        STOP RUN.
```

The compilation listing for the above program is presented in appendix B.

REVIEW QUESTIONS

1. Define program processing logic. What factors determine the way processing logic is set up in a program?

2. What is meant by top-down modular design? List the advantages of modular program code.

3. Define a COBOL paragraph. Which of the following are invalid paragraph names?

   100-READ   HERE   COMPUTE+IT   5000

4. What is meant by structured program design? Identify the steps necessary to implement top-down structured design.

5. How is the PERFORM command used to effect structured top-down design? How is the simple PERFORM different from the PERFORM . . . THRU command?

6. Write a statement for opening an indexed disk file, DISKFILE, that is to be accessed for input and output. Write a statement for closing three files—INFILE, OUTFILE, and WORKFILE.

7. Code two ways for reading records from the sequential file, IN-FILE, and depositing the record, IN-REC, into a hold area called HOLD-REC.

8. What is the function of the MOVE statement? How many types of moves are there? Identify them.

9. Code two ways for writing a record, OUT–REC, to a disk file from a work area called WORK–REC.

10. Write the FD statement for a print file, PRINTOUT, that will produce the following page characteristics: the body will have 50 lines, no footing, a top margin of 6 lines, and a bottom margin of 10 lines. The page width is 132 characters.

PROBLEMS

1. Alter the program from problem 1, Chapter 4, to produce on the printed report the literal "MALE" if the input field SEX contains an "M" or the literal "FEMALE" if the input field SEX contains an "F." Be sure to adjust your print layout to accommodate this change.

   Example: input field contains F—printed report shows FEMALE.

2. Write a program to read and list a stock portfolio file to determine whether some of the stocks should be sold. When the purchase price of the stock is less than the current price do not print any indicator. If the purchase price is greater than the current price print the indicator "SELL" on the detail line. Between each detail line skip a line and include in your heading lines the current date and page numbers.

Input layout

Position		Field name
21–24		# OF SHARES
27–31	(999V99)	CURRENT PRICE
35–39	(999V99)	PURCHASE PRICE
42–49		NAME OF STOCK

Output layout

Position		Field name
20–27		NAME OF STOCK
36–43	($$$$$.$$)	PURCHASE PRICE
46–52	($$$$$.$$)	CURRENT PRICE
58–61		# OF SHARES
70–74		SELL INDICATOR

7

SCREEN INPUT/OUTPUT OPERATIONS

In the last section of Chapter 6, a quick and easy program for building a test file on disk was presented. This presentation was mainly for the sake of expediency, so that you could create the data needed to run the program at the end of the previous section. Ordinarily, however, you will not use that kind of program to enter data into your system. For microcomputers, COBOL provides a very effective set of tools that enable the user to enter data through formats that can be displayed directly on the video screen. These formats, called *screen formats,* can be designed to meet each individual user's needs. Screen formats are defined in the DATA DIVISION and invoked in the PROCEDURE DIVISION. The screen formatting capability of COBOL for micros is perhaps one of its most useful and powerful features. In fact, it is this feature that distinguishes this species of COBOL from those used on large computer systems.

VIDEO DISPLAY TERMINALS

Screen formatting is done on a *video display terminal* (VDT), or *video monitor.* Video monitors come in an assortment of styles. There are monochrome video monitors for the more conservative person and polychrome monitors for the individual who prefers color. The monochrome variety comes mainly in white, green, or, lately, yellow phosphor against a dark background. At present, green phosphor seems to be the industry standard. In addition, monitors feature various levels of resolution, which is simply a measure of visual sharpness. The higher the resolution of a particular style of screen, the sharper is its picture. These attributes in combination can serve many different needs. While a high-resolution color monitor is nice for producing eye-catching special effects, a medium-resolution monochrome monitor is certainly adequate, and in fact preferred, for most business data processing needs. Accordingly, our discussion will focus on monitors of the latter type.

Much of what a monitor can do in terms of presenting data is a function of the programming language being used. Data can be presented in graphic (picture) form, in textual form, or in some combination of the two. COBOL permits only the presentation of textual-form data, but the clever programmer can use this form in very interesting ways to simulate graphics in a limited manner. In what follows, we shall concern ourselves only with the textual form of data presentation.

THE DISPLAY SCREEN

The display screen may be thought of as a matrix or grid having 24 horizontal lines and 80 vertical columns. (The number of lines and columns varies with the system; the 24 by 80 grid, however, is the most common.) If we multiply the number of lines by the number of columns, we obtain 1960, which is the total number of print positions on the screen. Each print position, or *screen cell,* as it is also called, may be thought of as made up of a small rectangular block capable of holding one character of text.

Any position on the screen can be referenced by combining its line and column numbers, thereby forming a pair of coordinates of the type (*x, y*), where *x* is the line number and *y* is the column number. For example, the pair of coordinates (3,10) would identify the print position occupying line 3 and column 10 on the screen. Like bytes of memory, individual screen cells may be strung together to form fields for holding text or data. To identify these fields, it is necessary to specify the coordinates of the first screen cell and the length of the string that occupies the field. In COBOL, strings may have up to 80 characters.

Figure 7-1 shows the upper left quadrant of a VDT screen pro-

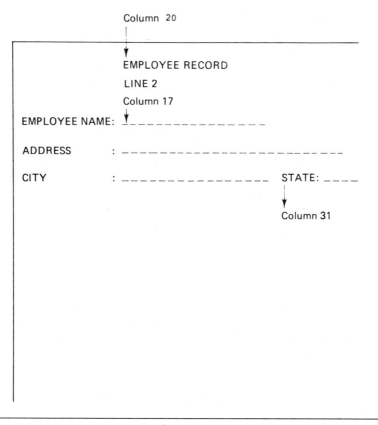

Figure 7-1
Video screen format for employee record

grammed for data entry. The text string EMPLOYEE RECORD is the name of the screen format to be filled in with data. Its starting coordinates are (2,20) and its length is 15. On line 5 is the first data field to be entered. It begins with the literal, EMPLOYEE NAME:, whose starting coordinates are (5,5) and whose length is 13, including the colon. The actual data field for recording the employee's name (denoted by the dashes) has starting coordinates (5,17) and length 20, so that it can accept a name of up to 20 characters in length. The address line begins at screen location (7,5) with the literal ADDRESS   :, of length 13, including the embedded blanks and the colon. It is followed by the data field for recording the employee's address, which starts at screen location (7,20) and is 25 characters long. We leave it to your deductive capacity to identify the coordinates and lengths of the city and state fields. As you can see, formatting the VDT screen is largely an exercise in coordinate geometry.

The whole idea in formatting a screen is to design it so that it looks exactly like a preprinted fill-in-the-blanks type form familiar to us all. To assist in that task, a blank screen format chart like that shown in Figure 7–2 (p. 138) is often used for planning and design. The chart consists of a grid with 24 lines and 80 columns to emulate the VDT screen. Use of such a chart, though not necessary, is highly recommended, as it can greatly facilitate the screen-design process by helping the programmer achieve the most aesthetic effects and revealing design problems that could lead to serious programming difficulties later. Using the chart is simply a matter of blocking out the data in the manner that best suits your needs or fancy.

Figure 7–3 (p. 139) shows a completed format chart for a data-entry screen designed to collect data for the record shown in Example 4–11. Notice that the chart looks much like an ordinary form. The constant fields EMPLOYEE NUMBER, EMPLOYEE NAME, etc. prompt for a particular piece of data. The data fields themselves are represented by 9's and x's, which indicate the type of data that is to be entered and the length of the entry. These 9's and x's will not, of course, appear on the programmed screen. They are used in the chart to show the characteristics of the data fields they represent, which helps in writing the program code to generate the screen format on the VDT.

Once the screen has been programmed, it may be used for both data entry and data retrieval. In the case of data entry—i.e., collecting data for writing to a disk file—when the screen format appears, only the constant literals are shown and the data fields are blank. It is your job to fill in those blank fields with the appropriate data so that it can be recorded in the file. In the case of data retrieval, when the screen format appears, not only do the constant literals show up, but also the data fields are filled in with the proper values from the data file being queried. Here, it is the program's job to fill in the data fields. All you have to do is watch.

Building a screen format on the VDT involves coding in both the DATA

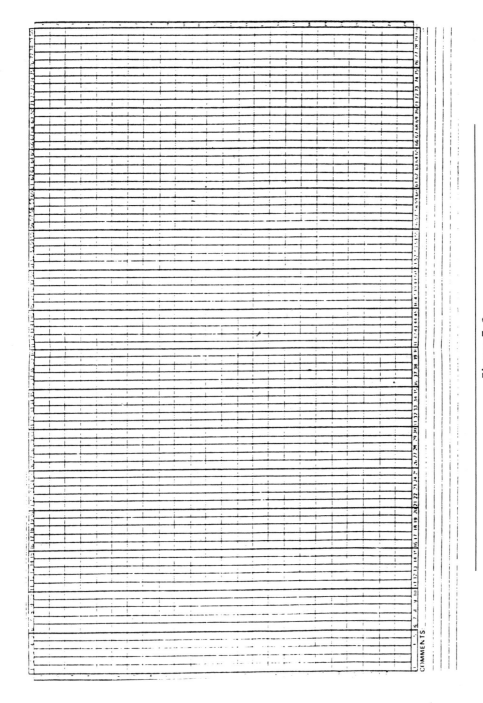

Figure 7-2
Screen format chart

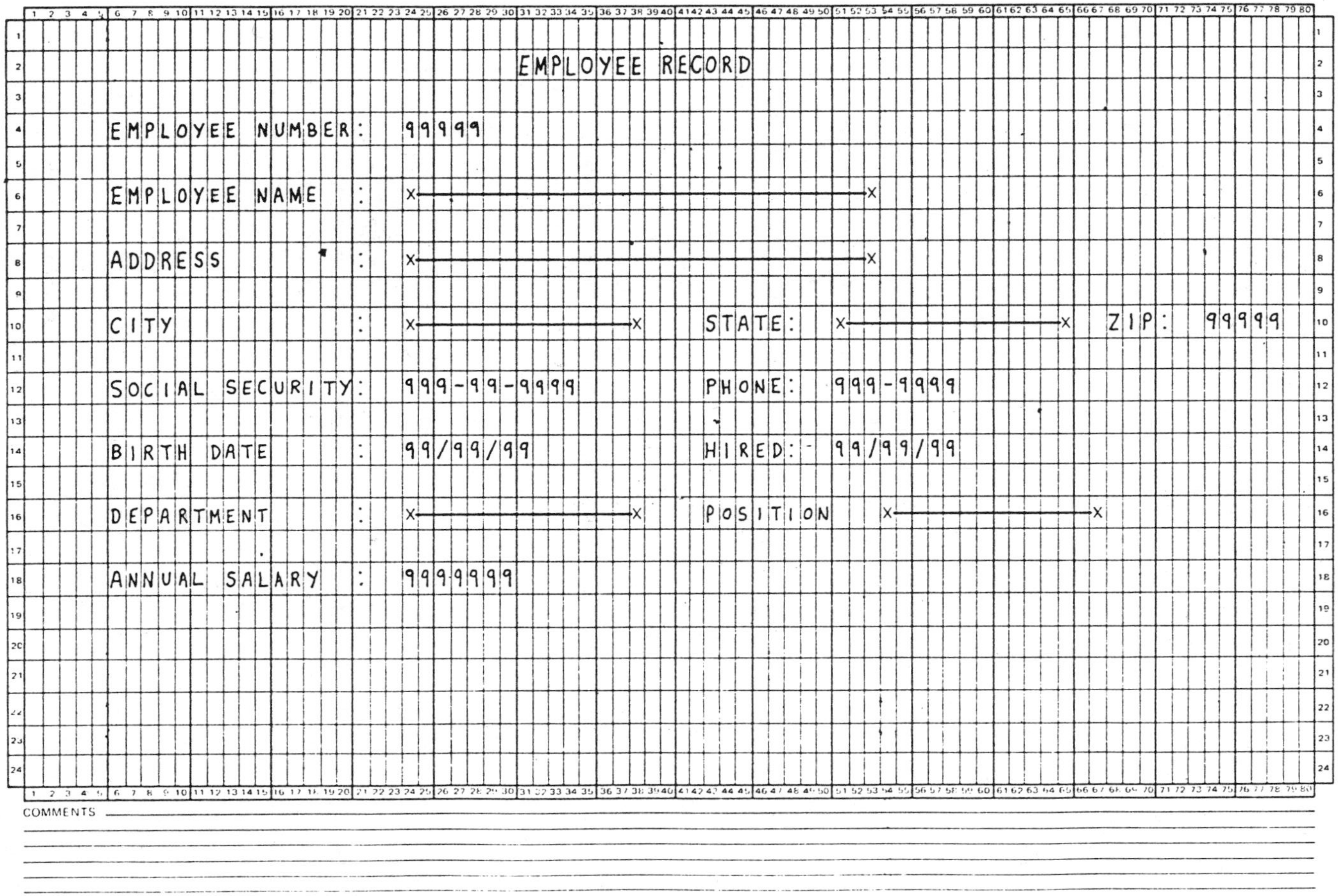

Figure 7-3
Screen format chart

139

DIVISION and the PROCEDURE DIVISION. The actual format of the screen is defined in the SCREEN SECTION of the DATA DIVISION, whereas the manipulations involved in ingesting data from or disgorging data to the screen are done in the PROCEDURE DIVISION. The interplay between the DATA DIVISION and the PROCEDURE DIVISION is much the same as that shown in Chapter 6 in the discussion of how files and printed reports are built. (See pp. 120-128.) We shall begin with a discussion of the SCREEN SECTION.

THE SCREEN SECTION

The SCREEN SECTION, which physically is the last section of the DATA DIVISION, is a little more complex than its sister sections. In addition to its intricate function as communicator between the VDT screen and the data fields within the program, the SCREEN SECTION incorporates numerous syntactical features that add to its complexity. For example, it has language elements that enable you to sound bells, highlight and underline video text, transmit messages that blink like Christmas tree lights, and, if you have a color monitor, create the most lavish display of psychedelic visual effects in an array of 15 different colors. In the interests of simplicity, we shall focus here only on the more practical of these aspects of the SCREEN SECTION, deferring until the end of the chapter a discussion of its more esoteric properties. Let us begin with the SCREEN SECTION's primary role as communications medium between you—the user—and your program.

As mentioned previously, the SCREEN SECTION enables you to construct screen formats in any number of ways for the purpose of collecting and displaying data in an organized, effective, and aesthetically pleasing manner. When data is collected through the use of a screen format, it is deposited in data fields defined in one of the other three sections of the DATA DIVISION, not the SCREEN SECTION. In like manner, when data is displayed through a screen format, it is obtained from data fields defined elsewhere in the DATA DIVISION, again, not in the SCREEN SECTION. The SCREEN SECTION, then, is not a repository of data in the COBOL program; rather, it is a conduit between the data fields defined elsewhere in the DATA DIVISION and the external world as represented by the screen format that appears on the VDT. This point, which may seem trivial now, will be seen to be important a little later.

The SCREEN SECTION is organized in much the same manner as are the FILE SECTION and the WORKING-STORAGE SECTION. There are two types of screen items: elementary items and group items. *Elementary items* are used to describe individual data-entry or display fields in the screen format. *Group items* name a collection of elementary items, which may be referenced by a single statement in the PROCEDURE DIVISION. Normally, a screen format consists of one group item that comprises all the elementary items that constitute the format. This group item, also called a GROUP SCREEN–DESCRIPTION ENTRY, has the general format

```
level-number    screen-name    [AUTO]    [SECURE]
    [REQUIRED]    [FULL].
```

where both the level-number and the screen-name conform to COBOL conventions—that is, the level-number must be an integer in the range 01 through 49, and the screen name must consist of 30 or fewer characters, etc. Although not required, it is advisable to use the level number 01 for all group screen-description entries. This practice will prevent confusion, especially if the program contains multiple screen formats, as do many programs. We shall defer explanation of the parameters following screen-name in the above format until after we have introduced the format of the elementary screen item.

The elementary screen item establishes the link between the data field entered or displayed on the VDT screen and its related field as defined in the FILE SECTION, WORKING–STORAGE SECTION, or LINKAGE SECTION of the DATA DIVISION. This item also contains all the parameters for defining the many features or attributes, as they are often called. The general format of an elementary screen item is

```
level-number[screen-name]
    [BLANK SCREEN]
    [LINE NUMBER IS [PLUS] integer-1]
    [COLUMN NUMBER IS [PLUS] integer-2]
    [BLANK LINE]
    *[BELL]
    *[UNDERLINE]
    *[REVERSE–VIDEO]
    *[HIGHLIGHT]
    *[BLINK]
     *[FOREGROUND–COLOR  integer-3]
     *[BACKGROUND–COLOR  integer-4]
     [VALUE IS literal-1]
     [PICTURE I PIC IS picture-string
          {[FROM literal 2/ identifier-1]
          [TO identifier-2] /
          [USING identifier-3]} ]
    *[BLANK WHEN ZERO]
    *[JUSTIFIED I JUST RIGHT]
    [AUTO]
    [SECURE]
    [REQUIRED]
    [FULL].
```

As is evident, saying that the SCREEN SECTION is somewhat complex is not overstating the case. Fortunately, not all of the clauses listed above are needed to make effective use of screen formats. Those most often used are the BLANK SCREEN, LINE, COLUMN, VALUE, and PICTURE clauses. Those marked with an asterisk produce attributes that may be nice, but are not necessary. The following comments apply to elementary screen items in general:

1. In a group item, it is necessary to use a screen-name; in an elementary item a screen-name need not be specified. If one is specified, however, it must conform to the COBOL naming conventions.
2. The level-numbers for elementary items must be greater than the level-number of the group item under which they appear.
3. The clauses associated with either group or elementary screen items may be listed in any order. No elementary screen item may exceed 80 characters in length.
4. Each item, along with its associated clauses, must be terminated by a period.

We next consider each particular elementary screen item, beginning with the last four since they apply to group screen-description entry as well. If specified with the group item, the AUTO, SECURE, REQUIRED, and FULL clauses behave as if they were also specified for every elementary item subordinate to the group screen item. In other words, if you desire to have any of these clauses apply to every elementary item attached to a group screen item, then code it at the group level; otherwise, code it at the elementary item to which you wish it to apply. In any event, these four clauses apply to data entry only.

AUTO is used for cursor control. When specified, it causes the cursor to skip automatically to the next data-entry field after the entry of the current field is completed. When the last data-entry field is input, the data typed into all the fields of the screen format are transferred to the internal data items specified in the respective PICTURE clauses.

SECURE provides feedback to the user. As data entered into a screen format is accepted by the processor, the characters typed in initially are echoed to indicate that they have been received successfully. This echoing happens rather quickly, so that if your eyes should shift from the screen momentarily, you might miss it. The SECURE clause suppresses the echoing of the input character and displays an asterisk instead, for each character accepted. That way, if you should turn away from the screen for a moment or two, then when you look at it again, you will see a string of asterisks in the data fields, indicating that the data has been accepted successfully.

REQUIRED checks whether data has been entered in a particular field. More often than not, the data fields in an entry screen format are mandatory, meaning that some nonblank data must be typed into them. The REQUIRED clause prevents you from skipping over mandatory fields during the data-entry process.

FULL means the same as REQUIRED, with the additional stipulation that the entire length of the field—that is, every input position—must be filled. This feature is a useful control for entering fields such as zip codes, which require an entry in each character position.

In order to understand the remaining clauses in the format of an elementary screen item, it is necessary to consider how screen formats are dealt with in the PROCEDURE DIVISION of a program since they have some bearing on the clauses used in the SCREEN SECTION. Although screen formats are defined in the SCREEN SECTION, they are transmitted to the VDT screen by COBOL commands coded in the PROCEDURE DIVISION. In other words, nothing happens to a screen format until an appropriate command is issued in the PROCEDURE DIVISION. Two such commands deal with formats: DISPLAY and ACCEPT. Their general formats are

    DISPLAY screen-name

and

    ACCEPT screen-name

respectively, where screen-name is the name specified in the group screen-description entry.

DISPLAY causes the screen format, screen-name, to be displayed on the VDT screen, together with the origin fields as specified in the PICTURE clauses of the elementary items. ACCEPT, on the other hand, causes data keyed into an entry screen format to be transmitted to the destination fields as defined by the PICTURE clauses of the elementary items. (This will become clearer when we consider the PICTURE clause below.) Use of these commands is determined by the particular processing task to be performed. For retrieving a record from a file simply for viewing on the VDT screen, just the DISPLAY command is needed. For entering data into the system via a screen format, both commands must be used. First the blank format must be transmitted to the screen using the DISPLAY command, and then the filled-in fields must be transmitted to the processing program using the ACCEPT command. Examples of these processes will be presented shortly.

Some of the clauses associated with screen formats affect the DISPLAY command, some affect the ACCEPT command, and some affect both. For example, the AUTO, SECURE, REQUIRED, and FULL clauses already discussed do not affect the DISPLAY statement since they are used within the context of data entry only. In our discussion that follows of the remaining clauses, we shall note whether and how these clauses affect the DISPLAY and ACCEPT commands. (Remember, the remaining clauses can be used only at the elementary level.)

BLANK SCREEN is used to clear the screen of any residual displays before the screen format is transmitted. While not required, it is advisable to include this entry as the first elementary entry in every screen format when you desire to print on a clear screen. BLANK SCREEN is to your VDT screen what an eraser is to a blackboard.

LINE NUMBER and COLUMN NUMBER work in conjunction to mark the starting screen coordinates for the elementary item in question. In other words, the cursor is positioned at a point on the screen specified by the LINE NUMBER and COLUMN NUMBER. For an 01-level group screen-description entry, the cursor is automatically positioned at line 1, column 1. The PLUS option in these clauses will position the cursor at the point specified by the value of integer plus the coordinate of the present cursor position. If LINE or COLUMN is not specified, then the cursor is placed at the next line or column, i.e., LINE PLUS 1 or COLUMN PLUS 1.

BLANK LINE erases the current line of the screen from the current cursor position to the end of the line. The cursor does not move from its current position.

VALUE IS literal-1 prints the exact contents of the literal on the screen, starting at the point specified by the line and column number when the DISPLAY screen-name command is issued. The literal must be bounded by quotes and cannot be a figurative constant. Contrary to its usage in the WORKING–STORAGE SECTION, this clause may not be used as part of a PICTURE clause. The ACCEPT statement ignores VALUE IS. VALUE IS is very useful for producing constant text on a screen format.

The PICTURE clause, which dominates the elementary item in the SCREEN SECTION just as it does in the other sections of the DATA DIVISION, specifies the format in which data is presented on the screen, except that it cannot be used with the VALUE IS clause. PICTURE or PIC is coded according to the rules that govern its use in WORKING–STORAGE; however, in the SCREEN SECTION its role is determined by the data conveyance mode. During execution of a DISPLAY statement, the contents of a FROM or USING field are moved to the item with the specified PICTURE clause in the screen format before being displayed on the VDT monitor. During execution of an ACCEPT statement, the data entered into the item described by the PICTURE clause is moved to the specified TO or USING field. In this manner, data is shifted between the SCREEN SECTION and its sister sections. No MOVE statements are required in the PROCEDURE DIVISION to effect the transfer of data, as they are required for transferring data between record description entries and print formats. (See Chapter 6.) There must, however, always be a tie between the screen item and a data item in either the FILE SECTION, the WORKING–STORAGE SEC-TION, or the LINKAGE SECTION.

Example 7-1   The following code consists of the screen-description entry and other DATA DIVISION and PROCEDURE DIVISION considerations for a data-entry screen format for inputting a user password and name:

```
DATA DIVISION.
                          •
                          •
                          •
WORKING-STORAGE SECTION.
01  TERMINAL-INPUT.
    05  USER-PASSWORD                 PIC  X(4).
    05  USER-NAME                     PIC  X(20).
                          •
                          •
                          •
SCREEN SECTION.
01  PASSWORD-SCREEN AUTO REQUIRED.
    05  BLANK SCREEN.
    05  LINE 2 COLUMN 5 VALUE
        "ENTER YOUR PASSWORD  = = >  ".
    05  LINE 2 COLUMN 29 PIC X(4)
        TO USER-PASSWORD.
    05  LINE 4 COLUMN 5 VALUE
        "ENTER YOUR NAME  = = >".
    05  LINE 4 COLUMN 29  PIC X(20)
        TO USER-NAME.
                          •
                          •
                          •
PROCEDURE DIVISION.
SIGN-ON ROUTINE.
    DISPLAY PASSWORD-SCREEN.
    ACCEPT PASSWORD-SCREEN.
                          •
                          •
                          •
```

In Example 7–1, a password and name are input through a screen for-mat. The format itself is simple, consisting of only two captioned lines. On line 2 of the screen, the prompt for entering the password appears. The cursor will be positioned one space to the right of the arrow (column 29 on the screen) and will remain there until data is entered. Up to four characters can be entered into this field, as denoted by the PIC X(4) clause. The password field and the name field that follows are mandatory, as specified by the REQUIRED parameter at the 01-level group screen-description entry. Once data has been entered in the password field, the cursor will skip automatically to line 4, column 29 of the screen, where it will be positioned to the right of the arrow following the name prompt. This automatic advancing of the cursor is the result of AUTO having been coded at the 01 level. When the return key is pressed after the name has been typed in, the system will accept the input data, transferring each item to its respective target field in the WORKING–STORAGE SECTION—the password entered to USER–PASSWORD, and the name to USER–NAME.

Example 7–2 is more sophisticated.

Example 7-2   Suppose that we wish to develop a program to collect data for the record layout shown in Example 4–11 using the screen format in Figure 7–3. All data fields shown on the format require an entry. In addition, we would like to verify each field as it is transferred to the processor. The ingested data fields are to be deposited directly into the internally defined data record. The code for this program is as follows:

```
                         •
                         •
                         •
DATA DIVISION.
FILE SECTION.
FD EMPLOYEE-FILE
                         •
                         •
                         •
        DATA RECORD IS EMPLOYEE-RECORD.
01  EMPLOYEE-RECORD.
      05  EMPLOYEE-NUMBER                 PIC 9(5).
      05  EMPLOYEE-NAME                   PIC X(30).
      05  ADDRESS                         PIC X(30).
      05  CITY                            PIC X(15).
      05  STATE                           PIC X(15).
      05  ZIP-CODE                        PIC 9(5).
      05  SOC-SEC-NUMBER                  PIC X(11).
      05  PHONE-NUMBER                    PIC X(8).
      05  BIRTH-DATE.
          10  BIRTH-MONTH                 PIC 99.
          10  FILLER                      PIC X.
          10  BIRTH-DAY                   PIC 99.
          10  FILLER                      PIC X.
          10  BIRTH-YEAR                  PIC 99.
      05  DATE-HIRED.
          10  MONTH-HIRED                 PIC 99.
          10  FILLER                      PIC X.
          10  DAY-HIRED.                  PIC 99.
          10  FILLER                      PIC X.
          10  YEAR-HIRED                  PIC 99.
      05  DEPARTMENT                      PIC X(15).
      05  POSITION                        PIC X(15).
      05  ANNUAL-SALARY                   PIC 9(7).
      05  FILLER                          PIC X(28).
                         •
                         •
                         •
SCREEN SECTION.
01  EMPLOYEE-SCREEN AUTO REQUIRED SECURE.
```

```
05  BLANK SCREEN.
05  LINE 2 COLUMN 31  VALUE
    "EMPLOYEE RECORD".
05  LINE 4 COLUMN 6 VALUE
    "EMPLOYEE NUMBER:    ".
05  LINE 4 COLUMN 24 PIC 9(5)
    USING EMPLOYEE-NUMBER.
05  LINE 6 COLUMN 6  VALUE
    "EMPLOYEE NAME: ".
05  LINE 6 COLUMN 24 PIC X(30)
    USING EMPLOYEE-NAME.
05  LINE 8 COLUMN 6  VALUE
    "ADDRESS      : ".
05  LINE 8 COLUMN 24 PIC X(30)
    USING ADDRESS.
05  LINE 10 COLUMN 6  VALUE
    "CITY          : ".
05  LINE 10 COLUMN 24 PIC X(15)
    USING CITY.
05  LINE 10 COLUMN 43  VALUE
    "STATE: ".
05  LINE 10 COLUMN 15 PIC X(15)
    USING STATE.
05  LINE 10 COLUMN 68  VALUE
    "ZIP: ".
05  LINE 10 COLUMN 74 PIC 9(5)
    USING ZIP-CODE.
05  LINE 12 COLUMN 6  VALUE
    "SOCIAL SECURITY :   ".
05  LINE 12 COLUMN 24 PIC X(11)
    USING SOC-SEC-NUMBER.
05  LINE 12 COLUMN 43  VALUE
    "PHONE: ".
05  LINE 12 COLUMN 51 PIC X(8)
    USING PHONE-NUMBER.
05  LINE 14 COLUMN 6 VALUE
    "BIRTH-DATE     : ".
05  LINE 14 COLUMN 24 PIC X(8)
    USING BIRTH-DATE.
05  LINE 14 COLUMN 43  VALUE
    "HIRED: ".
05  LINE 14 COLUMN 51 PIC X(8)
    USING DATE-HIRED.
05  LINE 16 COLUMN 6  VALUE
    "DEPARTMENT   :   ".
05  LINE 16 COLUMN 24 PIC X(30)
    USING DEPARTMENT.
05  LINE 16 COLUMN 43  VALUE
    "POSITION: ".
05  LINE 16 COLUMN 54 PIC X(15)
    USING DEPARTMENT.
05  LINE 18 COLUMN 6 VALUE
    "ANNUAL SALARY  : ".
05  LINE 18 COLUMN 24 PIC 9(7)
    USING ANNUAL-SALARY.
                    •
                    •
                    •
```

```
PROCEDURE DIVISION.
                          •
                          •
                          •
DATA-ENTRY-ROUTINE.
    MOVE SPACES TO EMPLOYEE-RECORD.
    DISPLAY EMPLOYEE-SCREEN.
    ACCEPT EMPLOYEE-SCREEN.
```

Notice in Example 7–2 that the USING option is employed in the PIC-TURE clause of the screen data items. This was done to enable the screen format to serve as both a data collection and data retrieval mechanism. In other words, we can use this screen for outputting data from or inputting data to a file. The USING option has the effect of the FROM option in the DISPLAY statement and the TO option in the ACCEPT statement. Dual-purpose screen formats of this kind can save you much toil.

Chapter 7 closes with an explanation of those elementary screen-item clauses that produce special effects.

BLANK LINE clears the current line from the current cursor position to the end. The cursor does not move.

BELL is used in conjunction with the ACCEPT EMPLOYEE–SCREEN statement. It sounds the system's speaker when the system is ready to ac-cept a data field from the screen format. BELL has no effect on output fields and is ignored by the DISPLAY screen-name statement. BELL is useful for waking up any terminal operator who is prone to falling asleep on the job.

HIGHLIGHT displays data fields on the screen in high intensity. It is useful for emphasizing significant data items.

BLINK, as its name implies, causes data items displayed on the screen to blink. Frequent and indiscriminant use of this feature has been known to produce dizziness in otherwise healthy computer users.

REVERSE–VIDEO inverts the colors appearing on the screen. The background becomes phosphorescent, and the foreground becomes dark. On the monochrome video display that uses green phosphor, the effect is dark characters on a field of bright green, producing a strain on the eyes. It is difficult to think of a practical business use for this feature.

UNDERLINE does exactly as it says, placing a line under a data item displayed on the screen. It is useful for emphasizing information that is sig-nificant. This feature is available only on the monochrome display and is ig-nored by the color display.

FOREGROUND–COLOR and BACKGROUND–COLOR are available only for color VDTs and systems equipped with graphics adapters. Consult your manufacturer's literature for details concerning the use of this feature.

BLANK WHEN ZERO is used for numeric display items, causing items with a value of zero to appear as blanks on the screen. It is used to suppress the printing of nonsignificant numeric fields.

JUSTIFIED is used for aligning operator-entered data with the right boundary of a data field. Normally, data is entered into a screen item from left to right. The JUSTIFIED clause causes the item entered to be shifted to the right, space permitting, and to be stored in such a manner that the rightmost character is aligned with the right margin of the receiving field. This feature is desirable for use with numeric data.

The last two clauses—BLANK WHEN ZERO and JUSTIFIED—may be used in the PICTURE of elementary items in the FILE SECTION, WORK-ING–STORAGE SECTION, and LINKAGE SECTION.

The SCREEN SECTION is a powerful feature that lends itself nicely to microcomputer applications. Once you learn to use it, you will find it indispensable.

REVIEW QUESTIONS

1. Describe the role of the SCREEN SECTION in the COBOL program. How is this section organized?

2. Explain the function of each of the following parameters in the screen descriptor:

   AUTO   SECURE   REQUIRED   FULL

3. Describe how the data items defined in the SCREEN SECTION are related to their corresponding data fields defined in the other sections of the DATA DIVISION.

4. How are the data elements defined on the screen received into the program? How are the data elements within the program sent to the screen?

5. What are the functions of LINE NUMBER and COLUMN NUMBER in the elementary screen items? How are the PICTURE and USING clauses used? What does the PLUS option do?

6. May the same screen descriptor be used for both input forms and output displays? Explain.

7. Code a screen descriptor for receiving data entries into the student record described in the program model at the end of the last chapter.

PROBLEMS

1. Design a screen layout using the first 10 lines to accept records which will be used to perform file maintenance on the employee file. File maintenance is the adding, removing, and changing of records. In order to change or remove any record, remember that the record must exist. Your assignment is to accept your transactions from the keyboard, to edit each field for correctness, and to write a record to an output file entitled "EMPTRN.DAT." The layout of the output file is:

Position	Field
1–3	ID NUMBER
4	INDICATOR
	A = ADD
	C = CHANGE
	R = REMOVE
5	CHANGE INDICATOR
	(used only if position 4 is C)
	N = NAME CHANGE
	R = RATE CHANGE
	J = SKILL INDICATOR
6–25	NEW INFORMATION

2. Develop a program to retrieve a record from the stock file. This program will use the query-response method of prompting the operator for tasks. You will develop your own screen design using the entire screen to request a transaction from the operator, test to ensure that data has been entered, search your input file for the correct record using the field NAME OF STOCK and, if the record is found, display that record. If the record does not exist, display the appropriate message to inform the operator that the record does not exist.

    The input record format is:

Position	Field name
21–24	# OF SHARES
27–31 (999V99)	CURRENT PRICE
35–39 (999V99)	PURCHASE PRICE
42–49	NAME OF STOCK

8

ARITHMETIC OPERATIONS

Much of what a program does consists in deriving computed results from numeric data and in making logical decisions based on the values of various data fields. Unlike FORTRAN, BASIC, and other algorithmic languages that feature a compact, algebra-like notation for performing arithmetic computations, COBOL makes use of the English-language computational verbs ADD, SUBTRACT, MULTIPLY, DIVIDE, and COMPUTE for executing arithmetic operations. This convention leads to somewhat cumbersome syntactical structures for effecting mathematical computations, especially if they involve any degree of complexity. However, for performing the ordinary computations found in the bulk of business applications, the syntax of COBOL works acceptably. On the other hand, the COBOL syntax used for logical operations is much like that found in other high-level computer languages. It relies mainly on the IF . . . THEN . . . ELSE construct, which should be familiar to anyone who has programmed in BASIC.

ARITHMETIC STATEMENTS

All arithmetic statements involve a recipient field, where the computed result is stored, and one or more operands that contribute to the result. These statements also provide mechanisms for rounding results and checking for errors during the computation. For example, consider the statement

```
ADD 1 TO REC-COUNTER
    ON SIZE ERROR DISPLAY "EXCEEDED 999 LIMIT".
```

In this statement, a numeric field, REC-COUNTER, with a PIC 999 clause associated with it, is repeatedly incremented by the numerical constant 1. Should REC-COUNTER be incremented to the point where its value exceeds the largest value permitted by its PICTURE clause, 999, the ON SIZE ERROR option will be invoked, causing the overflow message to be printed. We shall see other uses of this error-detection feature shortly. But first it is necessary to discuss each arithmetic statement in detail. We shall begin with the ADD statement.

The ADD statement is used to form the sum of two or more numeric values. Its general format is

```
ADD {numeric constant . . . }
    {data name-1}
{TO}              data-name-n [ROUNDED]
{GIVING}
        [ON SIZE ERROR imperative statement]
```

The values immediately following ADD may be signed constants or defined numeric data fields, both of which are called *summands*. Next is the required TO or GIVING option, followed by a single sum. If the TO option is used, the values of all the numeric operands preceding it are added to the value contained in the data field following it. When the GIVING option is used, at least two numeric operands must be included between ADD and GIVING. The values of the summands are added, and the result is placed in the data name following the GIVING option. In contrast to the case of the TO option, the summands are not added to the value of the data-name following the option. In other words, with the TO option, the value of the data field that follows the term is one of the summands contributing to the sum. With the GIVING option, any value in the data field following the term is ignored and replaced by the value of the computed sum. The TO and GIVING options are mutually exclusive and hence may not be used concurrently. The target of the TO option may be any display, packed, or binary item defined in the DATA DIVISION; the target of the GIVING option may be any of those that are valid for the TO option, as well as numeric report items. The GIVING option, then, has the effect of MOVEing the computed result to an edit field.

Example 8-1   The code

```
TENS-COUNTER PIC 000.
ADD 10 TO TENS-COUNTER.
```

adds a constant to a display numeric item. The value of TENS-COUNTER before addition is 50; the value after addition is 60.

Example 8-2   To add several numeric fields to form a sum, and to place the sum in a report item, the code

```
05   TOTAL-CREDITS        PIC S9(5)V99        Comp-3.
05   TOTAL-DEBITS         PIC S9(5)V99        Comp-3.
05   TOTAL-ADJUSTMENTS    PIC ZZZ,ZZZ.99CR.
```

```
ADD TOTAL-CREDITS TOTAL-DEBITS GIVING TOTAL-ADJUSTMENTS
```

may be used. The values of the fields before and after addition are:

Field	Value before addition	Value after addition
TOTAL-CREDITS	+73428.96	+73428.96
TOTAL-DEBITS	−12261.37	−12261.37
TOTAL ADJUSTMENTS	Immaterial	$6,167.59 CR

The following points are noteworthy:

1. One of the summands, TOTAL-DEBITS, contains a negative value. The ADD statement treats signed numbers the same way they are

treated in ordinary algebra: when numbers with different signs are added, (a) all positive summands are added; (b) all negative summands are added; (c) the absolute difference between the two intermediate sums is taken; and (d) the result is tagged with the sign of the sum that is larger.

2. The result, TOTAL–ADJUSTMENTS, is edited and ready for printing. The GIVING option functions the same way for each of the SUBTRACT, MULTIPLY, and DIVIDE commands.

3. Although only two summands are shown, the ADD . . . GIVING combination can employ up to any number of summands. This is a small but useful fact to know.

Whenever computations involve fractional amounts, the convention of most programming languages is to truncate the result by lopping off the nonsignificant decimal places. Suppose, for example, we are adding the numbers 12.31 and 10.26, and we wish to retain just one decimal place in the result. Carried out to two decimal places, the sum is 22.57; however, if we simply drop the digit 7, our result is 22.5, with one decimal place of precision, as desired. Note that truncation has no regard for the nearer fraction. That is, although 22.6 is nearer in value to 22.57 than is 22.5, truncation does not take such things into account. It is like an indiscriminate axeman chopping away excess without a thought to balance. Mathematically speaking, truncation is not desirable in most applications, as it can lead to an exaggerated error. Hence, it is better to round, since rounding does take into account the nearer fraction. If we round 22.57 instead of truncating it, the result is 22.6, a better representation of the number. The ROUNDED option in COBOL works according to the rounding rules of ordinary decimal arithmetic: fractional values greater than 5 are rounded up, and those less than or equal to 5 are rounded down, i.e., truncated. The ROUNDED option may be used with all arithmetic statements.

The ON SIZE ERROR option, as we have seen, checks for errors in the size of the result field. If the computed result is larger than the storage capacity of the retaining field, the instruction designated in the imperative statement following the ON SIZE ERROR option will occur. The ON SIZE ERROR option may be used with all arithmetic statements.

Example 8-3 The following code adds several numeric fields containing decimal values and uses the ROUNDED and ON SIZE ERROR options:

```
05   TOTAL-INTEREST      PIC S9(5)V9(4)     COMP-3.
05   TOTAL-DIVIDENDS     PIC S9(5)V9(4)     COMP-3.
05   TOTAL-INCOME        PIC ZZZ,ZZZ.99.

ADD TOTAL-INTEREST TOTAL-DIVIDENDS GIVING TOTAL-INCOME
ROUNDED ON SIZE ERROR MOVE ZEROS TO TOTAL-INCOME.
```

The values of the various fields before and after the addition are as follows:

	Field	Value before addition	Value after addition
	TOTAL–INTEREST	1673.6234	1673.6234
CASE 1	TOTAL–DIVIDENDS	2465.1435	2465.1425
	TOTAL–INCOME	immaterial	$4,138.77
	TOTAL–INTEREST	57342.1845	57342.1845
CASE 2	TOTAL–DIVIDENDS	63493.7525	63493.7525
	TOTAL–INCOME	immaterial	$.00

In Case 1, the decimal portion of the sum, .7659, is rounded to .77 in conformity with the PICTURE of the result field. In Case 2, the number of digits to the left of the decimal point in the sum exceeds the number of digits provided for in the PICTURE clause of the result field. (The dollar sign on the left does not count toward the total number of positions available for digits.) Hence, the error option is invoked.

The SUBTRACT statement[1] subtracts the value of one numeric item from the value of another numeric item and stores the result. Its general format is

```
                {data-name-1    }
SUBTRACT  {numeric-literal-1}. . . FROM

                {data-name-m  [GIVING]  data-name-n] }
                {numeric-literal-m  GIVING  data-name-n}

                [ROUNDED] [ON SIZE–ERROR imperative statement]
```

All of the subtrahends, i.e., the data names or numeric literals between SUBTRACT and FROM, are added algebraically, and their sum is subtracted from the minuend, i.e., the data name or literal following FROM. Notice the two forms of the GIVING option: in the one instance it is optional, in the other required. If this option is not used, the result of the computation or difference is stored in the data name following FROM. If it is used, the difference is stored in the named data item following GIVING. As is plain, the GIVING option is required when subtracting a quantity or quantities from a numeric literal or constant, since the difference must be stored in a named data item.

[1] In this and the other arithmetic statements that follow, the GIVING, ROUNDED, and ON SIZE ERROR options function the same way as they do for the ADD statement.

Example 8-4   The code

SUBTRACT .025 FROM DISCOUNT-RATE.

subtracts a constant from a display numeric item. If the file description of DISCOUNT-RATE is PIC V999 and its value before subtraction is .125, then its value after subtraction is .100.

Example 8-5   To subtract several numeric fields from a given field and place the difference in a report item, use the code

```
05  FED-TAX           PIC  S9(5)V99     COMP-3.
05  STATE-TAX         PIC  S9(5)V99     COMP-3.
05  FICA-TAX          PIC  S9(5)V99     COMP-3.
05  MISC-DEDUCTIONS   PIC  S9(5)V99     COMP-3.
05  GROSS-PAY         PIC  S9(5)V99     COMP-3.
05  NET-PAY-PRINT     PIX ***,***.99.
```

```
       SUBTRACT FED-TAX STATE-TAX FICA-TAX MISC-DEDUCTIONS
           FROM GROSS-PAY GIVING NET-PAY-PRINT.
```

The values of the fields before and after the subtraction are as follows:

Field	Value before subtraction	Value after subtraction
FED-TAX	230.50	230.50
STATE-TAX	15.60	15.60
FICA-TAX	32.25	32.25
MISC-DEDUCTIONS	10.00	10.00
GROSS-PAY	850.00	850.00
NET-PAY-PRINT	immaterial	****561.65

Notice the difference between Examples 8-4 and 8-5. In the former the result is stored in DISCOUNT-RATE, the field immediately following the FROM option. In the latter the result is stored in NET-PAY-PRINT, the field immediately following the GIVING option, and the value of GROSS-PAY is unchanged.

Example 8-6   The following code subtracts several data items from a constant value and places the result in another data field using the ROUNDED option.

```
05      RATE-1              PIC  V999     COMP-3.
05      RATE-2              PIC  V999     COMP-3.
05      REDUCTION-FACTOR    PIC  V99      COMP-3.
```

```
       SUBTRACT RATE-1 RATE-2 FROM 100 GIVING
           REDUCTION-FACTOR ROUNDED.
```

The values of the fields before and after the subtraction are given in the following table:

Field	Value before subtraction	Value after subtraction
RATE–1	.023	.023
RATE–2	.031	.031
REDUCTION FACTOR	immaterial	.95

Without the ROUNDED option, the value of REDUCTION–FACTOR would be .94.

Example 8-7   The code

```
05      TOTAL-CREDITS        PIC S9(3)V99      COMP-3.
05      TOTAL-DEBITS         PIC S9(3)V99      COMP-3.
05      DISBURSEMENTS        PIC S9(5)V99      COMP-3.

        SUBTRACT TOTAL-CREDITS TOTAL-DEBITS FROM DISBURSEMENTS.
```

subtracts numeric data items with different signs from a given item. The values of the fields before and after the subtraction are:

Field	Value before subtraction	Value after subtraction
TOTAL–CREDITS	+150.00	+150.00
TOTAL–DEBITS	–100.00	–100.00
DISBURSEMENTS	+500.00	+450.00

One might expect the above difference to be +250.00. However, the SUBTRACT statement employs the rules of ordinary algebra, i.e., if you subtract a negative number from any other number, the net effect is to add the two. In other words, in subtraction the signs of the subtrahends are reversed, and the remaining steps proceed as in addition. Negative subtrahends can cause some confusion. But if you understand their effect on the overall computation, you should have no difficulty interpreting results that are generated from them.

The MULTIPLY statement multiplies two numeric items together and stores the result, or product. Its general format is

```
                  {data name-1}
MULTIPLY          {numeric-literal 1}

BY                {data-name-2 [GIVING data-name-3]}
                  {numeric-literal-2 GIVING data-name-3}

[ROUNDED] [ON SIZE ERROR imperative statement]
```

Only one multiplier (data-name-1 or numeric-literal-1) and one multiplicand (data-name-2 or numeric-literal-2) occur in the statement. If the GIVING option is used, the product is stored in the data field immediately following the option. If it is omitted, the product is stored in the data field immediately following BY. In the latter case, the receiving operand must always be a named data field (data-name-2).

Example 8-8 The following code multiplies a display numeric field, DISCOUNT, with PIC 999V99, by a constant:

```
MULTIPLY .25 BY DISCOUNT.
```

If the value of DISCOUNT before the multiplication is 125.00, then its value after the multiplication is 31.25. Notice that in this type of situation the constant term must be placed before BY, and the named data field after it. This ordering may seem somewhat inappropriate, but it is necessary since the product will be placed in the named data field following BY. Had we written MULTIPLY DISCOUNT BY .25, the program would not have known where to store the product.

Example 8-9 To multiply signed numeric fields and place the product in an edited field, we may use the following code:

```
05    NUMBER-OF-DEBITS      PIC S9(3)           COMP-3.
05    DEBIT-AMOUNT          PIC S9(5)V99        COMP-3.
05    TOTAL-DEBITS-PRINT    PIC $$$,$$$.99-.

     MULTIPLY NUMBER-OF-DEBITS BY DEBIT-AMOUNT
         GIVING TOTAL-DEBITS-PRINT.
```

The values of the fields before and after the multiplication are as follows:

Field	Value before multiplication	Value after multiplication
NUMBER-OF-DEBITS	15	15
DEBIT-AMOUNT	−1240.00	−1240.00
TOTAL-DEBITS-PRINT	immaterial	$18,600.00−

The product in Example 8.9 is negative, as it should be. Like the SUBTRACT statement, the MULTIPLY statement applies the rules of ordinary algebra. Thus, multiplying a multiplier and multiplicand that have unlike signs yields a negative product, whereas multiplying those that have like signs yields a positive product. The size of the product in relation to the size of the multiplier and multiplicand is also important. A product can have only as many digits as the sum of the digits in the multiplier and multiplicand. In other words, if a multiplier N has n digits and a multiplicand M has m digits, then the product N times M can have no more than $n + m$ digits. This fact should be considered when planning data fields that will be used in multiplication applications. If the product field is not large enough to accommodate the largest possible result, problems can arise in multiplication in which the multiplier and multiplicand fields have as many digits as they are allowed. Accordingly, in multiplication applications it is always a good idea to make the product field at least as large as the sum of the lengths of the multiplier and multiplicand fields.

Finally, in multiplying decimal numbers, it is possible that some of the digits will be truncated. Since in multiplication the number of decimal places in the product is equal to the sum of the number of decimal places in the multiplier and multiplicand, if the number of decimal places specified in the product field is less than the sum of the numbers of places in the multiplier and multiplicand, the decimal portion of the product will be truncated. For example, suppose the multiplier has three decimal places in its PICTURE clause and the multiplicand has two. Suppose further that the PICTURE clause of the product has just four reserved decimal places. Then when the multiplication is performed, the computed product will contain five decimal places, but when this product is moved to the product field, the last digit will be lost. Fortunately, in many applications—e.g., in computations involving monetary fields—it is not necessary to maintain decimal precision beyond two places.

Example 8-10   The code

```
05      DISCOUNT-RATE      PIC  V99         COMP-3.
05      SELLING-PRICE      PIC  S9(3)V99    COMP-3.
05      DISCOUNT           PIC  9(3)V99     COMP-3.

        MULTIPLY DISCOUNT-RATE BY SELLING-PRICE
               GIVING DISCOUNT ROUNDED.
```

multiplies two decimal fields, yielding a product rounded to two decimal places of accuracy. The values of the fields before and after the multiplication are as follows:

Field	Value before multiplication	Value after multiplication
DISCOUNT-RATE	.12	.12
SELLING-PRICE	399.99	399.99
DISCOUNT	immaterial	48.00

If DISCOUNT were not rounded, its value would have been 47.99. Convince yourself of these results by working through the computation first without rounding and then with rounding.

The DIVIDE statement divides one numeric value by or into another and stores the result. Its general format is

```
DIVIDE  {data-name-1     }   {BY  }    {data-name-2     }
        {numeric-literal-1}  {INTO}    {numeric-literal-2}

        [GIVING data-name-3]     [ROUNDED]
                [ON SIZE ERROR imperative statement]
```

Notice the two forms of the statement: DIVIDE . . . BY and DIVIDE . . . INTO. In the BY form, the first operand (data-name-1 or numeric-literal-1) is the dividend, and the second operand (data-name-2 or numeric-literal-2) is the divisor. If the GIVING option is not used, the first operand must be a named numeric data field, and the quotient is stored there. If the GIVING option is used, the result is stored in data-name-3. In the INTO form, the first operand is the divisor, and the second operand is the dividend. If the GIVING option is not used with this form, the second operand must be a named numeric data field, and the quotient is stored there. If the GIVING option is used, the result is, of course, stored in data-name-3.

In division, zero may never be a divisor. If by chance your program attempts to use it as a divisor, the program will terminate abnormally. To guard against such a possibility, it is always a good practice to use the ON SIZE ERROR option in a DIVIDE statement, especially if the divisor is a data name. If the divisor is a nonzero numeric literal, you know you are safe. If, however, the divisor is a named data field extracted from an external data base, you can never be sure that it will not contain an unwanted zero. The action your program will take if it encounters a zero divisor is, of course, dependent on the application. Printing a message on the VDT screen to identify the error condition and the particular record containing the faulty field is a good practice.

Example 8–11   The following code divides a constant into a numeric data field, TOTAL–GRADE, and stores the result in that field:

```
        05  TOTAL-GRADE       PIC 9(5)V9 COMP-3.
CASE 1          DIVIDE TOTAL-GRADE BY 10.
CASE 2          DIVIDE 10 INTO TOTAL-GRADE.
```

If the value of TOTAL-GRADE before the division is 885, then its value after the division is 88.5.

In Example 8–11 the result is stored in the dividend field upon completion of the operation. Storage in this field may not always be desirable, however, as you may wish to preserve the contents of the dividend for subsequent use. If so, the GIVING option should be used, as shown in Example 8–12.

Example 8-12 The code

```
05  TOTAL-GRADE      PIC 9(5)V9 COMP-3.
05  AVERAGE-GRADE    PIC ZZZ.9
```

CASE 1   DIVIDE TOTAL-GRADE BY 10 GIVING AVERAGE-GRADE.

CASE 2   DIVIDE 10 INTO TOTAL-GRADE GIVING AVERAGE GRADE.

divides a constant into a numeric data field, TOTAL-GRADE, and stores the result in AVERAGE-GRADE. The following table shows the values of the fields before and after the division:

Field	Value before division	Value after division
TOTAL-GRADE	885	885
AVERAGE-GRADE	immaterial	88.5

In Examples 8-11 and 8-12 the divisor is a constant value. In most division problems, however, the divisor is a named data field, the value of which is either computed within the program or extracted from a data record. Hence, it is again advisable to use the ON SIZE ERROR option. Moreover, since division more often than not produces fractional values that you may wish to round off (e.g., values representing student grades or monetary amounts), use of the ROUNDED option is also advisable. Indeed, this option is more frequently seen in operations that involve division than in operations that do not.

Example 8-13 The following code uses a variable divisor and the extended options:

```
05  TOTAL-GRADE          PIC 9(5)V9 COMP-3.
05  NUMBER-OF-GRADES     PIC 99.
05  AVERAGE-GRADE        PIC ZZZ.
```

CASE 1   DIVIDE TOTAL-GRADE BY NUMBER-OF GRADES
           GIVING AVERAGE-GRADE ROUNDED
           ON SIZE ERROR DISPLAY "INVALID NUMBER OF GRADES".

CASE 2   DIVIDE NUMBER-OF-GRADES INTO TOTAL-GRADE
           GIVING AVERAGE-GRADE ROUNDED
           ON SIZE ERROR DISPLAY "INVALID NUMBER OF GRADES".

The values of the fields before and after the division are as follows:

Field	Value before division	Value after division
TOTAL-GRADE	885	88.5
NUMBER-OF-GRADES	10	10
AVERAGE-GRADE	immaterial	89

Note that AVERAGE-GRADE no longer carries any decimal places; it is calculated as a whole number and rounded to the nearest unit as required by the application.

MATHEMATICAL OPERATIONS AND THE COMPUTE STATEMENT

The four arithmetic statements so far presented are capable of handling most ordinary business-type computational problems. However, if a computation involves a number of mixed arithmetic operations or the process of exponentiation (raising a number to a power), then the use of these statements may generate a lengthy segment of program code. (See p. 166.)

The COMPUTE statement offers a welcome alternative to the four basic arithmetic commands when complicated computations must be performed.

The COMPUTE statement employs an algebra-like structure for setting up mathematical expressions. It also makes use of the following set of arithmetic operators, which are simply symbols that stand for the mathematical operations shown.

Operator	Operation
+	addition
−	subtraction
*	multiplication
/	division
**	exponentiation
=	storing a computed value

Right and left parentheses are used in conjunction with these operations to set up and evaluate mathematical expressions, much as they are used in ordinary algebra to indicate the order of operations. In COBOL, as in algebra, the operations proceed from left to right in accordance with the following hierarchy:

1. Exponentiation.
2. Multiplication and division.
3. Addition and subtraction.

The value resulting from the computation is stored after all of these operations that occur in the mathematical expression are performed.

As an example of the evaluation of a mathematical expression, consider

X = A * B + C ** 2 / D

The order in which the operations are performed to yield the value of the expression is as follows:

1. The value of C is raised to the second power, i.e., squared.
2. A and B are multiplied.
3. The value of C squared is divided by the value of D.
4. The product from step 2 is added to the quotient from step 3.
5. The result is stored in X.

Thus, if the variables have values

A = 2   C = 6
B = 6   D = 3

respectively, then, in accordance with the computation, the variable X contains 24.

Now let us see how the use of parentheses changes the order of the computation, and consequently, the result. Consider

X = A * (B + C) ** 2 / D

The order in which the operations are performed to yield the value of the expression is:

1. The sum of B and C is formed.
2. The sum is then squared.
3. The result from Step 2 is multiplied by A.
4. The result from Step 3 is divided by the value of D.
5. The final result is stored in X.

Using the same values as in the previous example, the variable X contains 864—quite a difference from that case! Thus, parentheses, depending on where they are placed in the expression, can radically affect the value of the computed result.

Parentheses may be *nested*—i.e., one parenthetical expression may be contained within one or more other parenthetical expressions. When such nesting occurs, the number of left parentheses must equal the number of right parentheses, as shown below:

```
(((exp 1)  exp2)  exp3)
```

The order of computation in nested parentheses is as follows: the expression in the innermost set of parentheses is evaluated first, that in the next innermost set second, and so forth. Thus, exp 1 would be evaluated first, exp 2 next, and exp 3 last. Parentheses, then, supersede the order of operations presented on p. 163.

The general format of the COMPUTE statement is

```
COMPUTE  data-name-1  [ROUNDED]. . . =

|data-name-2         |
|numeric literal     |   [ON  SIZE–ERROR  imperative  statement]
|arithmetic-expression|
```

The COMPUTE statement can be used to move one numeric field to another, as, for example,

```
COMPUTE  data-name-1  =  data-name-2
```

or to initialize a numeric data field with a numeric constant, as, for example,

```
COMPUTE  data-name-1  =  numeric  literal
```

or, most importantly, to calculate a numeric result and store its value, as, for example,

```
COMPUTE  data-name-1  =  arithmetic  expression.
```

In the last case—which is the only one of concern in this text—the arithmetic expression is a properly formed combination of numeric data fields, numeric literals, arithmetic operators, and parentheses. All data names and literals must be separated by an arithmetic operator with at least one blank on either side of it. When parentheses are used, the left parenthesis must be preceded by one or more spaces, and the right parenthesis must be followed by one or more spaces. If the data name or literal bears on explicit algebraic sign (not to be confused with the arithmetic operators for addition and subtraction), this sign must be placed immediately to the left of the item without an intervening space. Some examples of valid arithmetic expressions are:

```
PRINCIPAL * (1 + RATE) ** NUM-PERIODS
RATE / -2.55 + COMMISSION
(SIDEA ** 2 + SIDEB ** 2) ** .5
```

You may recognize the first example above as the expression for calculating the present value of an annuity. The mathematical formula for present value is:

$$PV = PR(L+r)^n \quad (8.1)$$

WHERE
N = number of periods
PV = present value of the annuity after N periods
PR = principal, or original amount
R = rate of interest

Using the naming conventions and mathematical operators of COBOL, formula 8.1 translates to:

```
PRESENT-VALUE = PRINCIPAL * (1+RATE) ** NUM-PERIODS
```

We had to compute present value and did not have the COMPUTE command. The code could become rather messy as you will see in the next example.

Example 8-14 Computing PRESENT VALUE using the normal arithmetic commands:

```
05  PRESENT-VALUE  PIC 9(7)V99    COMP-3.
05  PRINCIPAL       PIC 9(5)V99    COMP-3.
05  RATE            PIC V999       COMP-3.
05  NUM-PERIODS     PIC 9(3)       COMP-3.
05  P-RATE          PIC 9V999      COMP-3.
05  HOLD-AMOUNT     PIC 9(3)V99    COMP-3.

        ADD 1, RATE GIVING P-RATE.
        MOVE P-RATE TO HOLD-AMOUNT.
        SUBTRACT 1 FROM NUM-PERIODS.
        PERFORM EXPAND-RATE NUM-PERIODS TIMES.
        MOVE HOLD-AMOUNT TO PRESENT-VALUE.
        MULTIPLY PRESENT-VALUE BY PRINCIPAL ROUNDED.
            •           •
            •           •
            •           •
    EXPAND-RATE.
        MULTIPLY HOLD AMOUNT BY P-RATE ROUNDED.
            •           •
            •           •
            •           •
```

If we had used the more compact COMPUTE statement to calculate the present value, our work would be much simpler, as shown in the next example.

Example 8-15   The following COMPUTE statement calculates the value of PRESENT-VALUE:

```
COMPUTE PRESENT-VALUE ROUNDED = PRINCIPAL * (1 + RATE) **
    NUM-PERIODS.
```

The COMPUTE statement is a powerful tool for evaluating mathematical formulas in a COBOL program. Some programmers use it exclusively for arithmetic operations, even though it may be slightly less efficient in terms of speed of execution.

REVIEW QUESTIONS

1. Name the four basic arithmetic instructions. Construct an example of each.
2. Explain the role of the GIVING option following an arithmetic instruction. Give an example of an alternate method for achieving the same result with the MOVE statement.
3. Code the arithmetic statement necessary to sum three fields— FED-TAX, STATE-TAX, and LOCAL-TAX—depositing the result in the field TOTAL-TAX.
4. Code the arithmetic statement necessary to subtract the quantity in the field TOTAL-DEDUCTIONS from the field GROSS-PAY, depositing the difference in the field NET-PAY.
5. Code the arithmetic statement necessary to multiply the quantity in the field GROSS-SALES by the constant .05, depositing the result in the field COMMISSION. Include the code to handle an error in the case of an oversized product.
6. Code the arithmetic statement necessary to divide the field TOTAL-SCORES by the field NUMB-TESTS, placing the quotient in the field AVERAGE. Include the code to handle an error in the case of a zero divisor.
7. What are the advantages of the COMPUTE statement over the basic arithmetic statements?
8. Write a COMPUTE statement for each of questions 3 through 6 above. Round the results.

9. Write a compute statement for calculating the hypotenuse of a right triangle having legs A and B. The hypotenuse of a right triangle is equal to the square root of the sum of the squares of its legs.

10. Identify the errors in each of the following arithmetic statements:

```
ADD SUBTOTAL-A TO SUBTOTAL-B GIVING TOTAL-C.
MULTIPLY MINUTES BY 60.
SUBTRACT COST FROM SELLING-PRICE GIVING PROFIT.
DIVIDE ROUNDED TIME INTO DISTANCE GIVING RATE.
COMPUTE ROUNDED AREA = PI * RADIUS**2
```

PROBLEMS

1. Write a program to read a sales file containing the sales for one individual for three months. In the past, the returns per sales individual have averaged 2.145%. You are to produce a report showing total gross sales, the amount of returns, the net sales, and average sales per month for each individual.

   You must also produce a report total for all columns shown on the report. The report must contain headings with the date and page numbers, and two lines between each detail line. The layout of the output is up to you. The lengths of the output fields are shown.

The input is:

Position		Field name
1–20		NAME
26–30	(999V99)	SALES MONTH 1
31–35	(999V99)	SALES MONTH 2
36–40	(999V99)	SALES MONTH 3

The output lengths are:

Field name	Length	
NAME	20	
SALES MONTH 1	6	(ZZ9.99)
SALES MONTH 2	6	(ZZ9.99)
SALES MONTH 3	6	(ZZ9.99)
RETURNS	6	(ZZ9.99)
GROSS SALES	12	(Z,ZZZ,ZZ9.99)
NET SALES	12	(Z,ZZZ,ZZ9.99)
AVERAGE SALES	6	(ZZ9.99)

2. Write a program to produce a report from the stock portfolio file computing the average cost per share. Average cost per share is computed by adding all purchase prices and dividing by the total number of shares. At the end of the report, print a total value for the entire portfolio.

The input record format is:

Position	Field name
21–24	# OF SHARES
29–33 (999V99)	PURCHASE PRICE 1
34–38 (999V99)	PURCHASE PRICE 2
42–49	NAME OF STOCK

The output lengths for this report are:

Field name	Length
NAME OF STOCK	8
PURCHASE PRICE 1	6 (ZZ9.99)
PURCHASE PRICE 2	6 (ZZ9.99)
# OF SHARES	5 (Z,ZZ9)
TOTAL COST	10 (ZZZ,ZZ9.99)
AVERAGE COST PER SHARE	6 (ZZ9.99)

9

LOGICAL BRANCHING AND PROGRAM DECISIONMAKING

The single most striking feature of a computer language is its ability to make logical decisions. It is this feature that distinguishes a computer system from an ordinary calculating system. Within a computer program you may switch control from one procedure to another, bypass certain procedures on the basis of preselected conditions, or otherwise process information in whatever manner desired simply on the basis of binary logic. Binary logic is a two-pronged decisionmaking process: the outcome of every decision is either *yes* or *no* (or *true* or *false*), but not both. For example, is a certain input value equal to 56? If it is, then we select a certain action; if it is not, then we choose some other action. This process of choosing an action within a program is called *branching*. It is a feature common to all programming languages, and the mechanism for implementing it is much the same from one high-level language to another.

There are two kinds of branching: unconditional and conditional. *Unconditional* branching is the transfer of program control to a specified section or paragraph regardless of any external data or program conditions. It is accomplished by the use of a stand-alone GO TO statement, which you have already had occasion to use. *Conditional* branching, on the other hand, is the transfer of control to a specified section or paragraph upon satisfaction of external data or program conditions. Conditional branching employs the highly familiar IF . . . THEN . . . ELSE logical construct—e.g., if it rains, then I'll drive to work, or else I'll walk; if a certain data field equals 100, then program processing will stop, or else another record will be fetched. These elementary examples are depicted in the flowcharts of Figure 9–1 (p. 174).

LOGICAL OPERATORS

Most program decisions are the result of comparing two or more data values, either numeric or alphanumeric in nature. Numeric items may be compared with numeric items, and alphanumeric items with alphanumeric items. Neither, however, may be compared with the other.

For numeric items, a named data field containing a numeric value may be compared with either another such named data field or a numeric constant. The named data fields may be any of the three main kinds—display, packed decimal, or binary; that is, it is permissible to compare, e.g., a display and a binary item. For alphanumeric items, a named data field may be compared with an absolute character string (literal) enclosed in quotes. When numeric items are compared, the algebraic values of each field, including the sign, are considered. When alphanumeric items are compared, the binary configuration of each byte of each field is considered. In either case, there are only three possibilities when comparing two operands: the

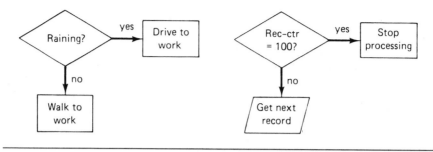

Figure 9-1
Flowcharts of two binary decisionmaking processes

first operand is less than the second; the two operands are equal; and the first operand is greater than the second. The symbols used by COBOL to determine which of these possibilities obtains are referred to as *logical operators.* For each logical operator, there is an equivalent COBOL English-like expression, as shown in Table 9-1.

The IF . . . THEN . . . ELSE construct, in which the logical operators are used, has the general format

```
IF {logical expression} THEN {imperative statement 1,
    imperative statement 2 . . . }  ELSE
    {imperative statement 3, imperative statement 4, . . . }.
```

The logical expression, which normally consists of a simple or compound comparison of operands, is assigned a truth value—*true* or *false*—after it is evaluated. If the value of the logical expression is *true,* the imperative statements following the word THEN (which is optional) are executed, and those following the word ELSE are ignored. If the value of the expression is *false,* the imperative statements following the word THEN are ignored, and those following the word ELSE are executed. Notice that more than one imperative statement may follow either or both of the THEN and ELSE options.

Table 9-1
Logical operators and their meanings

Operator	Equivalent COBOL syntax
<	IS LESS THAN
=	IS EQUAL TO
>	IS GREATER THAN

Example 9-1 Each of the following IF statements compares a named numeric data field with a constant.

        CASE 1:   IF REC-COUNTER < 100 THEN GO TO GET-NEXT-RECORD.

or, alternatively,

                IF REC-COUNTER LESS THAN 100 THEN GO TO
                GET-NEXT-RECORD.

        CASE 2:   IF STUDENT-AVG = 100 THEN DISPLAY 'NICE WORK'
                        PERFORM 100-ROUTINE
                        ELSE DISPLAY "SORRY, BETTER LUCK NEXT TIME"
                        PERFORM OTHER-ROUTINE.

or, alternatively,

                IF STUDENT-AVG EQUAL 100 THEN DISPLAY 'NICE WORK'
                        PERFORM 100-ROUTINE
                        ELSE DISPLAY "SORRY, BETTER LUCK NEXT TIME"
                        PERFORM OTHER-ROUTINE.

        CASE 3:   IF TAX-PAID > 1000.00 THEN
                        PERFORM EXCEPTION-ROUTINE,
                ELSE GO TO PRINT-LINE.

    or, alternatively,

                IF TAX-PAID GREATER THAN 1000.00 THEN
                        PERFORM EXCEPTION-ROUTINE,
                ELSE GO TO PRINT-LINE.

Notice the following points:

1. The ELSE clause need not be used, as indicated in case 1. If it is not used, no alternative action is required or desired in the event that the logical expression is false.

2. Each complete IF construct is required to end with a period. This requirement is important, as the period signals the end of the string of imperative statements belonging to the THEN or ELSE option. If the period is omitted or misplaced, strange and unpredictable results may occur.

3. The named data fields can be either display, packed decimal, or binary numeric items.

Example 9-2 The code

        IF CURRENT-AMOUNT < PREVIOUS-AMOUNT THEN GO TO ROUTINE-1.

        IF CURRENT-AMOUNT > PREVIOUS-AMOUNT THEN GO TO ROUTINE-2.
        ROUTINE-3.

        ADD CURRENT-AMOUNT TO TOTAL-AMOUNT.
                            •
                            •
                            •

tests two named numeric data fields and branches according to the truth or falsity of the indicated conditions. That is, the fields CURRENT–AMOUNT and PREVIOUS–AMOUNT are tested against each other to determine which one of the three possible relationships between them obtains, with a different course of action prescribed for each outcome. If the value of CURRENT–AMOUNT is less than the value of PREVIOUS–AMOUNT, then program control is directed to ROUTINE–1. If the value of CURRENT–AMOUNT is greater than the value of PREVIOUS–AMOUNT, then program control is directed to ROUTINE–2. If none of these two conditions is met, the two fields must contain identical values, the only remaining possibility. In that case, control "falls through" to ROUTINE–3.

Example 9–3   Each of the following IF statements compares a named alphanumeric data field with a literal, and branches according to the truth or falsity of the indicated condition.

```
CASE 1:    IF COURSE-TITLE = "FRENCH" THEN
                  PERFORM COMPUTE-FRENCH-GRADE.
```

or, alternatively,

```
           IF COURSE-TITLE EQUAL TO "FRENCH" THEN
                  PERFORM COMPUTE-FRENCH-GRADE.
```

```
CASE 2:    IF LAST-NAME < "Mbbbbbbbbbbbbbb" THEN
                  PERFORM NAME-ATHRUL-ROUTINE ELSE
                  PERFORM NAME-MTHRUZ-ROUTINE.
```

or, alternatively,

```
           IF COURSE-TITLE LESS THAN "Mbbbbbbbbbbbbbb" THEN
                  PERFORM NAME-ATHRUL-ROUTINE ELSE
                  PERFORM NAME-MTHRUZ-ROUTINE.
```

(*Note:* In the above operands, b represents a blank space.)

Observe that in each case above, the character string contained in the named data field is compared, byte by byte, with the character string contained in quotes. If each pair of corresponding bytes of the operands compared contains the same character for the entire length of the string, then the character strings themselves are considered to be equal. The test in case 2 is used to determine whether a certain last name falls either within the range A through L or within the range M through Z. In other words, it partitions a list of names into two components. The corresponding bytes of each operand are compared, and as soon as one of the bytes of the first operand is lower in the collating sequence than the corresponding byte of the second operand, the entire character string represented by the first operand is considered to be "less than," or lower, in the collating sequence than the character string represented by the second operand. Figure 9–2 shows how an alphanumeric comparison works.

```
                 OPERAND 1                    OPERAND 2
        Field:   LAST-NAME-1   PIC X(12)      LAST-NAME-2  PIC X(12).

        Contents:  A T K I N S E N              A T K I N S O N

        Logical expression:

           IF  LAST-NAME-1 <  LAST-NAME-2    THEN . . . .
```

Figure 9-2
Comparison of alphanumeric data items

In the figure, the first six bytes of each field match. However, the seventh byte of operand 1 does not match the seventh byte of operand 2: the character "E" is lower in the collating sequence than the character "O". At that point the comparison stops, and operand 1 is deemed less than operand 2, so that the value of the logical expression is *true*. Consequently, the imperative statement following the THEN option is executed.

So far, we have dealt with only three possible conditions in our data-comparison tests. Suppose, however, that we are interested in combining those tests into a single logical expression—that is, we would like to test whether a certain field is less than or equal to another field. There are several ways to do so. The most cumbersome is to use a compound logical expression of the form

```
   IF FIELD-1 < FIELD-2 OR FIELD-1 = FIELD-2 THEN . . .
```

Another way is to code two simple logical expressions in tandem using different comparison tests but the same conditional imperative statement, as follows:

```
   IF FIELD-1 < FIELD-2 THEN imperative statement 1.
   IF FIELD-1 = FIELD-2 then imperative statement 1.
```

The simplest way, however, is to use an alternative logical operator that includes the sense and meaning of both the < and = operators. We can do so by using the COBOL word NOT in conjunction with the > operator, thus:

```
   IF FIELD-1 NOT > FIELD-2 THEN imperative statement.
```

NOT > translates to *not greater than,* which means the same as less than or equal to. On the other hand, we may want to test whether a certain field is greater than or equal to another field. In this case, we could use the logical operator < preceded by the COBOL word NOT as follows:

```
   IF FIELD-1 NOT < FIELD-2 THEN imperative statement.
```

This statement has the same meaning as

    IF FIELD-1 > FIELD-2 OR FIELD-1 = FIELD-2 THEN imperative statement.

Now let us extend Table 9-1 to include the combined logical operators. Table 9-2 shows the new set of operators.

Frequently in data processing it is necessary to test whether the value of a particular data field lies within a range of values. For example, in a payroll application we may want to know whether an employee's gross salary is within a certain range for the purpose of computing taxes. Or we may want to know whether a student's average grade lies within a certain range for the purpose of assigning a better grade. These kinds of *range checks,* as they are called, can be accomplished by using compound logical expressions in conjunction with the various logical operators. A few examples will illustrate the point.

Example 9-4 Suppose it is necessary to check whether an employee's gross salary is greater than or equal to $10,000.00 and less than $20,000.00 in order to compute his taxes. The following test will accomplish that task:

    IF GROSS-SALARY NOT < 10000.0 AND < 20000.0
       THEN PERFORM TAX-COMPUTATION-2.

Another way of coding this statement is

    IF GROSS-SALARY < 20000.0 AND NOT < 10000.0
       THEN PERFORM TAX-COMPUTATION-2.

(Remember, NOT < has the sense of greater than or equal to.)
And a third way of coding the statement is

    IF GROSS-SALARY NOT LESS THAN 10000.0 AND LESS THAN 20000.0
       THEN PERFORM TAX-COMPUTATION-2.

Table 9-2
The logical operators of COBOL

Operator	Equivalent COBOL syntax	Meaning
<	IS LESS THAN	less than
=	IS EQUAL TO	equals
>	IS GREATER THAN	greater than
NOT <	IS NOT LESS THAN	greater than or equal to
NOT =	IS NOT EQUAL TO	not equal to
NOT >	IS NOT GREATER THAN	less than or equal to

Example 9-5   The following statement tests whether a student's grade is between 80 and 90 (greater than 80 but less than or equal to 90) for the purpose of assigning a letter grade:

```
IF STUDENT-GRADE > 80 AND NOT > 90 THEN MOVE 'B' TO FINAL
    GRADE.
```

Alternatively, the statement

```
IF STUDENT-GRADE GREATER THAN 80 AND NOT GREATER THAN 90
    MOVE 'B' TO FINAL-GRADE.
```

may be used.

Notice in both Example 9-4 and 9-5 that the range check includes one of the endpoints but excludes the other. In Example 9-4 we want to know whether the gross salary is greater than or equal to $10,000.00, thus including this value in the range of qualifying values. At the upper limit, we are only interested in values less than $20,000.00, but not that value itself. Therefore, $20,000.00 is not included in the range of qualifying values. Example 9-6 presents a range check in which we want to include both endpoints.

Example 9-6   The code

```
IF ACCOUNT-CODE NOT < 10 AND NOT > 20 THEN DISPLAY 'INVALID
    ACCOUNT CODE'.
```

checks a range of account codes for valid values. The check includes both endpoints, 10 and 20. This kind of range checking is very useful for the purpose of validating input data, a function that is particularly necessary in the data-entry process. When inputting new data to files, you want to be sure to test that data for valid values. If the input data is not correct or is otherwise invalid, it should be rejected. The process of performing integrity checks on data is often called *editing*. A good bit of the logic of a data-entry program involves editing.

THE LEVEL-88 ENTRY

The logical expressions introduced so far to evaluate data conditions within a program all require the use of explicitly defined logical operators. However, COBOL provides an easier means of testing data elements in the level-88 entry. A level-88 data item identifies a data field which, when referenced by its name within an IF statement, produces the effect of an "equal to" logical condition. In other words, it affords a compact way of testing whether a data field is equal to a particular value. A level-88 entry may be used as a subordinate item to any other level number except 77. Its general format is

```
nn   data-name-1        PIC ... VALUE IS literal
     88  data-name-2        VALUE IS literal
```

In effect, the 88-level item qualifies or modifies the data field to which it is subordinate. It is in reality a logical binary switch which can be tested for a true or false condition without the use of explicit logical operators.

Example 9-7 The following code uses an 88-level item as a binary switch for indicating an end-of-file condition:

```
01   END–OF–FILE          PIC XXX VALUE "NO".
     88  NO–MORE–RECORDS      VALUE "YES".

PROCEDURE ...
                              •
                              •
                              •
100–READ–RECORD.
     READ INFILE AT END MOVE "YES" TO END–OF–FILE.
                              •
                              •
                              •
     IF NO–MORE–RECORDS THEN GO TO 900–PROGRAM–EXIT.
```

Note that the stand-alone data item, END–OF–FILE, is set up in the program's WORKING-STORAGE SECTION and initialized with the value 'YES'. The value of END–OF–FILE remains 'NO' until such time that it is modified within the PROCEDURE DIVISION. Each time a record is read and processed, END–OF–FILE is tested for a 'YES' value. Without the 88-level entry, the test would take the form IF END–OF–FILE EQUAL TO "YES" THEN, etc. The 88-level data name replaces this logical expression, as shown in Example 9-7. IF NO–MORE–RECORDS returns a false result until the value of END–OF–FILE is changed to "YES" following the AT END option in the READ statement, at which time IF NO–MORE–RECORDS yields a true result and the action following the THEN clause takes place. The example is a bit artificial, but it does illustrate a possible use of an 88-level entry. Example 9-8 is more meaningful.

Example 9-8 The following code uses 88-level entries to test the value of a race-code field in a program for evaluating statistical data pertaining to students of a university:

```
05 STUDENT-RACE-CODE        PIC X.
   88  BLACK                VALUE "B".
   88  WHITE                VALUE "W".
   88  HISPANIC             VALUE "H".
   88  ASIAN                VALUE "A".
   88  OTHER                VALUE "O".
                               •
                               •
                               •
PROCEDURE DIVISION.
                               •
                               •
                               •
100-READ-FILE.
    READ STUDENT-FILE AT END GO TO 900-END-OF-JOB.
    IF BLACK ADD 1 TO BLACK-COUNTER.
    IF WHITE ADD 1 TO WHITE-COUNTER.
    IF HISPANIC ADD 1 TO HISPANIC-COUNTER.
    IF ASIAN ADD 1 TO ASIAN-COUNTER.
    IF OTHER ADD 1 TO OTHER-COUNTER.
                               •
                               •
                               •
```

In the example, STUDENT-RACE-CODE is part of the input record. Each of its possible values is described by a corresponding 88-level item. This type of data item is not only useful for divising compact conditional statements, but it also serves as meaningful data-field documentation.

NESTED IF . . . THEN . . . ELSE STATEMENTS

IF . . . THEN . . . ELSE statements can be strung together, or nested, to permit the formulation of elaborate compound conditional statements. So far, each IF . . . THEN . . . ELSE statement we have dealt with has ended with a period. We can, however, join a number of such statements together in the form

```
     IF logical expression-1 THEN imperative statement-1
ELSE IF logical expression-2 THEN imperative statement-2
ELSE IF logical expression-3 THEN imperative statement-3
ELSE imperative statement-4.
```

The above single nested IF . . . THEN . . . ELSE statement consists of a number of IF . . . THEN statements joined by the word ELSE. The principal advantages of this construction are that (1) the conditional test is conclusive—one and only one of the coded imperative statements will be executed; and (2) the test is terminated once a true condition is met—that is, once a logical expression evaluates to *true.* It should be noted that, in using nested IF . . . THEN . . . ELSE statements, (1) the condition tests should be mutually exclusive—i.e., no more than one of the logical expressions can be true; and (2) although the IF . . . THEN . . . ELSE statement format shows only three levels of nesting, any number of such statements can be nested.

Example 9-9 The code

```
IF BLACK ADD 1 TO BLACK-COUNTER ELSE
IF WHITE ADD 1 TO WHITE-COUNTER ELSE
IF HISPANIC ADD 1 TO HISPANIC-COUNTER ELSE
IF ASIAN ADD 1 TO ASIAN-COUNTER ELSE
    ADD 1 TO OTHER-COUNTER
```

uses a single nested IF . . . THEN . . . ELSE construct in place of the five conditional statements shown in Example 9-8. In this example, if the student is white, the test will end with the second test, whereas in Example 9-8 all tests will be performed even though only one yields a true result. Note the "catch-all" imperative following the last ELSE clause here. With it, no extraneous codes can slip by unprocessed, as they can in Example 9-8.

THE NEXT SENTENCE OPTION

One convenient way to choose among alternative actions when evaluating a logical condition is to skip to the next sentence of program code upon satisfaction of the condition. Such skipping is made possible by inserting the words NEXT SENTENCE within the IF construct as follows:

```
IF logical expression NEXT SENTENCE ELSE
    imperative statement.

(next program sentence).
```

If the logical expression evaluates to *true,* then control is directed to the next program sentence. In effect, NEXT SENTENCE replaces the THEN clause. This contrivance is particularly useful when several program steps are to be performed in the event that the logical expression evaluates to *true.*

Example 9-10 The following code uses the NEXT SENTENCE option:

```
IF SALARY < 10000.00 NEXT SENTENCE ELSE
    GO TO 2000-EXCESS-SALARY.

COMPUTE REFUND ROUNDED = SALARY * .05
                •
                •
                •
2000-EXCESS-SALARY.
```

If the employee's salary is less than ten thousand dollars, control is directed to the COMPUTE statement. Otherwise, control is passed to the paragraph called 2000–EXCESS–SALARY.

CLASS TESTS AND SIGN TESTS

It is often necessary within a program to test a data field for content—i.e., to determine whether it contains numeric or alphanumeric data. This type of test, known as a *class test,* is particularly important for testing data fields that are to be used in computations. If a given field does not contain purely numeric data, and an attempt is made to use the data in an arithmetic operation, the program will terminate abnormally. You may be inclined to say that a programmer should know beforehand what class of data a particular field contains. But this need not always be the case, especially if you are dealing with data on externally generated files. The class test takes the general form

IF data-name IS [NOT]   {NUMERIC
                          {ALPHABETIC   . . .

The NUMERIC test is valid for any data item not having an alphabetic picture. The ALPHABETIC test is valid for a group or character item having an alphanumeric PICTURE clause.

Example 9-11   The code

```
05  GROSS–SALARY PIC S9(5)V99 COMP3.
              •
              •
              •
IF GROSS–SALARY NOT NUMERIC THEN DISPLAY
    "NONNUMERIC SALARY FIELD".
```

tests a data item for numeric content.

Just as it is frequently useful to test a data name for numeric or alphabetic content, it is sometimes useful to test a numeric data item for an algebraic sign. The *sign test* is used for that purpose and has the following format:

IF data-name IS [NOT] {NEGATIVE}
                      {ZERO . . . }
                      {POSITIVE }

Example 9-12   The code

```
05 GROSS-SALARY PIC S9(5)V.99 COMP-3.
                   •
                   •
                   •
IF GROSS-SALARY ZERO THEN GO TO 900-ZERO-SALARY.
```

uses the sign test. The test is, in effect, the same as the test IF GROSS-SALARY = ZERO, etc. The sign test is an extension of an algebraic principle that states that every number is either positive, negative, or zero, three mutually exclusive conditions.

REVIEW QUESTIONS

1. Distinguish between conditional and unconditional branches. What part does branching play in the overall structure of a program?

2. Construct a flowchart to depict the logic involved in choosing from a McDonald's menu.

3. What are the six logical operators? Give two forms of each.

4. (T or F) The operator NOT $<$ has the same meaning as GREATER THAN OR EQUAL TO.

5. (T or F) The logical expression, A NOT = 4 AND NOT = 6, has the same meaning as A NOT = 4 OR NOT = 6. Explain.

6. What is an 88-level item? How is it used to effect conditional branching?

7. Distinguish between a class test and sign test. How may the class test be used to check data for validity?

8. In each of the following IF . . .THEN . . . statements, replace the compound logical expressions with simple expressions:

   ```
   IF A GREATER THAN B OR A EQUAL TO B THEN PERFORM
      ROUTINE-A.

   IF A LESS THAN C OR A EQUAL TO C THEN PERFORM ROUTINE-B.

   IF A GREATER THAN B OR A LESS THAN B THEN PERFORM
      ROUTINE-C.
   ```

9. Rewrite the following code using an IF . . . THEN . . . ELSE statement:

   ```
   IF A = B THEN PERFORM ROUTINE-C.
   IF A NOT = B THEN PERFORM ROUTINE-T.
   ```

10. Identify the errors or inconsistencies in the following IF statements:

IF A GREATER THAN C AND A EQUAL TO C THEN GO TO 100-WRITE.

IF A = B THEN NEXT SENTENCE PERFORM 200-COMPUTE-IT.

IF A < "BIG" OR NOT > "BIG" GO TO 3000-END-JOB.

IF A > THAN B AND C < D THEN PERFORM 200-ERROR.

IF C IS EQUAL TO D THEN GO TO 400-NEXT-READ.

IF A = C THEN PERFORM ROUTINE-C ELSE PERFORM ROUTINE-D ELSE PERFORM ROUTINE-E.

IF A > 4 OR A < 6 THEN PERFORM 100-READ ELSE PERFORM 200-WRITE.

IF X> 0 THEN DISPLAY "X IS NEGATIVE" ELSE
DISPLAY "X IS POSITIVE OR ZERO".

IF X < B AND B > 0 THEN DISPLAY "X IS POSITIVE".

IF X NOT = Y AND Y NOT > 0 THEN DISPLAY "X MUST BE NEGATIVE".

PROBLEMS

1. Create a departmental sales report which will read a sales input file and produce a breakdown of sales for each individual and a total for product line, with a store total. At the end of the report, produce a final total of all sales.

Input description

Position	Field name
1–20	NAME
26–34	SOCIAL SECURITY #
35–41 (99999V99)	SALES AMOUNT
50–51	STORE
52–53	PRODUCT LINE

Output description

(See output description on page 187.)

2. Produce a status report of your stock portfolio to determine the present value of your entire holdings. Compare the purchase price and the current price, and determine the percentage of increase or decrease in the value, of each individual stock. If the percentage of

decrease is 10% or more indicate this change by displaying the literal "SELL." If the percentage of increase is 15% or more, indicate this change by displaying the literal "BUY." At the end of the report, print the total purchase price for all stocks, the total current price for all stocks, and the percent of increase or decrease for the entire portfolio as a performance indicator.

Input description

Position	Field name
21–24	# OF SHARES
27–31 (999V99)	CURRENT PRICE
35–39 (999V99)	PURCHASE PRICE
42–49	NAME OF STOCK

Output description

(See output description on page 188.)

SALES REPORT   DATE XX-XX-XX

| STORE | PRODUCT | NAME | SOCIAL SECURITY | SALES |
| XX | XX | XXXXXXXXXXXXXXXXXXXX | XXX-XX-XXXX | $$$,$$$.99 |

TOTAL SALES OF $,$$$,$$$.99 FOR PRODUCT XX

TOTAL SALES OF $,$$$,$$$.99 FOR STORE XX

NEW PAGE

FINAL SALES TOTAL ALL STORES $$$,$$$,$$$.99

PORTFOLIO STATUS REPORT   DATE: XX-XX-XX

NAME OF STOCK	NUMBER OF SHARES	PURCHASE PRICE	CURRENT PRICE	PERCENTAGE	BUY/SELL
XXXXXXXXX	XXXX	222.99	222.99	XX.XX-	
OVERALL PORTFOLIO STATUS		2,222,229.99	2,222,229.99	XX.XX-	

10

ARRAYS AND ARRAY HANDLING

The concept of arrays and how to use them is one of the most difficult concepts in computer programming. COBOL provides for arrays of up to three dimensions. One-dimensional arrays are not very difficult to cope with, but two- and three-dimensional arrays sometimes make even seasoned programmers shudder. Nonetheless, arrays are important program constructs, and it is hard to envision an application that does not use them in one form or another.

THE CONCEPT OF AN ARRAY

An *array* is a sequence of fixed-length, contiguous memory locations. Arrays can be used to store numeric data or character data. Each location or element in an array is addressed relatively to the first element. A particular element is identified by an *index* or *subscript,* which is simply a numeric constant or variable whose value corresponds to the sequential position of that element. The name of an array element consists of the array name followed by the index enclosed in parentheses. The array name must conform to the COBOL convention for naming data fields. Figure 10–1 shows a one-dimensional array called TITLE.

In the figure, element 1 is referenced by the name TITLE (1), element 3 is called TITLE (3), and so forth. An array element can also be indexed by a variable containing a positive integer value less than or equal to the array

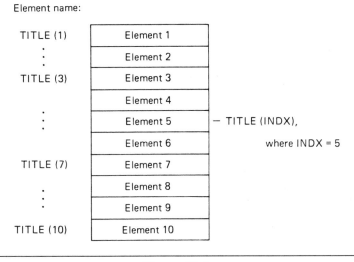

Figure 10-1
One-dimensional array consisting of ten elements or locations

size. Thus, we can reference any element in the array in Figure 10–1 with the name TITLE (INDX), where INDX is a numeric data item containing a value between 1 and 10. It is worth repeating that the value of an array index or subscript can never be less than one or more than the number of elements defined for the particular array.

An array may be pictured as a table or list of values. For example, the array TITLE in Figure 10–1 may be thought of as a list of book titles, motion picture titles, or titles of various job positions in a particular company. For the latter, the completed table (array) would be as shown in Figure 10–2.

In the figure, for each element of the table there is a corresponding value. For example, the value of TITLE (1) is PRESIDENT, the value of TITLE (3) is TREASURER, the value of TITLE (5) is GENERAL MANAGER, and so forth. To refer to any of the ten elements in this array, it is only necessary to use the array name followed by the number of the cell (in parentheses) occupied by the particular element in question. Remembering that it is also possible to refer to an array element using a variable subscript containing an appropriate value, we could also refer to any element in our table by TITLE (INDX), as previously indicated. If INDX contained the value 6, then TITLE (INDX) would refer to the element MANAGER, which occupies cell number 6 in the table.

Not all tables from ordinary experience can be represented by a one-dimensional list of values. Many tables—for example, tax tables and rate tables—require two dimensions, and hence, two subscripts, to reference their elements. Figure 10–3 shows a two-dimensional table.

In the figure, the table consists of five rows and five columns. The

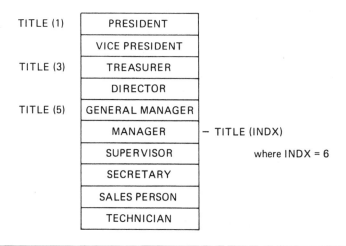

Figure 10-2
The array TITLE filled in with appropriate values

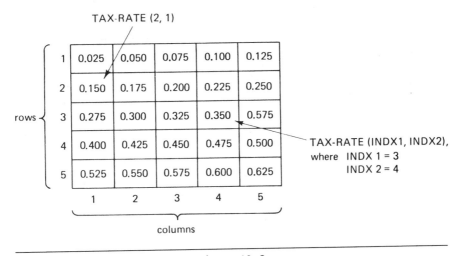

Figure 10-3
A two-dimensional table named TAX–RATE

rows, or horizontal entries, represent tax brackets and the columns, or vertical entries, represent numbers of dependents. Any element or location within this table is specified by using a pair of coordinates, the first of which indicates the row number and the second of which indicates the column number of the particular element. For example, .150 is contained in the cell located in the second row, first column. It is therefore referenced using the name of the array followed by the row and column coordinates in parentheses, thus: TAX–RATE (2, 1). The size of a two-dimensional array is the number of cells it contains, which happens to be equal to the number of rows multiplied by the number of columns. Hence, the table of Figure 10–3 is of size 5 × 5 = 25—i.e., the table has 25 cells. Note that the value of a row subscript can never exceed the number of rows contained in the array, and the value of a column subscript can never exceed the number of columns.

It is possible with two-dimensional tables to use variable subscripts, provided that the variables are numeric data fields. Thus, we can reference any element in the array of Figure 10–3 with the name TAX–RATE (INDX1, INDX2), where each of INDX1 and INDX2 contains an integer value between one and five. If INDX1 contained a value of 3 and INDX2 a value of 4, then TAX–RATE (INDX1, INDX2) would refer to .350 in the table.

Three-dimensional arrays do not occur frequently in normal applications. Often, they can be replaced by arrays with fewer dimensions. Figure 10–4 shows an extension of the two-dimensional array TAX–RATE of Figure 10–3 to include a third dimension, namely, marital status.

In the figure, the rows and columns continue to represent tax bracket

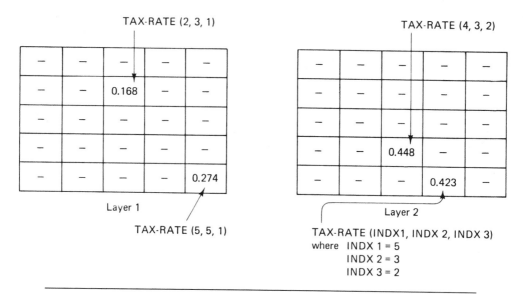

Figure 10-4
The array TAX-RATE extended to include a third dimension

and number of dependents, respectively. The layers represent marital status. A three-dimensional array requires an additional subscript to name the layer number. (In this case, there are only two layers.) As with arrays of fewer dimensions, the size of a three-dimensional array is equal to the number of cells it contains—in this case obtained by multiplying the number of rows by the number of columns by the number of layers. Thus, here TAX–RATE contains 5 × 5 × 2 = 50 cells. To reference a particular element, you use the array name followed by the row, column, and layer subscripts of that element, enclosed in parentheses. For example, the element .448 in the table is located in the fourth row, third column, second layer. It is therefore referenced by

TAX–RATE (4, 3, 2).

As with arrays of fewer dimensions, variable subscripts may be used. Thus, any element in the table of Figure 10–4 can be referenced by the name TAX–RATE (INDX1, INDX2, INDX3), where each of INDX1, INDX2, and INDX3 contains a numeric value in the appropriate range. If INDX1 contained 5, INDX2 4, and INDX3 contained 2, then TAX–RATE (INDX1, INDX2, INDX3) would refer to .423 in the table. Note that it is not necessary to use the particular names INDX1, etc. You can choose whatever names you want for variable subscripts, as long as they adhere to the COBOL rules for designating data fields.

DEFINING TABLES
IN THE COBOL PROGRAM

Using arrays or tables in a COBOL program involves coding considerations in both the DATA DIVISION and the PROCEDURE DIVISION. First, the tables and indexes, or subscripts, must be defined in the DATA DIVISION. A table may be part of a data record, or it can be set up as a separate entity in the WORKING–STORAGE SECTION of the program. A subscript can be any numeric data field, as long as its range of values is within the range of the table size. There is, however, a preferred method for defining subscripts. (See p. 198.)

Next, the table must be initialized with appropriate values, alphanumeric or numeric, as the case may be. This initialization can be done in either the DATA DIVISION or the PROCEDURE DIVISION, depending on the particular application.

Finally, the subscripts must be initialized and tested in the PROCEDURE DIVISION to make sure that the proper table entries are being referenced and that none of the subscripts exceeds the range of acceptable values.

There are several ways to do all of the above. Consider first how one-dimensional tables are defined. We can treat each element of the table as an occurrence of the table and say that the table "occurs" ten times, meaning that it contains ten cells or elements. Furthermore, we can think of each cell as having a finite length, which must be the same for all table cells. Again, the type of data that each table element is to contain must be the same for all cells. Thus, to define a table you must know (1) the number of times it occurs—that is, the number of cells it contains; (2) the length of each element or cell; and (3) the type of data each cell is to contain.

To specify the number of cells in a table, COBOL provides the OCCURS clause, which is a feature of the data descriptor. To specify the length and data type of the cells, the PICTURE clause is used. The general format of a table-defining data descriptor is

```
nn    data-name OCCURS k TIMES [INDEXED BY index-name]
                           PIC . . .
```

where nn is a level number between 02 and 49, and k is a positive numeric constant.

Level numbers 01 and 77 cannot be used in the OCCURS clause. Also, the INDEXED BY phrase is not required.

Example 10-1   Suppose that each cell of the table depicted in Figure 10–1 contains 15 alphanumeric characters. Then the code

```
01  ARRAY-TITLE.
    05  TITLE OCCURS 10  TIMES  PIC  X(15).
```

defines the table. Notice that level number 01 is used to define the group containing the array. Each element in the array is in turn defined as an 05-level data item, as COBOL does not allow you to name an array in an 01-level item. All stand-alone arrays must be defined in this manner. Arrays that are part of a data record or other data structure will by necessity be subordinate to the 01-level group item to which they belong. We shall discuss some of the techniques for initializing arrays with specific values after introducing the REDEFINES clause.

The REDEFINES clause, which is part of the data descriptor, is used to specify that a certain group or elementary data item will share the same internal memory area as another data item. Its general format is

```
nn    data-name-1  REDEFINES data-name-2  [PIC . . . ].
```

where nn is the level number of the redefining item. The level numbers of data-name-1 and data-name-2 can be any level numbers except 77 or 88, but must be the same. The redefined data item must be placed immediately after the data item it redefines.

Sometimes you may want a data item to take two different forms in a program. For example, you may want to treat the data as alphanumeric in one instance and numeric in another. Fields containing dates are frequently treated in that manner: in one instance you simply want to print the date, whereas in another you want to use the various components of the date in computations. The REDEFINES clause is ideal for such situations.

Example 10-2   The code

```
05  BIRTH-DATE             PIC  X(8).
05  BIRTH-DATE-R  REDEFINES  BIRTH-DATE.
    10  BIRTH-MONTH        PIC  99.
    10  FILLER             PIC  X     VALUE  "/".
    10  BIRTH-DAY          PIC  99.
    10  FILLER             PIC  X     VALUE  "/".
    10  BIRTH-YEAR         PIC  99.
```

redefines a date field. We can treat the redefined field, BIRTH-DATE, as a print item, or we can deal separately with any of the date components and use them in computations.

The REDEFINES clause may be used to initialize an array with a given set of values. When doing so, however, you must first define a list of values and then redefine the list, equating it with the array definition.

Example 10-3   The following code initializes the array of Example 10-1 with literal values:

```
01   JOB-TITLES.
     05  FILLER      PIC  X(15)    VALUE "PRESIDENT        ".
     05  FILLER      PIC  X(15)    VALUE "VICE PRESIDENT   ".
     05  FILLER      PIC  X(15)    VALUE "TREASURER        ".
     05  FILLER      PIC  X(15)    VALUE "DIRECTOR         ".
     05  FILLER      PIC  X(15)    VALUE "GENERAL MANAGER".
     05  FILLER      PIC  X(15)    VALUE "PLANT MANAGER    ".
     05  FILLER      PIC  X(15)    VALUE "SUPERVISOR       ".
     05  FILLER      PIC  X(15)    VALUE "SECRETARY        ".
     05  FILLER      PIC  X(15)    VALUE "SALESPERSON      ".
     05  FILLER      PIC  X(15)    VALUE "TECHNICIAN       ".
01   ARRAY-TITLE REDEFINES JOB-TITLES.
     05  TITLE OCCURS 10 TIMES PIC X(15).
```

The values that constitute the table are contained in the 01-level group item JOB-TITLES. There are ten elements, one for each cell in the table. Each element is spelled out exactly as it is to be stored in the table. In addition, each element is defined as an alphanumeric item and is allocated exactly 15 bytes. Immediately following the list of specific elements is the 01-level redefining item ARRAY-TITLE. This group item is sometimes called an *overlay*, because it occupies, or overlays, the same portion of computer memory as the group item JOB-TITLES. TITLE, the actual array name, is defined as occurring ten times, with each occurrence being exactly 15 bytes long. Each occurrence of TITLE corresponds to one element in the group item JOB-TITLES. For example, TITLE (1) contains the value "PRESIDENT   ", TITLE (2) contains the value "VICE PRESIDENT ", etc. With these values, the table is completely defined and initialized.

We next consider subscripts. Subscripts must be valid numeric items —either positive constants or data fields containing values within the range of the array size. If a data field is used, it must be either a display, packed decimal, or binary item. While not absolutely necessary, it is wise to define subscripts as binary data items, since binary subscripts tend to be more efficient from the standpoint of speed of execution. Data fields used to define variable subscripts can employ any level number except 88. Some examples of valid subscripts are:

```
77   INDX        PIC  S9(2)    COMP.

01   INDEX-A     PIC  9(5).

05   SUB-1       PIC  S9(3)    COMP-3.

77   A           PIC  9(2)     COMP      VALUE 0.
```

We are now ready to consider table manipulation in the PROCEDURE DIVISION. The task is to initialize the subscripts, vary them, and prevent them from exceeding their specified limit. How this task is accomplished depends largely upon the application. Suppose, for example, that we would like to display the list of values contained in the array TITLE. Suppose furthermore that we would like to number each item. The task is easily accomplished with a variant of the PERFORM statement, which we shall now discuss.

In Chapter 6 we showed how the PERFORM statement is used to produce iterations of a procedure. The number of iterations to be performed is explicitly stated with a numeric constant as follows:

```
PERFORM 100-ROUTINE-X 25 TIMES.
```

An extension of the PERFORM statement, called the PERFORM . . . VARYING statement, enables the programmer to control the iterative process by the use of numeric indexes. Now, manipulating an array is often an iterative process, in that it involves repetition of the same steps—steps that are controlled by the values assigned to the array subscripts. Accordingly, the PERFORM . . . VARYING statement is particularly suited to manipulating the array, providing a way of initializing and varying the subscript values through the desired range, and also preventing them from exceeding the prescribed limit. The general format of the PERFORM . . . VARYING statement is

```
PERFORM paragraph-name-1 [THRU paragraph-name-2] VARYING

    index-name
                FROM value-1  BY  value-2  UNTIL condition.
    data-name
```

Paragraph-name-1 is the name of the paragraph or section to be performed if the THRU option is not used. If the THRU option is used, paragraph-name-1 is the name of the first paragraph that is performed, and paragraph-name-2 is the name of the last paragraph performed. All paragraphs between the first and last are also performed. Index-name or data-name is the numeric data field containing the value to be varied. Value-1 is a numeric constant or data field indicating the beginning value of index-name or data-name, and value-2 is the amount by which index-name or data-name is varied during the process. Condition is an arithmetic or logical test that terminates the PERFORM . . . VARYING statement.

Example 10-4 The following code uses the PERFORM . . . VARYING statement to execute a group of paragraphs 10 times. The numeric data item J-COUNTER is used for control purposes.

```
PERFORM 100-ROUTINE-1 THRU 100-ROUTINE-5 VARYING
    J-COUNTER FROM 1 BY 1 UNTIL J-COUNTER > 10.
        •
        •
        •
```

```
100-ROUTINE-1.
    •
    •
    •
100-ROUTINE-5.
```

Processing begins with the data name, J-COUNTER, initialized with the value 1. J-COUNTER is incremented by 1 until its value reaches 11, at which time processing is completed. Each time J-COUNTER is incremented, the section of program code contained in ROUTINE-1 through ROUTINE-2 is performed. The net effect of the procedure is that this section of program code is performed 10 times. The same effect could be produced with the statement

```
PERFORM 100-ROUTINE-1 THRU 100-ROUTINE-2 10 TIMES.
```

However, if J-COUNTER is an index whose value is to be manipulated and referenced within the sections of performed program code, then the PERFORM...VARYING statement offers distinct advantages, as shown in the next example.

Example 10-5   The following code displays the contents of the array of Example 10-3 on the VDT screen using an index, J-COUNTER, together with the PERFORM...VARYING statement:

```
PERFORM 100-DISPLAY-ROUTINE VARYING J-COUNTER
    FROM 1 BY 1 UNTIL J-COUNTER > 10.
        •
        •
        •
100-DISPLAY-ROUTINE.
    DISPLAY LIN J-COUNTER COL 10 TITLE (J-COUNTER).
```

The code causes the ten elements of the array TITLE to be printed on the VDT screen in sequence, beginning on line 1. The displayed list will be aligned with column 10. As soon as the value of J-COUNTER reaches 11, the operation stops. If, instead, you wanted to print every other element of the array, starting with the first one, you could simply vary the index in the PERFORM...VARYING statement by 2 instead of 1, as follows:

```
PERFORM 100-DISPLAY-ROUTINE VARYING J-COUNTER
    FROM 1 BY 2 UNTIL J-COUNTER > 10.
```

The implications of the use of the PERFORM . . . VARYING statement in conjunction with arrays are far-reaching. (See the problems at the end of this chapter for some applications of the principles presented. The following example shows how to search a one-dimensional array for a specific value.

Example 10-6 The code

```
01  RECORD-FOUND        PIC 9        VALUE 0.
                         •
                         •
                         •
    PERFORM 100-SEARCH-ARRAY VARYING INDX
        FROM 1 BY 1 UNTIL INDX > 10 OR
        RECORD-FOUND = 1.
                     •
                     •
                     •
100-SEARCH-ARRAY.
    IF TITLE (INDX) = "GENERAL MANAGER" THEN
        MOVE 1 TO RECORD-FOUND.
```

uses the PERFORM . . . VARYING statement to search the array TITLE for the element GENERAL MANAGER. If this element is found (in this case of the table of Example 10-1 initialized with the values of Example 10-3, it will be), then the value 1 is moved to the field RECORD-FOUND, at which time the search is successfully terminated. If the element is not found, then the search is unsuccessfully terminated when the value of INDX exceeds 10. In this case the value of RECORD-FOUND remains zero, indicating that the element in question was not present in the table. A table search of this kind, where each element is examined in sequential order starting from the beginning of the array, is called a *linear search*.

TWO-DIMENSIONAL ARRAYS

The principles of defining one-dimensional arrays also apply to two-dimensional arrays, with the exception that there is an additional subscript to take care of. Accordingly, two-dimensional arrays are defined using two OCCURS clauses, as shown in Example 10-7.

Example 10-7 To define the two-dimensional array TAX-RATE shown in Figure 10-2, having five rows and five columns with each element consisting of three bytes, use the code

```
01  ARRAY-TAX-RATE.
    05  FILLER OCCURS 5 TIMES.
        10  TAX-RATE  OCCURS 5 TIMES PIC V999.
```

Notice that the first level of the array (the 05-level entry, which is actually the row indicator) is denoted by FILLER. This denotation is acceptable for two-dimensional arrays since the first level is never referenced by name. The second level of the array (the 10-level entry, which is the column indicator) does, however, bear a specific label, TAX-RATE, the name by which the array will be referenced. Note that the PICTURE clause is associated with the second-level entry. In other words, the array is capable of storing 25 numeric items composed of three digits each, preceded by an assumed decimal point.

Example 10–8 shows how a two-dimensional array can be initialized, as can a one-dimensional array, with the REDEFINES clause.

Example 10-8   The following code initializes the array TAX-RATE with the set of 25 values shown:

```
01  TAX-RATES.
    05  FILLER      PIC X(15)    VALUE "025050075010125".
    05  FILLER      PIC X(15)    VALUE "150175200225250".
    05  FILLER      PIC X(15)    VALUE "275300325350375".
    05  FILLER      PIC X(15)    VALUE "400425450475500".
    05  FILLER      PIC X(15)    VALUE "525550575600625".
01  ARRAY-TAX-RATE REDEFINES TAX-RATES.
    05  FILLER  OCCURS  5  TIMES.
        10  TAX-RATE  OCCURS  5  TIMES PIC V999.
```

Observe how the redefined group item containing the tax rates is arranged. There are five rows of FILLERs, each containing 15 characters of numeric data in character form. Each set of three digits in each of the five rows corresponds to a single element of the table. That is, a vertical line that ran from the top row to the bottom row separating each set of three digits would divide the data into five columns, thus completing the array. (See Figure 10–5.) There are accordingly twenty-five three-digit numbers: 025, 050, 075, and so forth. Each of these values is redefined in the array as a numeric item with an assumed decimal point at the beginning, so that the algebraic value

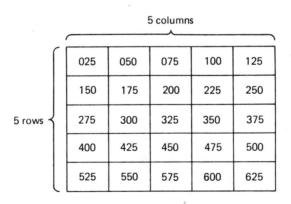

Tax-rate array contains 25 elements

Figure 10-5
Conceptualization of the two-dimensional array of Example 10-8

of the first element is .025, the second, .050, the third, .075, etc. Thus, the value, for example, of TAX–RATE (2, 1) is .150, and that of TAX–RATE (4, 3) is .450. Figure 10–5 shows the entire TAX–RATE array.

Two-dimensional arrays, of course, require two subscripts, which can be initialized and varied using the PERFORM . . .VARYING statement with an additional feature. Its general format is

```
PERFORM  paragraph-name-1  [THRU  paragraph-name-2]  VARYING

    index-name-1
                    FROM  value-1   BY   value-2   UNTIL  condition-1
    data-name-1

     AFTER

    index-name-2
                    FROM  value-3   BY   value-4   UNTIL  condition-2.
    data-name-2
```

This format is the same as the PERFORM . . . VARYING format shown earlier except for the addition of the AFTER clause, which permits the use of an additional index or subscript. The first FROM . . . BY . . . UNTIL line controls the first (row) index, and the second FROM . . . BY . . . UNTIL line controls the second (column) index. Example 10–9 shows how this form of the PERFORM . . . VARYING statement is used to manipulate two-dimensional arrays.

Example 10-9 The following code uses the PERFORM . . . VARYING . . . AFTER statement to display the contents of the array of Example 10–8 on the VDT screen:

```
    01 EDIT–OUT        PIC ZZ.999.
               •
               •
               •
       PERFORM 200–DISPLAY–RATES VARYING
          ROW–INDX FROM 1 BY 1 UNTIL ROW–INDX > 5
           AFTER
          COL–INDX FROM 1 BY 1 UNTIL COL–INDX > 5.
               •
               •
               •
    200–DISPLAY–RATES.
          MOVE TAX–RATE (ROW–INDX, COL–INDX) TO EDIT–OUT.
          MULTIPLY 8 BY COL–INDX  GIVING COL–NUMB.
          DISPLAY LIN ROW–INDX COL COL–NUMB EDIT–OUT.
```

Let us trace through the code of Example 10–9 to see how it works. First, ROW–INDX is set to the value 1. Then COL–INDX is varied from 1 by 1 until it is greater than 5. ROW–INDX is then incremented to the value 2, and COL–INDX is reset to 1 and again varied from 1 by 1 until it is greater than 5. Next, ROW–INDX is increased to the value 3, and COL–INDX is again reset to 1 and varied from 1 to 5. This process continues until ROW–INDX attains a value greater than 5. Each time an index is varied, the paragraph 200–DISPLAY–RATES is performed, with the following results.

First, the value of TAX–RATE (1, 1) is moved to the report item EDIT–OUT and the screen column coordinate is computed. The contents of EDIT–OUT are printed on line 1, column 8 of the screen, and the first iteration of the cycle is completed. Next, the value of TAX–RATE (1, 2) is moved to the report item. The screen column is recomputed, and the value of EDIT–OUT is printed on line 1, column 16 of the screen, and the second iteration is completed. The process continues in this manner until all twenty-five iterations of the cycle are completed. The result is shown in Figure 10–6.

As is plain from its context, the array TAX–RATE is intended to be used in computations, as is the case with many such tables. Any element of this array can be used as an arithmetic operand, as shown in Example 10–10.

Example 10-10 The code

```
COMPUTE TAXES ROUNDED = SALARY * TAX–RATE (ROW–INDX, COL–INDX)
```

uses the array TAX–RATE in an arithmetic computation. ROW–INDX and COL–INDX must be initialized with the proper values before the computation is performed.

THREE-DIMENSIONAL ARRAYS

In a three-dimensional array, the third dimension is usually represented as depth. It is also the third dimension referenced after the row and column; that is, in a three-dimensional array, the elements are referenced

.025	.050	.075	.100	.125
.150	.175	.200	.225	.250
.275	.300	.325	.350	.375
.400	.425	.450	.475	.500
.525	.550	.575	.600	.625

Figure 10-6
The output as produced on the VDT screen by the code of Example 10-9

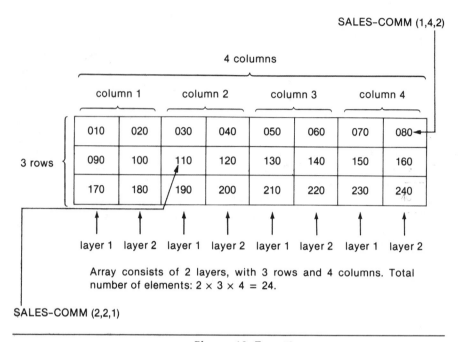

Figure 10-7
Conceptualization of a three-dimensional array

in the order row, column, layer. An array or table of three dimensions is defined quite simply by following the pattern used to define a two-dimensional array. (See Figure 10–7.)

Example 10-11   The code

```
01  ARRAY-SALES-COMM.
    05  FILLER  OCCURS  3  TIMES.
        10  FILLER  OCCURS  4  TIMES.
            15  SALES-COMM  OCCURS  2  TIMES  PIC  V999.
```

defines a three-dimensional array, SALES–COMM, consisting of three rows, four columns, and two layers. Since the table will be referenced at the third level of its occurrence, we need not specify data names for the first two levels, although we could if desired.

Initializing a three-dimensional table is done the same way as a two-dimensional table. It is simply a matter of preceding the table description with an image of its contents and redefining the image, as shown in Example 10–12.

Example 10-12   The code

```
01  SALES-COMMISSIONS.
    05  FILLER  PIC X(15)  VALUE "010020030040050060070080".
    05  FILLER  PIC X(15)  VALUE "090100110120130140150160".
    05  FILLER  PIC X(15)  VALUE "170180190200210220230240."
01  ARRAY-SALES-COMM REDEFINES SALES-COMMISSION.
    05  FILLER OCCURS  3  TIMES.
        10  FILLER OCCURS 4 TIMES.
            15  SALES-COMM  OCCURS  2  TIMES PIC V999.
```

uses the REDEFINES clause to initialize the table of Example 10-11 with appropriate values. The three 05-level entries under SALES-COMMISSIONS represent the three rows of the array. The columns and layers are a bit more difficult to conceptualize. The layers are actually embedded in the column entries. If we divide the three rows of FILLER entries into four columns of six digits each, we have both the column and layer specifications, as shown in Figure 10-7. The first three digits in each column represent the first layer of the column entry, and the second three digits the second layer of the same column. Thus, the value of the element SALES-COMM (1, 4, 2) in the table is .080, the value of the element SALES-COMM (2, 2, 1) is .110, and so forth.

To manipulate a three-dimensional array, COBOL provides yet a third extension to the PERFORM . . . VARYING statement in the form of an additional AFTER statement as follows:

```
PERFORM . . . . VARYING . . . . .
    . . . FROM . . . BY . . . UNTIL . . .
    AFTER
    . . . FROM . . . BY . . . UNTIL . . .
    AFTER
    . . . FROM . . . BY . . . UNTIL . . .
```

Using this extension of the PERFORM . . . VARYING statement is no different from using that for the two-dimensional case, except for the addition of a third subscript to control the depth references.

Example 10-13   The following code uses the PERFORM . . . VARYING statement to manipulate a three-dimensional array.

```
PERFORM 1000-COMPUTE-SALES-COMM VARYING
    INDX1 FROM 1 BY 1 UNTIL INDX1 > 3
    AFTER
    INDX2 FROM 1 BY 1 UNTIL INDX2 > 4
    AFTER
    INDX3 FROM 1 BY 1 UNTIL INDX3 > 2.
```

INDX1 is the row subscript, INDX2 the column subscript, and INDX3 the depth subscript. Within the paragraph 1000-COMPUTE-SALES-COMM, references to any of the elements of the array being manipulated (SALES-

COMM) would take the form SALES-COMM (INDX1, INDX2, INDX3). Several problems at the end of the chapter deal with three-dimensional arrays.

Up to now, the discussion of initialization of arrays has concentrated on how arrays with specific values are initialized statically from within the program. This method is fine for smaller arrays whose values are not likely to change often. However, with larger arrays with values likely to change frequently, it is better to store their values in an external disk file and to initialize the array dynamically using the READ statement. Example 10–14 shows how such dynamic initialization is done.

Example 10–14   The code below initializes a one-dimensional array whose values are stored on an external disk file. Each element of the array is assumed to contain a numeric code followed by an alphabetic description of the code. In other words, each element or occurrence of the array consists of two entries. The code consists of three digits, and the description consists of 15 characters. The maximum number of entries is 300.

```
DATA DIVISION.
FILE SECTION.
FD  ARRAY-ELEMENT-FILE
     DATA RECORD IS ARRAY-ELEMENT-RECORD.
01  ARRAY-ELEMENT-RECORD.
     02  ELEMENT-CODE      PIC 999.
     02  ELEMENT-DESC      PIC X(15).
                   •
                   •
                   •
WORKING-STORAGE SECTION.
01  END-OF-FILE-FLAG.      PIC XXX      VALUE "NO".
     88  NO-MORE-RECORDS                VALUE "YES".
                   •
                   •
                   •
01  INDX                   PIC 9(4)     COMP.
01  BIG-ARRAY.
     05  FILLER  OCCURS  300  TIMES.
          10  ARRAY-ELEMENT-CODE      PIC 999.
          10  ARRAY-ELEMENT-DESC      PIC X(15).
                   •
                   •
                   •
PROCEDURE DIVISION.
                   •
                   •
                   •
     PERFORM 1000-READ-AND-LOAD-ARRAY VARYING INDX
          FROM 1 BY 1 UNTIL NO-MORE-RECORDS.
                   •
                   •
                   •
1000-READ-AND-LOAD-ARRAY.
     READ ARRAY-ELEMENT-FILE AT END MOVE "YES" TO
          END-OF-FILE-FLAG.
```

```
MOVE ELEMENT-CODE TO ARRAY-ELEMENT-CODE (INDX).
MOVE ELEMENT-DESC TO ARRAY-ELEMENT-DESC (INDX).
```

As many elements as are required by an application may be included within a particular occurrence of an array, in accordance with the constraints of computer memory.

There are countless ways to employ arrays and tables within a program. Appendix C introduces further uses of arrays and explains some techniques for searching them for specific values. Appendix C presents a sample program that uses arrays extensively.

REVIEW QUESTIONS

1. What is a table or array? Distinguish between a one-, two-, and three-dimensional table.

2. What is the purpose of subscripts? How are they used in the case of a two-dimensional table? A three-dimensional table?

3. Write the code to define a one-dimensional table that is to be used for storing the names of the states. Each element of the table is to contain 14 characters, and the table is to contain a maximum of 50 entries.

4. Explain the role of the PERFORM . . . VARYING . . . statement in table handling. Write the program code to load values into the above table from a sequential disk file using the PERFORM . . . VARYING . . . statement.

5. A calendar for any given year may be thought of as a three-dimensional table, with the pages representing the months, the rows on each page representing the weeks, and the columns on each page representing the days of the week. Explain how a three-dimensional array may be used to store an annual calendar.

6. Write the code to define the table you explained in the previous exercise.

7. Write the program code to print the contents of the table using the PERFORM . . . VARYING . . . statement.

PROBLEMS

NOTE: For these three problems, THERE ARE DELIBERATE ERRORS in the input file. Design your programs to test each of the fields for correctness. Do not change the data in order to make your program work. Make your program work to handle any data.

1. Using the crime table shown below you are to produce a detail report of all persons arrested. The input data contains:

Position	Field name
1–20	DEFENDANT NAME
21–24	OFFENSE CODE
25	SEX OF DEFENDANT
26	REGION OF ARREST

The output requires that you interpret the OFFENSE CODE, ensure that it is correct, determine the correct classification, and print the name, offense code and classification, sex of defendant, and region of arrest (see p. 209).
The crime table is:

100	Homicide
200	Rape
300	Robbery
400	Aggravated assault
500	Burglary
600	Theft (except auto)
700	Auto theft
800	Other assaults
900	Arson—catastrophe
1000	Forgery—counterfeiting
1100	Fraud
1200	Embezzlement
1300	Stolen property
1400	Vandalism
1500	Weapons
1600	Prostitution
1700	Sex offenses
1800	Narcotic-drug laws
1900	Gambling

2. This problem is a variation of problem 1. Instead of printing a detail line for each defendant, read the entire data file and produce a summary report containing only the offense code, classification, and the number of males and females that have been arrested for that classification. The output requirement is shown on p. 210.

3. This problem will allow the reader to test his or her skills by designing a three-dimensional table or array to accomplish this function. This variation is to read the entire data file, interpret each of the input fields for correctness, and produce a printed report showing the offense code, classification, and the number of males and females that have been arrested for these offense codes broken down by five regions. The output requirement is shown on p. 211.

NATIONAL CRIME REPORT

DATE: XX-XX-XX

REMARKS
LINE NO.
WORD NO.
PRINT POSITION

CRIME CODE
NAME
CLASSIFICATION
SEX
REGION

209

NATIONAL CRIME REPORT   DATE XX-XX-XX

CRIME CODE	CLASSIFICATION	MALES	FEMALES
XXXXX	XXXXXXXXXXXX X XXXXXXXXXXXX	2,229	2,229

REMARKS

LINE NO.

WORD NO

PRINT POSITION

NATIONAL CRIME REPORT

DATE XX-XX-XX

CRIME CODE	CLASSIFICATION	REGION 1		REGION 2		REGION 3		REGION 4		REGION 5	
		MALE	FEMALE	MALE	FEMALE	MALE	FEMALE	MALE	FEMALE	MALE	FEMALE
XXXXX	XXXXXXXXXXXXXXXXXXXXXXXX	XXXX	XXX	XXXX	XXX	XXXX	XXX	XXXX	XXX	XXXX	XXX

LINE NO. — WORD NO — PRINT POSITION — LINE NO. — REMARKS

11

FILES AND FILE PROCESSING

A *file* is a collection of records related to a given application. A *record* is a collection of data items or fields that are related to a given event or transaction. Records are composed of *characters,* which, taken together, have a given meaning. These relationships are reflected in the COBOL *data hierarchy:* (1) the file is described by SELECT and FD statements; (2) the record is the 01 level; (3) a field is any level between 02 and 49 and consists of a subset of the characters from A to Z, numbers, and special characters.

FILE ORGANIZATION AND ACCESS

Many systems have two generic types of file organization: sequential and random. A *sequential* file is generally organized either in the order in which the records have been entered or in ascending order of a unique identifier. For the file at the end of Chapter 6, the initial order was one record after another. The data listing shows, however, that the students' social security numbers (the unique identifier, or key) are in ascending order. For most applications, sequential files are generally in some sort of identifier order.

A *random* file is a file whose records are in no particular order but do have a unique identifier. Records may be retrieved from such a file only by means of that identifier; if you elected to retrieve all the records of a random file, from first to last, there would be no rhyme or reason to the sequence of the records retrieved.

A third type of file organization is *indexed,* which is an organization that provides access to data either sequentially or randomly. Records organized as indexed can be retrieved one at a time or from beginning to end by using a series of pointers. Indexed organization provides an alternative to sequential and random organizations, giving you the best of both worlds.

File access is the technique used to retrieve data. A program that states

ACCESS IS SEQUENTIAL

is requesting that all records in the file be retrieved one after the other, from beginning to end. A program that states

ACCESS IS RANDOM

is requesting that records be retrieved in no particular order, regardless of how the file is organized. A program that states

ACCESS IS DYNAMIC

Table 11-1
File organization and types of access

File organization	File access allowed
Sequential	Sequential
Random	Dynamic, random
Indexed	Dynamic, random, sequential

is requesting that records be retrieved from some point in the file (not the beginning) and continue to be retrieved one after the other (sequentially). Table 11-1 lists the types of file access allowed with each type of file organization.

FILE MAINTENANCE

File maintenance is the updating—i.e., the adding, removing, and changing—of records in a file. Particularly for a file in which data is kept in order of entry, records must periodically be purged to make more space available.

File maintenance on sequential files is accomplished by passing every record in the master file and comparing each record with transactions that will update the master. During this process an output file is created, which will then become the master file. For a file that is organized in either indexed or dynamic mode, it is not necessary to process every record in the file to perform maintenance. You may choose to retrieve only records that have to be changed or deleted, and add new records. However, this type of maintenance on indexed files requires that a file reorganization or "reorg" be periodically performed. A *reorg* is the task of copying the file from one medium to another and dropping the records you no longer need.

SEQUENTIAL PROCESSING AND SEQUENTIAL FILE MAINTENANCE

As explained earlier, sequential processing is the technique of retrieving records sequentially, i.e., one after another. In Chapter 6, we coded a program to enter records sequentially into a file and another program to retrieve the records sequentially from that file.

Students' social security numbers, arranged in ascending sequence

Identifier	Transaction type
191000006	CHANGE—major
191000008	CHANGE—admission date
191000012	REMOVE
191000016	CHANGE—name
191000020	REMOVE
191000031	ADD
191000032	ADD
191000033	ADD

Figure 11-1
Record identifiers and types of transaction for updating master file

(low to high), were used as the identifier for the file, and both programs performed sequential processing using that identifier.

Suppose now that during the semester some students dropped out, some changed their major, and new students were admitted. These events are called *transactions,* and we can gather them all together and process them sequentially against the master file. Figures 11–1 through 11–3 show that student master file, the transactions to be processed, and the updated student file, respectively.

```
ABARA,ROSALIND        1910000010801801
APPLEBAUM,CARLA       1910000020801822
ARNHOLD,DEBORAH       1910000030110833
ATKINSON,TRACEY       1910000040105835
BAILEY,PATRICIA       1910000050110804
BARR,THOMAS           1910000060921815
COHEN,JILL            1910000080223826
DESANCTIS,PAUL        1910000090302825
DEVERENT,MICHAEL      1910000100910790
FREDERICO,ALICIA      1910000110402794
FREEDMAN,LAUREEN      1910000121008827
HABER,JEFF            1910000130501822
HARDING,PHEBE         1910000140301817
HATHAWAY,LARRY        1910000150301838
HELLER,KAREN          1910000160207804
HODULIK,DEBORAH       1910000170401814
IACOVELLI,MICHAEL     1910000180918815
MCKNIGHT,GREGORY      1910000190201828
NEBORAK,JOANNE        1910000200501830
PALMER,DOROTHY        1910000210304824
RACCOSTA,CATHY        1910000220920811
ROEBERG,LISA          1910000230520830
SUHOSKEY,VIRGINIA     1910000241019827
SWENK,DIANE           1910000250301835
VENUTO,JOANN          1910000260309813
WOODS,JOAN            1910000270910829
ZOMORIODIAN,ALI       1910000280820823
```

Figure 11-2
Student master file

STUDENT LISTING

DATE: 840411

NAME	SOCIAL SECURITY NUMBER	ADMISSION DATE	CURRICULUM CODE
ABARA, ROSALIND	191-00-0001	08/01/80	1
APPLEBAUM, CARLA	191-00-0002	08/01/82	2
ARNHOLD, DEBORAH	191-00-0003	01/10/83	3
ATKINSON, TRACEY	191-00-0004	01/05/83	5
BAILEY, PATRICIA	191-00-0005	01/10/80	4
BARR, THOMAS	191-00-0006	09/21/81	8
COHEN, JILL	191-00-0008	04/30/83	6
DESANCTIS, PAUL	191-00-0009	03/02/82	5
DEVERENT, MICHAEL	191-00-0010	09/10/79	0
FREDERICO, ALICIA	191-00-0011	04/02/79	4
HABER, JEFF	191-00-0013	05/01/82	2
HARDING, PHEBE	191-00-0014	03/01/81	7
HATHAWAY, LARRY	191-00-0015	03/01/83	8
HALLER, KAREN	191-00-0016	02/07/80	4
HODULIK, DEBORAH	191-00-0017	04/01/81	4
IACOVELLI, MICHAEL	191-00-0018	09/18/81	5
MCKNIGHT, GREGORY	191-00-0019	02/01/82	8
PALMER, DOROTHY	191-00-0021	03/04/82	4
RACCOSTA, CATHY	191-00-0022	09/20/81	1
ROEBERG, LISA	191-00-0023	05/20/83	0
SUHOSKEY, VIRGINIA	191-00-0024	10/19/82	7
SWENK, DIANE	191-00-0025	03/01/83	5
VENUTO, JOANN	191-00-0026	03/09/81	3
WOODS, JOAN	191-00-0027	09/10/82	9
ZOMORIODIAN, ALI	191-00-0028	08/20/82	3
BELSKY, KATHLEEN	191-00-0031	02/07/81	7
SEA, DOROTHEA	191-00-0032	04/29/83	5
CROWE, JOHN	191-00-0033	07/26/83	0

Figure 11-3
Updated student file (master and transactions combined)

RANDOM FILE MAINTENANCE

As with sequential files, updating a random file requires a master file and a transaction file. However, it is not necessary to have a third, new student file: the transactions are used to change the master file records exactly where they appear in the master data file.

Figures 11-4 and 11-5 show the old and updated student master files, respectively, for updating a random indexed file with the transactions shown in Figure 11-1.

FILE BACKUP

When doing either sequential or random file maintenance, be sure to make a copy of your master file *before* you begin. If a data file is destroyed, the recovery procedure is extremely unpleasant if a backup was not taken

```
                               STUDENT LISTING
                                                    DATE: 840411
                               SOCIAL SECURITY    ADMISSION    CURRICULU'
                NAME               NUMBER            DATE         CODE

          ABARA,ROSALIND          191-00-0001      08/01/80       1
          APPLEBAUM,CARLA         191-00-0002      08/01/82       2
          ARNHOLD,DEBORAH         191-00-0003      01/10/83       3
          ATKINSON,TRACEY         191-00-0004      01/05/83       5
          BAILEY,PATRICIA         191-00-0005      01/10/80       4
          BARR,THOMAS             191-00-0006      09/21/81       5
          BELSKY,KATHLEEN         191-00-0007      81/07/81       4
          COHEN,JILL              191-00-0008      02/23/82       6
          DESANCTIS,PAUL          191-00-0009      03/02/82       5
          DEVERENT,MICHAEL        191-00-0010      09/10/79       0
          FREDERICO,ALICIA        191-00-0011      04/02/79       4
          FREEDMAN,LAUREEN        191-00-0012      10/08/82       7
          HABER,JEFF              191-00-0013      05/01/82       2
          HARDING,PHEBE           191-00-0014      03/01/81       7
          HATHAWAY,LARRY          191-00-0015      03/01/83       8
          HELLER,KAREN            191-00-0016      02/07/80       4
          HODULIK,DEBORAH         191-00-0017      04/01/81       4
          IACOVELLI,MICHAEL       191-00-0018      09/18/81       5
          MCKNIGHT,GREGORY        191-00-0019      02/01/82       8
          NEBORAK,JOANNE          191-00-0020      05/01/83       0
          PALMER,DOROTHY          191-00-0021      03/04/82       4
          RACCOSTA,CATHY          191-00-0022      09/20/81       1
          ROEBURG,LISA            191-00-0023      05/20/83       0
          SUHOSKEY,VIRGINIA       191-00-0024      10/19/82       7
          SWENK,DIANE             191-00-0025      03/01/83       5
          SEA,DOROTHEA            191-00-0027      83/10/82       4
          ZOMORIODIAN,ALI         191-00-0028      08/20/82       3
```

Figure 11-4
The student master file before updates

before beginning maintenance. A backup should be made no matter how long it takes. If you made only a minor change to a program, be sure to back up your file or work with a test file so that you do not lose data. Innumerable times someone has said only one line of code was changed and ended up with a two-day recovery procedure.

You may back up or copy your files using the DOS COPY function or a program that you may purchase, such as COPYIIPC. If you are using sequential files and doing a sequential file update, you must also remember to copy the updated master file under the old master name so that the next time you process a group of transactions you are updating the correct version of the master file.

When you are copying index sequential files, be sure to copy both the prime data and the index file. You may elect to use the "wildcard" character to copy both files or copy each file individually.

```
                         STUDENT LISTING
                                          DATE:  840411
                         SOCIAL SECURITY   ADMISSION   CURRICULU▌
              NAME          NUMBER           DATE        CODE

    ABARA,ROSALIND        191-00-0001      08/01/80        1
    APPLEBAUM,CARLA       191-00-0002      08/01/82        2
    ARNHOLD,DEBORAH       191-00-0003      01/10/83        3
    ATKINSON,TRACEY       191-00-0004      01/05/83        5
    BAILEY,PATRICIA       191-00-0005      01/10/80        4
    BARR,THOMAS           191-00-0006      09/21/81        5
    BELSKY,KATHLEEN       191-00-0007      81/07/81        4
    COHEN,JILL            191-00-0008      02/23/82        6
    DESANCTIS,PAUL        191-00-0009      03/02/82        5
    DEVERENT,MICHAEL      191-00-0010      09/10/79        0
    FREDERICO,ALICIA      191-00-0011      04/02/79        4
    FREEDMAN,LAUREEN      191-00-0012      10/08/82        7
    HABER,JEFF           191-00-0013      05/01/82        2
    HARDING,PHEBE         191-00-0014      03/01/81        7
    HATHAWAY,LARRY        191-00-0015      03/01/83        8
    HELLER,KAREN          191-00-0016      02/07/80        4
    HODULIK,DEBORAH       191-00-0017      04/01/81        4
    IACOVELLI,MICHAEL     191-00-0018      09/18/81        5
    MCKNIGHT,GREGORY      191-00-0019      02/01/82        8
    NEBORAK,JOANNE        191-00-0020      05/01/83        0
    PALMER,DOROTHY        191-00-0021      03/04/82        4
    RACCOSTA,CATHY        191-00-0022      09/20/81        1
    ROEBURG,LISA          191-00-0023      05/20/83        0
    SUHOSKEY,VIRGINIA     191-00-0024      10/19/82        7
    SWENK,DIANE           191-00-0025      03/01/83        5
    SEA,DOROTHEA          191-00-0027      83/10/82        4
    ZOMORIODIAN,ALI       191-00-0028      08/20/82        3
    ATKINSON,WILLIAM      191-00-0031      04/01/84        3
    DESANCTIS,PAUL        191-00-0032      05/01/83        6
```

Figure 11-5
Updated master file (same as physical data file on disk)

COBOL AND SEQUENTIAL FILES

COBOL processes sequential files in a straightforward manner. In the FILE–CONTROL paragraph, you must use the SELECT statement to identify the device you are using. With a sequential file the SELECT clause would be

```
SELECT filename ASSIGN TO DISK
ACCESS MODE IS SEQUENTIAL
ORGANIZATION IS SEQUENTIAL
FILE STATUS IS status-field.
```

The ACCESS and ORGANIZATION statements are optional; however, you may prefer to use them to take advantage of COBOL's self-documenting features. The FILE STATUS clause is also optional and refers to a two-character field in either the WORKING–STORAGE SECTION or LINKAGE SEC-

TION. The field contains one of the following codes that indicate the results of an I/O operation made against a data file:

File status codes	Meaning
00	Successful operation or completion
10	End-of-file condition
21	Key not in sequence
22	Attempt to write a duplicate record
23	No record found
24	Disk space full
30	Permanent error
91	File structure destroyed

Some of these codes will be explained in great detail; others are self-explanatory.

The DATA DIVISION entries for a sequential file are as follows:

```
FD   filename
     LABEL RECORDS ARE STANDARD
     VALUE-OF-FILE-ID "file label.file extension"
     RECORD CONTAINS _____ CHARACTERS
     DATA RECORD IS data-record.
```

In file processing, an FD entry must appear for every file named in a SELECT statement. Also, a sequential file on diskette requires the statement LABEL RECORDS ARE STANDARD in its FD, and the clause ASSIGN TO DISK in the SELECT statement. The VALUE-OF-FILE-ID clause is the actual file label of your data file on disk. The name must match exactly; otherwise you cannot access the data file. It must contain the file label and the file extension of the data file. For example, the file used on p. 217 is called "STUDENT.DAT". The file label is STUDENT and the file extension is DAT, with a period separating the label from the extension. Refer to your operating system manual for a more detailed explanation of file names.

RECORD CONTAINS is used only for purposes of documentation and will provide a warning message after your compile only if the stated number of characters differs from the computed length of the data record (01 group-item length, or total length of all elementary items under the group item 01).

The PROCEDURE DIVISION contains all access verbs to any data file. In COBOL, a file must be opened in the PROCEDURE DIVISION before any function can be performed on it. For sequential data files, any of the following options of the OPEN verb may be used:

```
OPEN INPUT filename
OPEN OUTPUT filename
```

```
OPEN I–O filename
OPEN EXTEND filename
```

Your choice of option affects which of the verbs you can use during the processing of the file.

A data file opened by OPEN INPUT must exist, or the program will terminate abnormally. To create a sequential file, the verb OPEN OUTPUT must be used. When it is, any file on disk with the same file name is destroyed when the new file is written. Hence, make sure that the file being opened is not a master file that is needed for any further processing. If it is needed, a backup copy of it should be made before using OPEN OUTPUT.

If a program is going to read and change records in a sequential file, the file must be opened using OPEN I–O. When this form of the OPEN statement is used, the file must exist on disk or the program will terminate abnormally. The last form of the OPEN verb is OPEN EXTEND. When a file is opened with this format, the file must exist and records will be added at the end of the data records as if the file were opened in OUTPUT mode.

Examples 11–1 through 11–4 show how the various formats of the OPEN statement and the FILE STATUS feature of the FD clause are jointly used. We shall assume that the following SELECT and FD clauses have been coded for all of the example, and all other necessary COBOL code has been written.

```
SELECT STUDENT-FILE ASSIGN TO DISK
    ACCESS MODE IS SEQUENTIAL
    ORGANIZATION IS SEQUENTIAL
    FILE STATUS IS STUDENT-FILE-STATUS.

FD  STUDENT-FILE
    LABEL RECORDS ARE STANDARD
    VALUE-OF-FILE-ID "STUDENT.DAT"
    RECORD CONTAINS 80 CHARACTERS
    DATA RECORD IS STUDENT-RECORD.
```

Example 11-1   The following code OPENs a sequential file for read-only input and checks the file status.

```
OPEN-FILES.
    OPEN INPUT STUDENT-FILE.
    IF STUDENT-FILE-STATUS = "00" GO TO OPEN-EXIT.
    IF STUDENT-FILE-STATUS = "30"
        DISPLAY "FILE DOES NOT EXIST" GO TO END-PROGRAM.
    DISPLAY "ERROR ON OPENING FILE STUDENT-FILE"
    DISPLAY "FILE STATUS RETURN CODE IS ",
        STUDENT-FILE-STATUS, GO TO END-PROGRAM.
OPEN-EXIT. EXIT.
```

Checking is done by placing a return code in the file-status field at run time, and this code may be integrated by the program for further processing decisions. In this instance the test is for successful execution of the OPEN statement, implying that the file was found and made available. If the file-status return code is 30, the file does not exist on the default disk. Such a failure could be caused by the wrong disk being inserted or by the file being lost or destroyed in past processing. Investigation is required to determine what happened. In the example, for all error codes other than 30, we have elected to display on the screen both the return code and a message alerting the user to a problem. The user must then refer to his manual for an interpretation of the particular return code he incurs. An alternative would have been to integrate each of the return codes at one time, but there is really no need to do so so early in the program.

Example 11-2 The following code OPENs a data file for output processing and checks the file status.

```
OPEN-FILES.
     OPEN OUTPUT STUDENT-FILE.
     IF STUDENT-FILE-STATUS = "00" GO TO OPEN-EXIT.
     DISPLAY "ERROR ON OPENING FILE STUDENT-FILE"
     DISPLAY "FILE STATUS RETURN CODE IS ",
          STUDENT-FILE-STATUS, GO TO END-PROGRAM.
OPEN-EXIT. EXIT.
```

In this situation there can only be a test for a return code of 00. If a file is opened for output, and the file already exists, then the old file is destroyed and an entry is made for the new file. Hence, in creating files, be careful not to destroy the current version of the file. Remember, creating a file implies that the new version of the data is the latest; all other versions are no longer considered to be valid or current. Accordingly, the best alternative available in this form of the OPEN verb is to test whether the file has been successfully opened, and if not, terminate the program and display the file return code.

Example 11-3 The following code OPENs a data file for I-O processing and checks the file status.

```
OPEN-FILES.
     OPEN I-O STUDENT-FILE.
     IF STUDENT-FILE-STATUS = "00" GO TO OPEN-EXIT.
     IF STUDENT-FILE-STATUS = "30"
        DISPLAY "FILE DOES NOT EXIST" GO TO END-PROGRAM.
     DISPLAY "ERROR ON OPENING FILE STUDENT-FILE"
     DISPLAY "FILE STATUS RETURN CODE IS ",
          STUDENT-FILE-STATUS, GO TO END-PROGRAM.
OPEN-EXIT. EXIT.
```

The code reads and rewrites records to a data file. When OPEN I-O is used, the file must exist; otherwise 30 is the status return code. In this example, all other codes are displayed, and the user must determine the appropriate corrective action to be taken.

Example 11-4   The code

```
OPEN-FILES.
    OPEN EXTEND STUDENT-FILE.
    IF STUDENT-FILE-STATUS = "00" GO TO OPEN-EXIT.
    DISPLAY "ERROR ON OPENING FILE STUDENT-FILE"
    DISPLAY "FILE STATUS RETURN CODE IS ",
        STUDENT-FILE-STATUS, GO TO END-PROGRAM.
OPEN-EXIT. EXIT.
```

OPENs a sequential data file for EXTENDed processing—i.e., records will be added to the end of the file—and checks the file status. If we receive any return code other than 00, a message will be displayed and the processing will be terminated.

You may feel that Examples 11-1 through 11-4 represent a lot of superfluous code, but checking return codes will eliminate or reduce the number of files you lose. Essentially, the most valuable asset in any data processing environment is the data files; some cannot be replaced under any circumstances.

The COBOL CLOSE verb is relatively straightforward. However, after you CLOSE any data file, you should inspect the file return code. If you do not receive a completion code that indicates success, you may have a problem with the file. For example, it may be that after having created or added records to the file, you fill up the disk. Depending on the particulars of the situation, you may lose up to 256 characters of data, which in Examples 11-1 through 11-4 is over three data records. You must CLOSE the data file in order to transfer as much data as possible to the disk. To recover the data file, use the rebuild function that is available with COBOL.

In sequential processing, depending upon the OPEN option selected, only certain processing verbs are valid. For instance, in Example 11-1 STUDENT-FILE was opened with the INPUT option; therefore the only processing verb that could be used was READ. The format of the READ statement was presented earlier; it only remains to say that the AT END condition is equivalent to a return code of 10. Thus, instead of testing the file-status field for a return code of 10, you only need use the AT END option.

Example 11-2 used the OUTPUT option of the OPEN verb; consequently, only the WRITE verb could be used for the data file. For processing a sequential data file on disk, neither the ADVANCING option nor any of the other print-file options should be used. The only difficulty you may encounter in using the WRITE verb for a sequential file is a boundary error, which indicates that the disk is full (file status 30). Make sure to test the file-status field for a boundary error after each WRITE. If you encounter an error, close the file to eliminate loss of data and notify anyone who uses the file with a message directing him to take appropriate action.

In Example 11–3 the file was opened using the I–O option of the OPEN command. With this option, the operative processing verbs are READ and REWRITE. The WRITE verb may not be used here because the ORGANIZA-TION clause specifies SEQUENTIAL. REWRITE, which may be used only after a successful READ, has as its format

    REWRITE record-name [FROM data-name]

Remember that with sequential file organization, if you REWRITE a record that is longer than the record read, you will lose some of the data characters of the new record. You can only REWRITE the same number of characters as has been read. On the other hand, if you REWRITE a record that is smaller than the record read, the system will replace the remaining charac-ters with any characters it chooses up to the next data record. Accordingly, be cautious when using REWRITE to avoid unpleasant surprises.

In Example 11–4 the file was opened in EXTEND mode, which posi-tions the record pointer to the first available point after the last data record. The only processing verb available with the EXTEND option of the OPEN command is WRITE. Remember, EXTEND only adds records to the end of the file; it does nothing to any of the existing records.

Table 11–2 summarizes all the options connected with the OPEN verb, together with the appropriate processing verbs, for sequential organization of files.

SEQUENTIAL FILE MAINTENANCE WITH COBOL

This section presents the core of a COBOL program to process a master file and transaction file, and create an updated master file. The pro-gram deals with our familiar student file discussed at length in this and previous sections. Only the code necessary to execute the update function is presented; the rest of the program is left to the reader to fill in as his or

Table 11-2
Options of the OPEN verb and file-processing capabilities

Processing verbs	Open option			
	INPUT	OUTPUT	I-O	EXTEND
READ	X		X	
WRITE		X		X
REWRITE			X	

her particular application dictates. (One completed version of the program is given in Appendix C.) The program shown here requires three data files—two for input, and one for output. The transaction file is assumed to have been created by another program. To perform a sequential update properly, both the transaction and master files must be arranged in the same sequence.

The ENVIRONMENT DIVISION entries for the program are:

```
SELECT STUDENT-FILE ASSIGN TO DISK
   ACCESS MODE IS SEQUENTIAL
   ORGANIZATION IS SEQUENTIAL
   FILE STATUS IS STUDENT-FILE-STATUS.

SELECT TRANSACTION-FILE ASSIGN TO DISK
   ACCESS MODE IS SEQUENTIAL
   ORGANIZATION IS SEQUENTIAL
   FILE STATUS IS TRANSACTION-FILE-STATUS.

SELECT UPDATED-STUDENT-FILE ASSIGN TO DISK
   ACCESS MODE IS SEQUENTIAL
   ORGANIZATION IS SEQUENTIAL
   FILE STATUS IS STUDENT-UPDATE-STATUS.
```

STUDENT-FILE is the master file containing current information concerning students. TRANSACTION-FILE contains the changes that must be made to STUDENT-FILE to reflect the current status of all students. UPDATED-STUDENT-FILE will contain the results of combining STUDENT-FILE and TRANSACTION-FILE.

The DATA DIVISION entries for these files are:[1]

```
FD  STUDENT-FILE
    LABEL RECORDS ARE STANDARD
    VALUE-OF-FILE-ID IS "STUDENT.DAT"
    RECORD CONTAINS 80 CHARACTERS
    DATA RECORD IS STUDENT-RECORD.

01  STUDENT-REC
                        •
                        •
                        •
    05  STUDENT-SSN             PIC 9(9).
                        •
                        •
                        •

FD  TRANSACTION-FILE
    LABEL RECORDS ARE STANDARD
    VALUE-OF-FILE-ID IS "TRNSACT.DAT"
    RECORD CONTAINS 80 CHARACTERS
    DATA RECORD IS TRANSACTION-RECORD.
```

[1] Note that the VALUE-OF-FILE-ID clause does not specify a drive. In that case the system expects to find the files on the default drive. The general format of the VALUE-OF-FILE-ID clause is: VALUE-OF-FILE-ID {drive:filename.filespec}

```
01   TRANSACTION-REC.
                      •
                      •
                      •
     05   TRANSACTION-SSN          PIC 9(9).
                      •
                      •
                      •

FD   UPDATED-STUDENT-FILE
     LABEL RECORDS ARE STANDARD
     VALUE-OF-FILE-ID IS "UPDSTDT.DAT"
     RECORD CONTAINS 80 CHARACTERS
     DATA RECORD IS UPDATED-STUDENT-RECORD.

01   UPDATED-STUDENT-REC.
                      •
                      •
                      •
     05   UPDATED-STUDENT-SSN      PIC 9(9).
                      •
                      •
                      •
```

Next, the PROCEDURE DIVISION statements are presented:

```
OPEN-FILES.
     OPEN INPUT STUDENT-FILE.
     IF STUDENT-FILE-STATUS = "00" GO TO OPEN-TRANS-FILE.
     IF STUDENT-FILE-STATUS = "30"
        DISPLAY "STUDENT FILE DOES NOT EXIST"
        GO TO END-PROGRAM.
     DISPLAY "ERROR ON OPENING STUDENT FILE "
     DISPLAY "FILE STATUS RETURN CODE IS ",
            STUDENT-FILE-STATUS, GO TO END-PROGRAM.
OPEN-TRANS-FILE.
     OPEN INPUT TRANSACTION-FILE.
     IF TRANSACTION-FILE-STATUS = "00"
            GO TO OPEN-UPDATE-FILE.
     IF TRANSACTION-FILE-STATUS = "30"
        DISPLAY "TRANSACTION FILE DOES NOT EXIST"
        GO TO END-PROGRAM.
     DISPLAY "ERROR ON OPENING TRANSACTION FILE"
     DISPLAY "FILE STATUS RETURN CODE IS ",
            TRANSACTION-FILE-STATUS, GO TO END-PROGRAM.
OPEN-UPDATE-FILE.
     OPEN OUTPUT UPDATED-STUDENT-FILE.
     IF STUDENT-UPDATE-STATUS = "00" GO TO OPEN-EXIT.
     DISPLAY "ERROR ON OPENING UPDATED STUDENT FILE"
     DISPLAY "FILE STATUS RETURN CODE IS ",
            STUDENT-UPDATE-STATUS, GO TO END-PROGRAM.
OPEN-EXIT. EXIT.
                      •
                      •
                      •

         PERFORM READ-MASTER-RTN.
         PERFORM READ-TRANSACTION-RTN.
         PERFORM COMPARE-AND-PROCESS UNTIL
            UPDATE-COMPLETE = "YES".
```

```
COMPARE-AND-PROCESS.
        IF STUDENT-SSN = TRANSACTION-SSN PERFORM
            UPDATE-RTN.
        IF STUDENT-SSN IS LESS THAN TRANSACTION-SSN
            PERFORM WRITE-MASTER-RECORD.
        IF STUDENT-SSN IS GREATER THAN TRANSACTION-SSN
            PERFORM ADD-TRANSACTION-RTN.

UPDATE-RTN.
*  THIS ROUTINE WILL MOVE THE TRANSACTION DATA TO THE OLD
*  MASTER RECORD AND WRITE THE UPDATED RECORD FROM THE OLD
*  RECORD AREA. IT WILL THEN PERFORM ROUTINES
*  READ-MASTER-RTN AND READ-TRANSACTION-RTN.

WRITE-MASTER-RECORD.
*  SINCE THERE ARE NO CHANGES TO THIS MASTER RECORD, THE
*  RECORD MUST BE WRITTEN TO THE UPDATED-STUDENT-FILE. THEN
*  THE NEXT STUDENT RECORD IS READ BY ROUTINE READ-MASTER-
*  RTN.

ADD-TRANSACTION-RTN.
*  CONTROL PASSES TO THIS ROUTINE WHEN THE TRANSACTION
*  RECORD IS TO BE ADDED TO THE MASTER FILE. THE ROUTINE
*  BUILDS AN UPDATED-STUDENT-RECORD, WRITES THE RECORD, AND
*  READS THE NEXT TRANSACTION RECORD, USING ROUTINE READ-
*  TRANSACTION-RTN
```

No code is shown for routines UPDATE-RTN, WRITE-MASTER-RECORD, and ADD-TRANSACTION-RTN. The comments suffice to explain what each one does. Note that the appropriate CLOSE statements for each file must be coded at the end of the PROCEDURE DIVISION. Make sure to test the file-status return codes for each.

To close the discussion on sequential files and sequential file maintenance in COBOL, line-sequential file organization must be mentioned. *Line-sequential* files contain the carriage-return, line-feed delimiter for every record contained in the data file. Line-sequential organization is necessary for files, like EDLIN, that are created outside a COBOL program. With this type of organization, you cannot use the COMP-0 or COMP-3 options for any data item. All other verbs and rules that apply to SEQUENTIAL organization, however, also apply to line-sequential organization, although, whereas the ORGANIZATION clause is optional for sequential files, the statement ORGANIZATION IS LINE SEQUENTIAL is mandatory for line-sequential files.

COBOL AND INDEXED SEQUENTIAL FILES

Indexed sequential files allow a program to retrieve data records either sequentially or in random fashion. In the former case, processing may begin either at the beginning of, or later on in, the file. Like a sequentially organized file, an indexed sequential file must be created. Actually, two files are created: the *primary data file,* in which the actual data records are placed; and the *index file,* which contains pointers to each of the data records. If the index file is destroyed, you can recover by reading the data portion of the file one record after the other. (Refer to your COBOL manual for the format of each key record in the index portion of the file.) Again, as with sequential files, care must be taken with indexed sequential files to ensure that you are working with the most current copy and that you have a backup of the file on some other disk.

ENVIRONMENT DIVISION entries for indexed sequential files

A general format for the FILE–CONTROL SECTION of the ENVIRON-MENT DIVISION for indexed sequential files is:

```
SELECT filename ASSIGN TO DISK
[ACCESS MODE IS SEQUENTIAL:RANDOM:DYNAMIC]
ORGANIZATION IS INDEXED
RECORD KEY IS key-field-in-record
FILE STATUS IS status-field.
```

This SELECT statement is the same as the general format for a sequential file, with two exceptions: the ACCESS MODE statement and the RECORD KEY clause. With *indexed sequential* files, data may be retrieved in one of three ways: one record after another, in no particular sequence, and starting somewhere in the file and either retrieving one record or a series of records one after the other. The selection of one of these ACCESS MODEs depends on the needs of the application, and if the statement is not specified the default is SEQUENTIAL. As for the RECORD KEY clause, the data field specified in it (1) must be the unique identifier of each record, (2) must appear in the same position of each record, (3) can be either a group or elementary alphanumeric item, (4) must contain 60 or fewer characters, and (5) must not contain any null characters (binary zeros).

The FILE STATUS clause is basically the same as that for sequential files. However, with INDEXED files you can use the FILE STATUS field to enhance the processing options of your program.

DATA DIVISION entries for indexed sequential files

In the DATA DIVISION, the entries that apply to sequential files also apply to indexed sequential files. The general format is

```
FD   filename
     LABEL RECORDS ARE STANDARD
     VALUE-OF-FILE-ID IS "file label.file extension"
```

RECORD CONTAINS _____ CHARACTERS
DATA RECORD IS data-record.

The LABEL RECORDS and VALUE–OF–FILE–ID clauses are required.

The ENVIRONMENT DIVISION and the DATA DIVISION are connected by the RECORD KEY clause in the former. The key-field-in-record must be described and must appear in the 01 description of the data record. If the FROM option in the READ and WRITE statements is used, the key-field must be identified in the record description. As an elementary item, the key-field would look like the following:

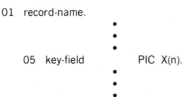

Used in this manner, the key-field is really no different from any other group item. It just has been identified in the SELECT statement as the field that will be used to retrieve data.

As a group item, the key-field would look like the following:

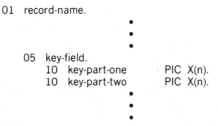

In either situation, the key-field must be of length less than or equal to 60 characters, and must be an alphanumeric field containing no null characters.

The PROCEDURE DIVISION
for indexed sequential files

The significant difference between sequential and indexed sequential files is contained within the PROCEDURE DIVISION. Let us begin with the OPEN and CLOSE statements. In processing indexed sequential files, you may not use the EXTEND option of the OPEN verb; all other options are permissible. The CLOSE verb, on the other hand, is the same for *indexed sequential* files as for sequential files.

Table 11-3
Processing verbs for indexed sequential processing

ACCESS MODE	Type of OPEN	Processing verbs				
		READ	WRITE	REWRITE	START	DELETE
SEQUENTIAL	INPUT	X			X	
	OUTPUT		X			
	I-O	X		X	X	X
RANDOM	INPUT	X				
	OUTPUT		X			
	I-O	X	X	X		X
DYNAMIC	INPUT	X			X	
	OUTPUT		X			
	I-O	X	X	X	X	X

The remaining forms of the OPEN verb and the processing verbs for record access depend on the ACCESS MODE clause of the SELECT statement. Table 11-3 shows all the verbs that can be used for indexed sequential processing with each type of ACCESS MODE and OPEN statement option. Let us consider each of the modes in turn.

ACCESS MODE IS SEQUENTIAL When ACCESS MODE IS SEQUENTIAL is expressed, or when it is implied by stating ORGANIZATION IS INDEXED, the processing of records in a sequential manner is the same as that when ORGANIZATION IS SEQUENTIAL or ORGANIZATION IS LINE SEQUENTIAL is stated. The difference appears with the use of the START verb.[2] The START verb is used to begin processing records in a sequential fashion at some point in the file other than the first record. The general format of the START statement is

```
START filename
    [KEY IS GREATER THAN: NOT LESS THAN:
        EQUAL TO key-field]
    [INVALID KEY imperative statement . . . ]
```

The record key sought must be moved to the key-field before the statement is executed, and the file must be opened in either INPUT or I-O mode only.

If the KEY phrase is not stated, COBOL assumes that you are looking for a record with a value equal to the value place in the key-field. If the GREATER THAN option is selected, processing will begin at the next record

[2] The READ format is identical to that for sequential processing.

with a value greater than the key specified in the key-field. If the option NOT LESS THAN is chosen, processing will begin at the record containing a value equal to or greater than the value specified. When using the START command, be sure to interrogate the FILE STATUS field for a NO RECORD FOUND condition (file status 23) or EOF (file status 10).

For a file opened in OUTPUT mode, the only verb permissible is WRITE. With WRITE, records must be processed in ascending sequence; otherwise INVALID KEY condition (file status 21) is generated. The general format for the WRITE statement is

```
WRITE  record-name [FROM data-name-1]
       [INVALID KEY imperative statement . . . ]
```

Before WRITE is executed, a unique key must be placed in the key-field of the record, or else an invalid key condition (file status 22) or a disk full error (file status 24) will occur.

For indexed sequential files for which ACCESS MODE IS SEQUENTIAL, REWRITE and DELETE may also be used. To *REWRITE* a record is to change the contents of an existing record; to *DELETE* a record is to permanently remove it from a file. The general format of the REWRITE statement is

```
REWRITE  record-name [FROM data-name]
         [INVALID KEY imperative statement]
```

In order to REWRITE any record using ACCESS MODE IS SEQUENTIAL, the most recently issued input/output command to a data file must have been a successful READ. If the key value of the record being rewritten and the key value of the last record read disagree, an INVALID KEY condition will occur.

Like REWRITE, the DELETE verb will logically remove a record from a file. DELETE requires that the most recently issued input/output command to the file be a successful READ. The general format for the DELETE statement is

```
DELETE  file-name  RECORD
        [INVALID KEY imperative statement . . . ]
```

For a file for which ACCESS MODE IS SEQUENTIAL, the INVALID KEY option is not necessary because the most recently issued command to the file was automatically a successful READ.

ACCESS MODE IS RANDOM   When ACCESS MODE IS RANDOM is specified, the format for the READ statement is different. The general format is

```
READ filename RECORD [INTO data-name-1]
    [INVALID KEY imperative statement . . . ]
```

Notice that the AT END phrase is not used. The INVALID KEY clause specifies an action to be performed if the desired key does not exist in the file. The appropriate file status return code is 23 (RECORD NOT FOUND). You may elect to perform a routine to notify the user that the record does not exist, or continue to process, depending on the needs of the application.

The general format for a WRITE statement when ACCESS MODE IS RANDOM is specified is

```
WRITE record-name [FROM data-name-1]
    [INVALID KEY imperative statement . . . ]
```

This format is the same as that for ACCESS MODE IS SEQUENTIAL. An IN-VALID KEY condition will occur when ACCESS MODE IS RANDOM if the record key is not unique (file status 22) or the allocated disk-file space has been used (file status 24).

The formats of the READ and WRITE statements are the same if the file has been opened in either INPUT, OUTPUT, or I–O mode. If the file has been opened in I–O mode, two additional commands are available: REWRITE and DELETE. The general format of the REWRITE statement is

```
REWRITE record-name [FROM data-name]
    [INVALID KEY imperative statement]
```

This format is the same as the REWRITE statement for ACCESS IS SE-QUENTIAL. The only significant difference between the two is that in AC-CESS MODE IS RANDOM no previous successful READ is necessary. The INVALID KEY condition will appear if there is no valid key in the file that is equal to the key you are rewriting.

The general format of the DELETE statement is

```
DELETE filename RECORD
    [INVALID KEY imperative statement . . . ]
```

The record to be deleted is associated with a record that already exists in the data file. Since the READ statement does not have to be issued when ACCESS MODE IS RANDOM, an INVALID KEY condition will exist if the record is not available in the data file.

ACCESS MODE IS DYNAMIC   When an indexed file is accessed us-ing the ACCESS MODE IS DYNAMIC option, most of the processing verb formats and rules are the same as for ACCESS MODE IS SEQUENTIAL and ACCESS MODE IS RANDOM. Accordingly, we shall only highlight the differences from those options, beginning with the INPUT option of the OPEN command.

When a file is OPENed with INPUT, the only verbs permitted are READ and START. The format of the READ statement[3] for processing a data file sequentially from any point within the file with ACCESS MODE IS DYNAMIC is

```
READ filename [NEXT] RECORD [INTO data-name-1]
     [AT END imperative statement . . . ].
```

For processing a data file randomly, the format for the READ statement is

```
READ filename RECORD [INTO data-name-1]
     [INVALID KEY imperative statement . . . ].
```

This format is the same as for processing a file using ACCESS MODE IS RANDOM, so the same rules apply.

When an indexed sequential file is opened for OUTPUT and ACCESS MODE IS DYNAMIC, the only permissible processing verb is WRITE. The general format and rules are the same as for ACCESS MODE IS SEQUEN-TIAL and ACCESS MODE IS RANDOM.

An indexed sequential file opened in I–O mode has every processing verb available. The READ format is the same as the READ format for sequential or random access, whichever is used; similarly for the WRITE format. The REWRITE verb for ACCESS MODE IS DYNAMIC has the same general format as that for ACCESS MODE IS RANDOM. The START and DELETE verbs have the same general format as well.

The chapter concludes with Examples 11–5 through 11–22, which show coding for various processing operations for the various options associated with the different access modes for indexed sequential processing.

Example 11–5   The following is code for the ENVIRONMENT DIVISION for indexed files for which ACCESS MODE IS SEQUENTIAL:

```
SELECT STUDENT–FILE ASSIGN TO DISK
  ACCESS MODE IS SEQUENTIAL
  ORGANIZATION IS INDEXED
  FILE STATUS IS STUDENT–FILE–STATUS.

FD STUDENT–FILE
  LABEL RECORDS ARE STANDARD
  VALUE–OF–FILE–ID IS "STUDENT.DAT"
  RECORD CONTAINS 80 CHARACTERS
  DATA RECORD IS STUDENT–RECORD.
```

[3] The START command has the same rules and format as stated for ACCESS MODE IS SEQUENTIAL.

```
01  STUDENT-RECORD.
                    •
                    •
                    •
    05  STUDENT-NUMBER          PIC  X(5).
                    •
                    •
                    •
```

Example 11-6   The following PROCEDURE DIVISION code opens an indexed file for INPUT and checks the file status. This code is the same for every type of ACCESS mode.

```
OPEN-FILES.
    OPEN INPUT STUDENT-FILE.
    IF STUDENT-FILE-STATUS = "00" GO TO OPEN-EXIT.
    IF STUDENT-FILE-STATUS = "30"
      DISPLAY "FILE DOES NOT EXIST" GO TO END-PROGRAM.
    DISPLAY "ERROR ON OPENING FILE STUDENT-FILE"
    DISPLAY "FILE STATUS RETURN CODE IS ",
        STUDENT-FILE-STATUS, GO TO END-PROGRAM.
OPEN-EXIT. EXIT.
```

Example 11-7   The code

```
READ-AND-PROCESS.
    READ STUDENT-FILE RECORD AT END
        MOVE "NO" TO MORE-RECORDS,
        GO TO READ-AND-PROCESS-EXIT.
```

reads an indexed file that has been opened with the INPUT or I-O option when ACCESS MODE IS SEQUENTIAL.

As is evident, there are no real differences between indexed sequential files and sequential files.

Example 11-8   The following code illustrates the use of the START and READ verbs with an INVALID KEY clause for an indexed sequential file for which ACCESS MODE IS SEQUENTIAL and the OPEN statement option is either INPUT or I-O:

```
SELECTIVE-PROCESSING.
    MOVE "12345" TO STUDENT-NUMBER.
    START STUDENT-FILE KEY IS EQUAL TO STUDENT-NUMBER
    INVALID KEY PERFORM ERROR-ROUTINE.
                    •
                    •
                    •
    READ STUDENT-FILE RECORD AT END
        MOVE "NO" TO MORE-RECORDS,
        GO TO READ-AND-PROCESS-EXIT.
```

```
ERROR-ROUTINE.
    IF STUDENT-FILE-STATUS = "23"
    DISPLAY "RECORD NOT FOUND", STUDENT-NUMBER
    GO TO GET-NEXT-KEY.
```

Example 11-9 The code below illustrates the correct usage of the WRITE statement when ACCESS MODE IS SEQUENTIAL and the data file is opened for OUTPUT.

```
CREATE-OUTPUT-RECORD.
    WRITE STUDENT-RECORD FROM WORK-RECORD
        INVALID KEY GO TO ERROR-ROUTINE.

ERROR-ROUTINE.
    IF STUDENT-FILE-STATUS = "21"
    DISPLAY "KEYS OUT OF SEQUENCE" GO TO
    GET-NEXT-KEY.
    IF STUDENT-FILE STATUS = "22"
    DISPLAY "DUPLICATE KEY " GO TO
    GET-NEXT-KEY
    IF STUDENT-FILE-STATUS = "24"
    DISPLAY "DISK FULL, PERFORMING CLOSE ROUTINE"
    GO TO CLOSE-OUTPUT-FILE.
```

Example 11-10 The code

```
READ-AND-PROCESS.
    READ STUDENT-FILE RECORD AT END
        MOVE "NO" TO MORE-RECORDS,
        GO TO READ-AND-PROCESS-EXIT.
                    •
                    •
                    •
        DELETE STUDENT-FILE RECORD.
                    •
                    •
                    •
```

shows how the READ and DELETE verbs are used when ACCESS MODE IS SEQUENTIAL and the data file is opened with the I-O option.

Example 11-11 The following code illustrates the usage of the READ and REWRITE verbs when ACCESS MODE IS SEQUENTIAL and the data file is opened with the I-O option:

```
READ-AND-PROCESS.
    READ STUDENT-FILE RECORD AT END
        MOVE "NO" TO MORE-RECORDS,
        GO TO READ-AND-PROCESS-EXIT.
                    •
                    •
                    •
        REWRITE STUDENT-RECORD.
                    •
                    •
```

Example 11-12   The following is code for the ENVIRONMENT DIVISION for indexed files for which ACCESS MODE IS RANDOM:

```
SELECT STUDENT-FILE ASSIGN TO DISK
   ACCESS MODE IS RANDOM
   ORGANIZATION IS INDEXED
   FILE STATUS IS STUDENT-FILE-STATUS.
```

Example 11-13   The following PROCEDURE DIVISION code reads an indexed file when the OPEN verb option is INPUT or I-O and when ACCESS MODE IS RANDOM:

```
READ-AND-PROCESS.
      MOVE SEARCH-KEY TO STUDENT-NUMBER.
      READ STUDENT-FILE RECORD
            INVALID KEY GO TO ERROR-ROUTINE.


ERROR-ROUTINE.
      IF STUDENT-FILE-STATUS = "23"
         DISPLAY "RECORD NOT FOUND", SEARCH-KEY
         GO TO GET-NEXT-KEY.
```

Example 11-14   The following code shows the usage of the WRITE verb when ACCESS MODE IS RANDOM and the data file is opened for OUTPUT or I-O:

```
CREATE-OUTPUT-RECORD.
      WRITE STUDENT-RECORD FROM WORK-RECORD
            INVALID KEY GO TO ERROR-ROUTINE.

ERROR-ROUTINE.
      IF STUDENT-FILE STATUS = "22"
         DISPLAY "DUPLICATE KEY " GO TO
         GET-NEXT-KEY.
      IF STUDENT-FILE-STATUS = "24"
            DISPLAY "DISK FULL, PERFORMING CLOSE ROUTINE"
            GO TO CLOSE-OUTPUT-FILE.
```

Example 11-15   The code below shows how the REWRITE verb is used when ACCESS MODE IS RANDOM and the data file is opened with the I-O option.

```
            MOVE SEARCH-KEY TO STUDENT-NUMBER.
            REWRITE STUDENT-RECORD FROM WORK-RECORD
                  INVALID KEY GO TO ERROR-ROUTINE.

ERROR-ROUTINE.
      IF STUDENT-FILE-STATUS = "23"
         DISPLAY "RECORD NOT FOUND", STUDENT-NUMBER
         GO TO GET-NEXT-KEY.
```

Example 11-16   The code below uses the DELETE verb when ACCESS MODE IS RANDOM and the data file is opened with the I-O option.

```
        MOVE SEARCH-KEY TO STUDENT-NUMBER.

    DELETE STUDENT-FILE RECORD
            INVALID KEY GO TO ERROR-ROUTINE.

ERROR-ROUTINE.
    IF STUDENT-FILE-STATUS = "23"
        DISPLAY "RECORD NOT FOUND", STUDENT-NUMBER
        GO TO GET-NEXT-KEY.
```

Example 11-17   The following is code for the ENVIRONMENT DIVISION for indexed files for which ACCESS MODE IS DYNAMIC:

```
SELECT STUDENT-FILE ASSIGN TO DISK
    ACCESS MODE IS DYNAMIC
    ORGANIZATION IS INDEXED
    FILE STATUS IS STUDENT-FILE-STATUS.
```

Example 11-18   The following PROCEDURE DIVISION code reads an indexed file when the OPEN verb option is INPUT or I-O and when ACCESS MODE IS DYNAMIC (i.e., the records are to be retrieved randomly):

```
READ-AND-PROCESS.
    MOVE SEARCH-KEY TO STUDENT-NUMBER.
    READ STUDENT-FILE RECORD
        INVALID KEY GO TO ERROR-ROUTINE.

ERROR-ROUTINE.
    IF STUDENT-FILE-STATUS = "23"
        DISPLAY "RECORD NOT FOUND", SEARCH-KEY
        GO TO GET-NEXT-KEY.
```

Example 11-19   The following code illustrates the use of the START and READ verbs with an INVALID KEY clause for an indexed sequential file for which ACCESS MODE IS DYNAMIC and the OPEN statement option is either INPUT or I = O (i.e., records are to be retrieved sequentially):

```
SELECTIVE-PROCESSING.
    MOVE "12345" TO STUDENT-NUMBER.
    START STUDENT-FILE KEY IS EQUAL TO STUDENT-NUMBER
    INVALID KEY PERFORM ERROR-ROUTINE.
                        •
                        •
                        •
    READ STUDENT-FILE NEXT RECORD AT END
        MOVE "NO" TO MORE-RECORDS
        GO TO READ-AND-PROCESS-EXIT.

ERROR-ROUTINE.
    IF STUDENT-FILE-STATUS = "23"
        DISPLAY "RECORD NOT FOUND", STUDENT-NUMBER
        GO TO GET-NEXT-KEY.
```

Example 11-20   The code below shows the usage of the WRITE verb when ACCESS MODE IS DYNAMIC and the data file is opened for OUTPUT or I-O.

```
CREATE-OUTPUT-RECORD.
    WRITE STUDENT-RECORD FROM WORK-RECORD
        INVALID KEY GO TO ERROR-ROUTINE.

ERROR-ROUTINE.
    IF STUDENT-FILE STATUS = "22"
        DISPLAY "DUPLICATE KEY " GO TO
    GET-NEXT-KEY.
    IF STUDENT-FILE-STATUS = "24"
        DISPLAY "DISK FULL, PERFORMING CLOSE ROUTINE"
        GO TO CLOSE-OUTPUT-FILE.
```

Example 11-21   The following code shows how the REWRITE verb is used when ACCESS MODE IS DYNAMIC and the data file is opened with the I-O option:

```
MOVE SEARCH-KEY TO STUDENT-NUMBER.

REWRITE STUDENT-RECORD FROM WORK-RECORD
    INVALID KEY GO TO ERROR-ROUTINE.

ERROR-ROUTINE.
    IF STUDENT-FILE STATUS = "23"
        DISPLAY "RECORD NOT FOUND", STUDENT-NUMBER
        GO TO GET-NEXT-KEY.
```

Example 11-22   The following code illustrates the usage of the DELETE verb when ACCESS MODE IS DYNAMIC and the data file is opened with the I-O option:

```
MOVE SEARCH-KEY TO STUDENT-NUMBER.

DELETE STUDENT-FILE RECORD
    INVALID KEY GO TO ERROR-ROUTINE.

ERROR-ROUTINE.
    IF STUDENT-FILE STATUS = "23"
        DISPLAY "RECORD NOT FOUND", STUDENT-NUMBER
        GO TO GET-NEXT-KEY.
```

REVIEW QUESTIONS

1. Identify the three file access modes and distinguish between them.
2. (T or F)   A random file that is to be accessed dynamically may be opened in the INPUT mode.
3. (T or F)   A random file that is to be accessed sequentially may be opened in the I-O mode.
4. What is the function of the DYNAMIC access mode? What type of files may it be used with?

5. Write the code for a SELECT statement to declare an indexed disk file that is to be accessed randomly. Include the file status specification.

6. What is the difference between a sequential and a line sequential file? Write the code for a SELECT statement to declare a line sequential file.

7. (T or F) A READ statement must precede a REWRITE statement.

8. (T or F) A READ statement must precede a DELETE statement.

9. Explain the function of the START statement. How are this statement and the NEXT option of the READ command related?

10. Frequently within an application, it is desirable to "browse" through a file. ("Browsing" means to read the file sequentially from a certain point and display the retrieved records.) Explain how file browsing may be implemented using the DYNAMIC access mode in conjunction with the START and READ . . . NEXT commands.

PROBLEMS

1. Using the data file from Appendix B, create a sequential disk file entitled "EMPSEQ.DAT," and produce a screen display showing:

```
RECORDS READ FROM INPUT FILE        XXX
RECORDS WRITTEN TO EMPSEQ.DAT       XXX
```

Input layout

Position	Field name
1–20	NAME
25	SEX
26–29	SALARY
50–54	ID NUMBER

Output layout

Position	Field name
1–5	ID NUMBER
6–25	NAME
26–29	SALARY
30	SEX

The record length for this file is only 30 characters.

2. Using the file created in problem 1 ("EMPSEQ.DAT") and the transaction file created in problem 1, Chapter 7 ("EMPTRN.DAT"), perform file maintenance on file "EMPSEQ.DAT." Remember that when doing a sequential update, you must create an output file. (You decide what the value of the file ID is for this one.) When your program is complete, display on the screen:

```
INPUT RECORDS READ              ZZ9
TRANSACTION RECORDS READ        ZZ9
RECORDS ADDED                   ZZ9
RECORDS CHANGED                 ZZ9
RECORDS REMOVED                 ZZ9
OUTPUT RECORDS WRITTEN          ZZ9
```

In order to check your program remember:
Records added + changed + removed = transaction records
Input records + records added − removed = output records.

3. Using file "EMPSEQ.DAT" as input, create an indexed sequential file entitled "EMPIND.MST." Use the same input record and output record definition and display the same output as the program from problem 1.

4. Develop a program in which you will perform file maintenance on the indexed sequential file "EMPIND.MST." You may use the same transactions from the data file "EMPTRN.DAT" for this task. Type the transaction file using the DOS command entitled TYPE EMPTRN.DAT > LPT1 (for those who have a parallel printer), which will produce a hard copy listing.

Your objective in this program is to use random updating techniques for this indexed sequential file. Refer back to the chapter for some helpful hints for these techniques.

Your input should come from the keyboard, which will require you to design a screen layout to accept data from the keyboard.

The output display screen after all maintenance is completed is:

```
INPUT RECORDS READ              ZZ9
TRANSACTION RECORDS READ        ZZ9
RECORDS ADDED                   ZZ9
RECORDS CHANGED                 ZZ9
RECORDS REMOVED                 ZZ9
OUTPUT RECORDS WRITTEN          ZZ9
```

12

ADVANCED SEARCHING TECHNIQUES, SORTING, AND SUBPROGRAMS

Three procedures of considerable importance in data processing are table searching, file sorting, and interprogram communications. Chapter 10 dealt with how to search tables or arrays using the linear search. Recall that this technique searches for a specific element in the table by looping through the table sequentially until either the desired element is found or the table is exhausted. While useful for short tables (about 15 elements or fewer), the linear search is slow and inefficient for tables of greater length. For longer tables, there exists a much more efficient technique called the *binary search.* In this chapter we shall show how to implement this technique in the COBOL program.

File sorting is even more important than table searching. Data files on a computer system are arranged in sequence by file key in the case of indexed files, and by physical record number in the case of sequential files. For some applications of the data file, the existing sort sequence may be acceptable. For other applications, however, it may be necessary to arrange or sort the file in some other order before processing. On large computer systems sorting is easily accomplished by utility programs designed specifically for that purpose. These sort utilities are extremely powerful and efficient, but they require large amounts of disk space. On microcomputer systems disk space is rather scarce, prohibiting or severely limiting the use of general-purpose sort-utility programs. Versions of COBOL for large-scale systems include a SORT verb that permits the programmer to access the general sort utility from within the program. The version of COBOL for microcomputers that is the subject of this text, however, does not include the SORT verb. Hence, other techniques for sorting disk files must be used. These techniques are the second topic of this chapter.

While not as widely used or needed as either table searching or file sorting, interprogram communications is nonetheless important. In writing computer applications involving a number of programs, it is often necessary to code common algorithms and processing tasks that can be used by more than one program. In such situations it is advantageous to code those tasks in a separate program, thereby creating an object-code module—called a subprogram—that can be accessed and utilized by a higher-level program module. This way, the common tasks need only be written once, thus avoiding the development of redundant code. A discussion of methods for effecting communication between separate program modules concludes the chapter.

THE BINARY SEARCH

The binary search employs a simple algorithm commonly used in the puzzle introduced by the statement, "Think of a number between one and one thousand, and I will tell you what it is in at most ten tries. All that you must do is reveal whether the number I choose is greater than, less than, or equal to the number you are thinking of." Readers who are familiar with this game know how the search algorithm works. Let us consider an example.

Suppose that, in response to the above statement, the participant secretly selects the number 687. The puzzler begins by mentally adding one to the number of elements and dividing that number (1001 in this case) by two. She arrives at the quotient, 500, and discards the remainder, one. This quotient becomes her first guess. The participant replies by stating that his number is greater than 500. The puzzler then adds the number 500 to 1001 and again divides the result by two, yielding the quotient, 750, and the remainder, one, which she again discards. This quotient becomes her second guess. The participant replies that his number is less than 750. Now the puzzler adds 500 to 750 and divides by two, yielding the quotient, 625, and the remainder, zero. The participant replies that his number is greater than 625. The puzzler then adds 625 to 750 and divides by two, yielding the quotient, 687, and the remainder, one, which she again discards. This quotient becomes her third and final guess, for now the participant must admit that the number he had chosen was indeed 687! In three educated guesses she has determined his secretly selected number. Under no circumstances would she have required more than ten guesses, provided that the participant's selection was within the required range. In fact, even if it hadn't been, she would have been able to detect his deception within the stipulated ten tries.

Notice in the above example that the puzzler arrived at each guess simply by dividing the range of values between one and 1000 into successive halves. (Ergo the name binary search.) To do this successfully, she had to employ a few steps that were not altogether obvious. We shall explain those steps shortly. The important point to keep in mind is the nature of the algorithm, which homes in on the desired item by narrowing the possible choices to successively smaller ranges of values. The concept is relatively simple. The translation of that concept to a programming language is a little more complex. In what follows, we shall examine the binary search algorithm in detail and present the COBOL code necessary to implement it.

To implement the binary search, it is necessary to arrange all possible values of the qualifying items, whether alphabetic or numeric, in ascending order within a table or array and to determine the number of items in the table. We begin the search with the complete table and keep dividing it into successive halves until either the desired item is found or the search is exhausted. The whole table and each of its subdivisions has a lower limit, an upper limit, and a midpoint. The lower limit marks the starting point of the search, and the upper limit marks the ending point. The midpoint identifies the particular element within the table that contains the specific value to be interrogated.

The algorithm is initiated by priming the lower and upper limits with appropriate values and then calculating the midpoint. After that, the algorithm passes through a cycle of iterations aimed at finding the desired value.

To prime the algorithm, the programmer must

1. Move zero to the lower limit.
2. Add one to the number of elements in the table and move the result to the upper limit.
3. Compute the midpoint by adding the lower limit to the upper limit and dividing the sum by two. The resulting quotient is the midpoint. Discard the remainder.

To implement the iterative portion of the algorithm, the programmer must then proceed as follows:

4. Interrogate the midpoint. If it is equal to the lower limit, then the search has been exhausted, meaning that the desired item was not found in the table. Accordingly, exit from the routine.
5. Compare the desired item to the value contained in that element of the table indexed by the midpoint.
6. If the desired element is less than the value of the midpoint element, then move the midpoint to the lower limit and return to step 3. This means that the desired item must be contained in the lower half of the section just searched.
7. If the desired item is greater than the value of the midpoint element, then move the midpoint to the upper limit and return to step 3. This means that the desired item must be contained in the upper half of the section just searched.
8. The desired item is equal to the value of the midpoint element; hence the search is successful. Accordingly, exit from the routine.

These processing steps are transformed into COBOL program code in Example 12-1.

Example 12-1 Suppose that you are programming a mailing list application that employs the standard two-letter postal state abbreviation codes. A one-dimensional table containing all the postal codes and names of the fifty states has been prepared for the purpose. The codes are arranged in ascending alphabetical order. As part of your program, you must validate the state codes as they are entered from the terminal keyboard. A binary search algorithm to accomplish the validation task is as follows:

```
      FILE SECTION.
            •
            •
            •
      01  RECORD-IN.
          05  NAME-IN              PIC  X(20).
                •
                •
                •
          05  STATE-CODE-IN        PIC  XX.
                •
                •
                •
      WORKING-STORAGE SECTION.
      77  LOWER-LIMIT              PIC  S999      COMP-3.
      77  UPPER-LIMIT              PIC  S999      COMP-3.
      77  MIDPOINT                 PIC  S99       COMP.
      77  HOLD-STATE-CODE          PIX  XX.
      01  STATE-TABLE.
          05  FILLER OCCURS 50 TIMES.
              10  STATE-CODE       PIC  XX.
              10  STATE-NAME       PIC  X(15).
      01  ITEM-FOUND-FLAG          PIC  XXX.
          88  ITEM-FOUND                          VALUE "YES".
              •
              •
              •
      PROCEDURE DIVISION.
            •
            •
            •
      PERFORM 300-SEARCH-SETUP THRU 300-SEARCH-EXIT.
      IF ITEM-FOUND THEN NEXT SENTENCE
          ELSE
          PERFORM 400-STATE-CODE-ERROR.
              •
              •
              •
      300-SEARCH-SETUP.
          MOVE "NO " TO ITEM-FOUND.
          MOVE ZERO  TO LOWER-LIMIT.
          MOVE 51    TO UPPER-LIMIT.
          PERFORM 300-BINARY-SEARCH UNTIL
              ITEM-FOUND OR MIDPOINT = LOWER-LIMIT.
          GO TO 300-SEARCH-EXIT.
      300-BINARY-SEARCH.
          COMPUTE MIDPOINT = (LOWER-LIMIT + UPPER-LIMIT) / 2.
          MOVE STATE-CODE (MIDPOINT) TO HOLD-STATE-CODE.
          IF STATE-CODE-IN < HOLD-STATE-CODE THEN
              MOVE MIDPOINT TO UPPER-LIMIT
          ELSE
          IF STATE-CODE-IN > HOLD-STATE-CODE THEN
              MOVE MIDPOINT TO LOWER-LIMIT
```

```
        ELSE
            MOVE "YES" TO ITEM-FOUND-FLAG.
    300-SEARCH-EXIT.
        EXIT.
            •
            •
            •
```

Table searches of this kind may also be accomplished using the SEARCH and SEARCH ALL verbs which are available with most versions of COBOL for microcomputers. For more information on the use of these commands, refer to the reference manual for your particular compiler. The main advantages of the binary search technique shown above are that it can be used with all COBOL compilers and that it demonstrates the workings of an important programming algorithm.

SORTING INDEXED FILES

Recall from Chapter 11 that indexed files are stored in ascending order by the file or record key. If the key is numeric, then the records are stored in ascending order by number; if the key is alphanumeric, then the records are stored in ascending order by collating sequence.

Suppose, then, that you have an indexed file keyed on some numeric identifier, but you would like to reorder or sort it on some other field or fields within the record. An economical way to do this using microcomputer COBOL would be to create a cross-reference file indexed on the basis of the desired sort fields. This file would contain two segments: an index consisting of the desired sort fields, and a data element containing the index or record key of the file to be sorted. The latter would point to the corresponding record in the parent file, i.e., the file to be sorted. Figure 12–1 shows the relationship between the two files.

The cross-reference file is built from the parent file. For each record in the parent file, there is a corresponding record in the cross-reference file. The records in the cross-reference file are arranged in the order of the desired sort sequence. The cross-reference file is then read sequentially, i.e., in its natural order by record key. As each cross-reference record is read, the corresponding record in the parent file is retrieved randomly using the key stored in the second segment of the cross-reference record. The result is that the records from the parent file are retrieved in the order of the keys of the cross-reference records. Example 12–2 shows how to structure the cross-reference record. A complete sample program for sorting an indexed file using this technique is found in Appendix C.

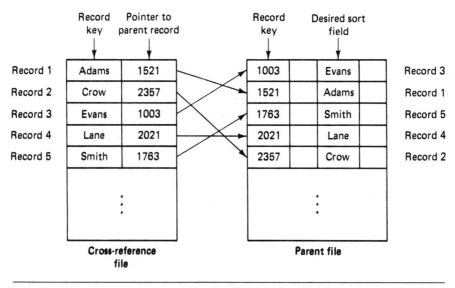

Figure 12-1
Relationship between cross-reference file and parent file

Example 12-2 Suppose that you have an indexed personnel file keyed on social security number which you would like to sort by name in preparation for printing. Suppose further that the record key of the personnel file (the parent file) is named SOC–SEC–NUMB, and the last and first names of the employee are stored in separate fields named LAST–NAME and FIRST–NAME, respectively. Then the cross-reference record may be structured as follows:

```
01  CROSS-REF-RECORD.
    05  SORT-KEY.
        10  LAST-NAME          PIC  X(20).
        10  FIRST-NAME         PIC  X(10).
        10  SEQUENCE-NUMB      PIC  999.
    05  SOC-SEC-NUMB           PIC  X(11).
```

The first segment of the cross-reference record consists of the group item SORT-KEY, containing the fields from the parent file that are to be sorted. The second segment consists of the elementary item SOC–SEC–NUMB, which points to the corresponding employee record in the personnel file. Notice that an additional field, SEQUENCE–NUMB, has been appended to the cross-reference record key. This field is necessary because some names in the employee file may not be unique, thus causing a potential problem with duplicate record keys when writing the cross-reference file to disk. SEQUENCE–NUMB starts at one with the first cross-reference record and is incremented by one for each new record created. In this way, duplicate keys are avoided.

The above technique may not be applied for sequential or line-sequential files. For these kinds of files, a utility or user-written memory sort must be employed. To ensure that your COBOL applications have file-sorting capability, it is a good practice to make all permanent disk files indexed files.

SUBPROGRAMS

As mentioned earlier, subprograms are used for implementing common algorithms and processing tasks. Subprograms may be written in other computer languages (Assembler, BASIC, and FORTRAN, for example) but we shall consider only those written in COBOL. A subprogram is coded and structured in the same way as an ordinary COBOL program, except for some small but important differences.

If data is to be passed to or from the subprogram, as is frequently the case, then the LINKAGE SECTION (see Chapter 4) must be included in the main program, immediately after the WORKING–STORAGE SECTION. In addition, a USING clause followed by the list of data elements to be passed—called the parameter list—is appended to the PROCEDURE DIVISION statement. Finally, the EXIT PROGRAM statement is used to return processing control to the calling program, the higher-level program that invokes the subprogram.

The subprogram is identified by its PROGRAM–ID name and compiled and linked in the same way as an ordinary COBOL program. The calling program invokes the subprogram by means of the CALL . . . USING statement followed by the parameter list, if there is one. Data elements passed to and received from the subprogram are defined in the WORKING–STORAGE SECTION. Once the subprogram has completed its task, control passes back to the calling program and processing continues with the statement immediately following the CALL statement. Within the calling program, the same or different subprograms may be invoked as often as desired. Also, subprograms may be invoked by other subprograms. Figure 12–2 shows the relationship between the calling program and the subprogram.

Let us now consider the syntax and grammar of those elements needed for invoking and using subprograms. The only item needed in the calling program is the CALL . . . USING statement, which has the general format

CALL "subprogram-name" USING data-name-1 . . . data-name-n.

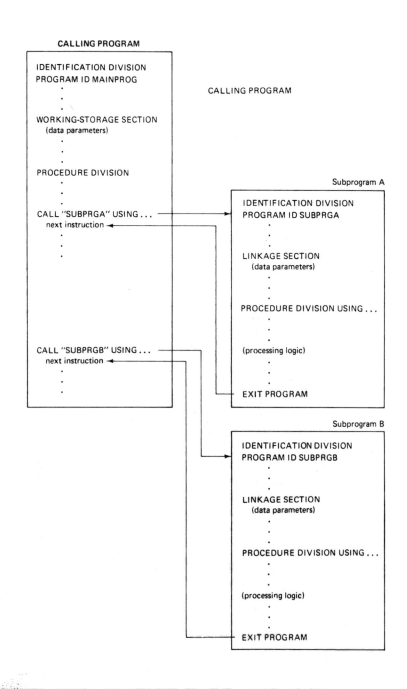

Figure 12-2
Relationship between calling program and subprogram.

Subprogram-name is the name specified in the subprogram's PROGRAM–ID clause. The name must be enclosed in quotes. Data-name-1 through data-name-n constitute the parameter list—that is, the list of data elements whose values are exchanged between the calling program and the subprogram. These elements are defined in the WORKING–STORAGE SECTION. The USING clause is not needed if no data is to be communicated between program and subprogram modules.

For the subprogram, the LINKAGE SECTION, the USING clause in the PROCEDURE DIVISION statement, and the EXIT PROGRAM statement are required. The first two of these need not be used if there is no parameter list.

The LINKAGE SECTION, as previously mentioned, appears immediately after the WORKING–STORAGE SECTION and is coded in exactly the same way as the latter, except that the VALUE clause may be specified only for 88-level items.

The USING clause occurs in the PROCEDURE DIVISION statement in the subprogram, which has the general format

        PROCEDURE DIVISION USING data-name-1 . . . data-name-n.

Data-name-1 through data-name-n constitute the list of exchange parameters and are defined in the LINKAGE SECTION. These items exactly parallel the parameters in the CALL . . . USING statement of the calling program. The number of parameters in the two lists must be the same, and the corresponding parameters must have the same lengths. The reason is that the association between items in the respective lists is made on the basis of their position, as opposed to their symbolic names.

The EXIT PROGRAM statement returns processing control to the calling program. Like the EXIT statement, the EXIT PROGRAM statement must be placed in a paragraph by itself; if placed in the main program, it is ignored. Example 12–3 illustrates these subprogram concepts and techniques.

Example 12-3   Validation of dates is a very common data processing task. In performing any kind of processing involving calendar dates, it is necessary to ensure that the dates are valid—i.e., that they fall within the range of acceptable values. For example, you wouldn't want a date of 12/32/84 to show up in the records of your data files. Hence, it is advantageous to edit dates for validity, and since this kind of edit checking is generally useful across a range of applications, validation of dates is an ideal candidate for inclusion in a subprogram. The instructions necessary to call such a subprogram, followed by a fully coded subprogram to do the date editing, are as follows:

Calling Program:

```
IDENTIFICATION DIVISION.
PROGRAM-ID. MAINPROG.
        •
        •
        •
DATA DIVISION.
        •
        •
        •
WORKING-STORAGE SECTION.
        •
        •
        •
01  DATE-CHECK          PIC 9(6).
01  DATE-ERROR          PIC X.
        •
        •
        •
PROCEDURE DIVISION.
        •
        •
        •
    CALL "DATECHK" USING DATE-CHECK DATE-ERROR.
    IF DATE-ERROR NOT = "0" THEN . . .
        •
        •
        •
```

The Called Subprogram:

```
IDENTIFICATION DIVISION.
PROGRAM-ID. DATECHK.
ENVIRONMENT DIVISION.
DATA DIVISION.
WORKING-STORAGE SECTION.
01  INDX                    PIC 99      COMP.
01  MONTH-DAY-TABLE         PIC X(48)   VALUE
    "013102280331043005310630073108310930103111301231".
01  MONTH-DAY-TABLE-R       REDEFINES  MONTH-DAY-TABLE.
    05  FILLER OCCURS 12 TIMES.
        10  MON-TAB         PIC 99.
        10  DAY-LIM         PIC 99.
01  WS-YEAR                 PIC 99.
01  WS-WORK                 PIC 99.
LINKAGE SECTION.
01  DATE-HOLD               PIC 9(6).
01  DATE-HOLD-R REDEFINES  DATE-HOLD.
    05  MM-HOLD             PIC 99.
    05  DD-HOLD             PIC 99.
    05  YY-HOLD             PIC 99.
01  DATE-ERROR              PIC X.
PROCEDURE DIVISION USING DATE-HOLD DATE-ERROR.
    MOVE "0" TO DATE-ERROR.
```

```
        IF  DATE-HOLD  NOT  NUMERIC  THEN
            GO  TO  BAD-DATE.
        DIVIDE  YY-HOLD  BY  4  GIVING  WS-YEAR  REMAINDER  WS-WORK.
        IF  WS-WORK  =  0  THEN
            MOVE  29  TO  DAY-LIM  (2)
        ELSE
            MOVE  28  TO  DAY-LIM  (2).
        IF  MM-HOLD  <  1 OR  >  12  THEN
            GO  TO  BAD-DATE.
        IF  DD-HOLD  NOT  <  1  AND  NOT  >  DAY-LIM  (MM-HOLD)  THEN
            GO  TO  GET-OUT.
    BAD-DATE.
        MOVE  "1"  TO  DATE-ERROR.
    GET-OUT.
        EXIT  PROGRAM.
```

In this rather lengthy example, a date is passed to the subprogram and an error code is returned to the calling program depending on the results of the subprogram's processing action. Notice the following points:

1. In the calling program the date parameter, DATE-CHECK, to be passed to the subprogram is defined in the WORKING-STORAGE SECTION, as is the error code, DATE-ERROR, returned by the subprogram. These parameters are also included in the CALL statement following the USING clause. The name of the subprogram in the CALL statement is enclosed in quotes.

2. The values in the data fields of the parameter list at the time the CALL statement is issued are communicated to the data fields DATE-HOLD and DATE-ERROR, respectively, in the LINKAGE SECTION of the subprogram. Note that the parameters need not have the same names, as they occupy the same locations in computer memory, which in fact is how the association between respective parameters is made.

3. The data parameters as defined in the LINKAGE SECTION of the subprogram are listed in the USING clause of the PROCEDURE DIVISION statement. They must be listed in the same order as they are listed in the CALL statement of the calling program. Otherwise the parameters passed from the calling program will not be sent to the appropriate entries in the subprogram, resulting in faulty processing.

4. The field DATE-ERROR is initialized in the subprogram with the value 0, indicating that the date is valid. The contents of DATE-HOLD are then examined. If there is an error, the fact is signalled by moving a value of 1 to the error flag, DATE-ERROR. If there is no error, the value 0 remains in the error flag. In either case, the EXIT PROGRAM statement is executed and control is passed back to the main program along with the value deposited in

the error flag field. Processing in the calling program resumes with the statement IF DATE-ERROR NOT = "0" THEN . . . , and appropriate action is taken on the basis of the contents of the error return code.

In designing an application, it is a good idea to identify common programming tasks and build a library of subprograms to perform those tasks. Such foresight at the front end of your project not only can spare you much programming effort in the long run, but also can save you much of one of your microcomputer's most valuable resources—disk space.

REVIEW QUESTIONS

1. Compare the linear search and the binary search. What are the limitations and advantages of each?

2. Example 12-1 presents a method of coding the binary search routine. What would happen if a value of 1 were moved to the LOWER-LIMIT instead of the value zero? What would happen if a value of 50 were moved to the UPPER-LIMIT? If your version of COBOL features the SEARCH and SEARCH ALL commands, refer to your COBOL manual to see how these commands can be used to accomplish the same results as the search routine in Example 12-1.

3. At the end of the chapter, we suggested the use of the memory sort for sequential files, if they are small enough. One famous algorithm for doing this is the bubble sort, which loads the sort keys into a memory array and forces the values in their proper order toward the top of the array. In the case of an ascending sort, this process involves comparing each value in the array to every other value beneath it and replacing the particular value under examination with the smallest value found. Try your hand at coding a routine for performing a bubble sort. (Hint: you will need an array large enough to hold the entire file to be sorted, and also two variable subscripts.)

PROBLEMS

1. Using the program you have created in problem 1, Chapter 10, change the sequential search routine of the classification table to include the SEARCH verb. All definitions are the same.

WORD NO.		REMARKS
LINE NO.		
PRINT POSITION	LINE NO.	

ALPHABETICAL EMPLOYEE LIST   DATE: XX-XX-XX

NAME
XXXXXXXXXXXXXXXX

PAY
RATE
XX.XX

SEX
X

257

2. Using the file constructed in problem 3, Chapter 11 ("EMPIND. MST"), retrieve all data records and build a table in storage consisting of NAME and EMPLOYEE #. The file is retrieved in EMPLOYEE # sequence and your task is to produce a listing of the employee file in alphabetic sequence (NAME) (see p. 257). Write your sorted table to an output disk file entitled "SORTED.FILE." Once the sorted file is constructed, open it as an input file and, using the EMPLOYEE # portion of the sorted record, retrieve the correct record from the "EMPIND.MST" file, and print a detail line.

APPENDIX A

COBOL
RESERVED WORDS

We have taken the time to research COBOL reserved words. Some of the reserved words listed here are not implemented in IBM® Personal Computer COBOL, but the reader should take note of them and not use them as a data name, paragraph name or section name in any COBOL program. This will make any program written using this version of COBOL transportable from one compiler to another.

Symbol	Denotes
@	Reserved words required by IBM Personal Computer COBOL.
:	Standard COBOL reserved words not implemented in personal computer COBOL. (Use of these words should be avoided as programmer-supplied names in a COBOL program.)

COBOL reserved words

	ACCEPT		CH		DEBUGGING
	ACCESS		CHAIN	:	DEBUG-CONTENTS
	ADD		CHAINING	:	DEBUG-ITEM
	ADVANCING		CHARACTER(S)	:	DEBUG-LINE
	AFTER	:	CLOCK-UNITS	:	DEBUG-NAME
	ALL		CLOSE	:	DEBUG-SUB-1
	ALPHABETIC	:	COBOL	:	DEBUG-SUB-2
:	ALSO	:	CODE	:	DEBUG-SUB-3
	ALTER		CODE-SET		DECIMAL-POINT
:	ALTERNATE	@	COL		DECLARATIVES
	AND		COLLATING		DELETE
	ARE		COLUMN		DELIMITED
	AREA(S)		COMMA		DELIMITER
	ASCENDING	:	COMMUNICATION		DEPENDING
@	ASCII		COMP		DESCENDING
	ASSIGN		COMPUTATIONAL	:	DESTINATION
	AT		COMPUTATIONAL-0	:	DISABLE
	AUTHOR	@	COMPUTATIONAL-3	@	DISK
	AUTO		COMPUTE		DISPLAY
@	AUTO-SKIP		COMP-0		DIVIDE
		@	COMP-3		DIVISION
@	BACKGROUND-COLOR		CONFIGURATION		DOWN
@	BEEP		CONTAINS	:	DUPLICATES
	BEFORE	:	CONTROL(S)		DYNAMIC
	BELL		COPY		
	BLANK	:	CORR(ESPONDING)	:	EGI
	BLINK		COUNT		ELSE
	BLOCK		CURRENCY	:	EMI
	BOTTOM			@	EMPTY-CHECK
	BY		DATA	:	ENABLE
			DATE		END
	CALL		DATE-COMPILED		END-OF-PAGE
:	CANCEL		DATE-WRITTEN	:	ENTER
:	CD		DAY		ENVIRONMENT
:	CF	:	DE(TAIL)		EOP

COBOL reserved words (continued)

EQUAL	: LAST	: POSITION
@ ERASE	LEADING	POSITIVE
ERROR	LEFT	@ PRINTER
ESCAPE	@ LEFT–JUSTIFY	: PRINTING
: ESI	: LENGTH	: PRINT–SWITCH
: EVERY	@ LENGTH–CHECK	PROCEDURE(S)
EXCEPTION	LESS	PROCEED
@ EXHIBIT	: LIMIT(S)	PROGRAM
EXIT	@ LIN	PROGRAM–ID
EXTEND	LINAGE	@ PROMPT
	LINAGE–COUNTER	
FD	LINE(S)	: QUEUE
FILE	: LINE–COUNTER	QUOTE
FILE–CONTROL	LINKAGE	: QUOTES
@ FILE–ID	LOCK	
FILLER	LOW–VALUE(S)	RANDOM
: FINAL		: RD
FIRST	MEMORY	READ
FOOTING	MERGE	@ READY
FOR	: MESSAGE	: RECEIVE
@ FOREGROUND–COLOR	MODE	RECORD(S)
FROM	MODULES	REDEFINES
@ FULL	MOVE	: REEL
	: MULTIPLE	: REFERENCES
: GENERATE	MULTIPLY	RELATIVE
GIVING		RELEASE
GO	@ NAMES	: REMAINDER
GREATER	NATIVE	REMOVAL
: GROUP	NEGATIVE	: RENAMES
	NEXT	REPLACING
: HEADING	: NO	: REPORT(S)
@ HIGHLIGHT	@ NO–ECHO	: REPORTING
HIGH–VALUE(S)	NOT	@ REQUIRED
	NUMBER	RERUN
IDENTIFICATION	NUMERIC	RESERVE
IF		RESET
IN	OBJECT–COMPUTER	RETURN
INDEX	OCCURS	: REVERSED
INDEXED	OF	@ REVERSE–VIDEO
: INDICATE	: OFF	: REWIND
INITIAL	OMITTED	REWRITE
: INITIATE	ON	: RF
INPUT	OPEN	: RH
INPUT–OUTPUT	: OPTIONAL	RIGHT
INSPECT	OR	@ RIGHT–JUSTIFY
INSTALLATION	ORGANIZATION	ROUNDED
INTO	OUTPUT	RUN
INVALID	OVERFLOW	
IS		SAME
I–O	PAGE	SCREEN
I–O–CONTROL	: PAGE–COUNTER	: SD
	PERFORM	SEARCH
JUST(IFIED)	: PF	SECTION
	: PH	SECURE
KEY	PIC(TURE)	SECURITY
	PLUS	: SEGMENT
LABEL	POINTER	: SEGMENT–LIMIT

COBOL reserved words (continued)

	SELECT	@	SWITCH–4		UNTIL
:	SEND	@	SWITCH–5		UP
	SENTENCE	@	SWITCH–6	@	UPDATE
	SEPARATE	@	SWITCH–7		UPON
	SEQUENCE	@	SWITCH–8		USAGE
	SEQUENTIAL	:	SYMBOLIC		USE
	SET		SYNC(HRONIZED)	@	USER
	SIGN				USING
	SIZE	:	TABLE		
	SORT		TALLYING		VALUE(S)
	SORT–MERGE	:	TAPE		VARYING
:	SOURCE	:	TERMINAL		
	SOURCE–COMPUTER	:	TERMINATE		WHEN
	SPACE(S)	:	TEXT		WITH
@	SPACE–FILL		THAN		WORDS
	SPECIAL–NAMES		THROUGH		WORKING–STORAGE
	STANDARD		THRU		WRITE
	STANDARD–1		TIME		
	START		TIMES		ZERO((E)S)
	STATUS		TO	@	ZERO–FILL
	STOP		TOP		
	STRING	@	TRACE		+
:	SUB–QUEUE–1,2,3		TRAILING		–
	SUBTRACT	@	TRAILING–SIGN		*
:	SUM	:	TYPE		/
:	SUPPRESS				**
@	SWITCH–1	@	UNDERLINE		>
@	SWITCH–2	:	UNIT		<
@	SWITCH–3		UNSTRING		=

APPENDIX B

PROBLEM DATA FILE

```
1234567891123456789212345678931234567894123456789512345678961234567897 12
```

J	CCCCE	1600F2189215102277181AMHES	01102
D	HEHHAH	1600F1234318512840221BNKAM	01105
K	LILLLE	1000M2079505680928733CIGNA	01108
A	EEEES	0200M3112508681308107CHYSLR	01111
M	CCACCE	0200M4258320413140242DOWJN	01114
N	RORE	1700F4149011701765143EXXON	01117
T	SSSSISS	1200M4337626114161312FAIRCHD	01120
R	LULELL	1300M5100607631175094GNMILLS	01123
C	SISSSIES	0800F1579745477217530GMTR	02126
H	WIWWOW	1400M1912372631109884HEWPK	02129
S	CACCOC	2000M5756659729338697IBM	02132
B	DADDOD	1400M2466736395817429JOHNJN	02135
B	JOJEJ	1400F3639650027917586KELLOG	02138
F	WIWWEWW	0100M2720656728898663LEHVAL	02141
A	COWWIWW	0100M1200816042420191MGTAST	02144
R	BIZZ	1000F3130010181535125NABSCB	02147
E	CUCCICCCAC	1000M4407631795036357ORION	02150
S	SSOESAS	1200M4316624683898294POLARID	02153
P	POPPPAP	1700M6393630644861362RCA	02156
J	HEAHHEH	1700F2435734095417400STREGIS	02159
A	EAAAS	0300M1385229954756355SEARS	02162
F	EEEIE	1900M1103238313124189TEXINST	03165
H	MMMAMM	1900M1992378631197891UPJOHN	03168
E	WIWW	1400M1822364971010875VIACOM	03171
A	BBOBB	1400M2515740276417472WUNION	03174
J	SSISS	0700M3684653728458629XEROX	03177
C	JOJEJ	0800M1142991162416627ZENITHR	03180
R	AAAAA	1200M1113748188135181ALTAIRCP	03183
C	WAWWEW	0300M5532332630475540BEECHM	03186
B	AAAIAA	0800F2139510931650134CHEROKE	03189
F	FUFFEF	0400M5210316802540200DBEER	03192
G	PAPPEP	1800F5121094314201163FTHAWAI	03195
J	WIWWIAWW	1300F4246319462990232GENESB	03198
A	WIWWIW	0400M4163212981952157INFODAT	03201
S	ABAA	0500F2947710110888495LORIMR	03204
E	BABEB	0500F1228318082765216MICROS	03207
F	JOJJJ	0100F4282322313461263NISSAN	03210
A	FOFE	0100M3358627764423331PEOPBNK	04213
B	SSEASSS	0500M4459735815717422ROUSE	04216
A	YEYYIY	0600F4507739626317465SUMMA	04219
H	MIMMOM	0900F1603747427517552TANDEM	04222
B	JOJJJOJ	0600M155414339689750UNCTYGS	04225
J	BIBB	0700M3531741576617487VAFST	04228
C	SAUSSESS	1400M1702655228657864WASHSCI	04231
L	SSSSS	0800M2563744177017516XICOR	04234
L	HHHE	0900F1648650728018595ZIEGLER	04237
S	RERER	0600F5902371751098883AMBRND	04240
M	BBOBB	0900M5107038645128369DIGEQ	04243

APPENDIX C

SAMPLE WORKING PROGRAMS

Program 1
Create data file

```
    1          IDENTIFICATION DIVISION.
    2          PROGRAM-ID. CREAT.
    3          ENVIRONMENT DIVISION.
    4          INPUT-OUTPUT SECTION.
    5          FILE-CONTROL.
    6              SELECT STUDENT-FILE ASSIGN TO DISK
    7                  FILE STATUS IS FILE-STATUS-CODE
    8                  ACCESS IS SEQUENTIAL
    9                  ORGANIZATION IS SEQUENTIAL.
   10          DATA DIVISION.
   11          FILE SECTION.
   12          FD  STUDENT-FILE
   13              LABEL RECORDS ARE STANDARD
   14              VALUE OF FILE-ID "STUDENTS.MST"
   15              RECORD CONTAINS 80 CHARACTERS
   16              DATA RECORD IS STUDENT-REC.
   17              COPY STDREC.COB.
   18          01  STUDENT-REC.
   19              05  STUDENT-NAME            PIC X(20).
   20              05  STUDENT-SSN             PIC 9(9).
   21              05  ADMISSION-DATE.
   22                  10  ADMIT-MONTH         PIC 99.
   23                  10  ADMIT-DAY           PIC 99.
   24                  10  ADMIT-YEAR          PIC 99.
   25              05  CURRICULUM-CODE         PIC X.
   26              05  FILLER                  PIC X(44).
   27          WORKING-STORAGE SECTION.
   28          01  WORK-AREA.
   29              05  REPLY           PIC X VALUE " ".
   30              05  FILE-STATUS-CODE   PIC XX VALUE "  ".
   31              05  NAME-WORK       PIC X(30).
   32              05  SSN-WORK        PIC 9(9).
   33              05  ADMDT-WORK      PIC 9(6).
   34              05  CURCDE-WORK     PIC X.
   35          SCREEN SECTION.
   36          01 STUDENT-SCREEN.
   37              05 BLANK SCREEN.
   38              05 LINE 3 COLUMN 2 VALUE
   39                  'ENTER NAME (QUIT TO END)'.
   40              05 LINE 3 COLUMN 30 PIC X(30) TO NAME-WORK AUTO.
   41              05 LINE 5 COLUMN 2 VALUE
   42                  'SOCIAL SECURITY NUMBER'.
   43              05 LINE 5 COLUMN 30 PIC X(9) TO SSN-WORK AUTO.
   44              05 LINE 7 COLUMN 2 VALUE
   45                  'ADMISSION DATE'.
   46              05 LINE 7 COLUMN 30 PIC X(6) TO ADMDT-WORK AUTO.
   47              05 LINE 9 COLUMN 2 VALUE
   48                  'CURCULUM CODE'.
   49              05 LINE 9 COLUMN 30 PIC X TO CURCDE-WORK AUTO.
   50          PROCEDURE DIVISION.
   51          BEGIN-PROGRAM.
   52              DISPLAY "IS THIS A RESTART? ENTER Y OR N"
   53              ACCEPT REPLY.
   54              IF REPLY = "Y" PERFORM RESTART-OPEN ELSE
   55                  PERFORM FIRST-OPEN.
   56          MAIN-LOOP-PROCESSING.
   57              DISPLAY STUDENT-SCREEN.
   58              ACCEPT STUDENT-SCREEN.
   59              IF NAME-WORK = "QUIT" GO TO CLOSE-FILE.
   60              MOVE NAME-WORK TO STUDENT-NAME,
   61              MOVE SSN-WORK TO STUDENT-SSN,
```

Program 1 (continued)

```
CREAT   COB                           18:17:55    02-Jan-84    PAGE   2
Line Number Source Line    IBM Personal Computer COBOL Compiler    Version 1.00

     62            MOVE ADMDT-WORK TO ADMISSION-DATE,
     63            MOVE CURCDE-WORK TO CURRICULUM-CODE,
     64            WRITE STUDENT-REC.
     65            GO TO MAIN-LOOP-PROCESSING.
     66        MAIN-LOOP-EXIT. EXIT.
     67        FIRST-OPEN.
     68            OPEN OUTPUT STUDENT-FILE.
     69        FIRST-EXIT. EXIT.
     70        RESTART-OPEN.
     71            OPEN EXTEND STUDENT-FILE.
     72        RESTART-EXIT. EXIT.
     73        CLOSE-FILE.
     74            CLOSE STUDENT-FILE.
     75            STOP RUN.
```

Program 2
List data file

```
LSTSTDNTCOB                          18:16:01    02-Jan-84    PAGE   1
Line Number Source Line    IBM Personal Computer COBOL Compiler   Version 1.00

     1          IDENTIFICATION DIVISION.
     2          PROGRAM-ID. CREAT.
     3          ENVIRONMENT DIVISION.
     4          INPUT-OUTPUT SECTION.
     5          FILE-CONTROL.
     6              SELECT STUDENT-FILE ASSIGN TO DISK
     7                  FILE STATUS IS FILE-STATUS-CODE
     8                  ACCESS IS SEQUENTIAL
     9                  ORGANIZATION IS SEQUENTIAL.
    10              SELECT PRINT-FILE ASSIGN TO PRINTER.
    11          DATA DIVISION.
    12          FILE SECTION.
    13          FD  STUDENT-FILE
    14              LABEL RECORDS ARE STANDARD
    15              VALUE OF FILE-ID "STUDENTS.MST"
    16              RECORD CONTAINS 80 CHARACTERS
    17              DATA RECORD IS STUDENT-REC.
    18              COPY STDREC.COB.
    19          01  STUDENT-REC.
    20              05   STUDENT-NAME             PIC X(20).
    21              05   STUDENT-SSN              PIC 9(9).
    22              05   ADMISSION-DATE.
    23                  10   ADMIT-MONTH          PIC 99.
    24                  10   ADMIT-DAY            PIC 99.
    25                  10   ADMIT-YEAR           PIC 99.
    26              05   CURRICULUM-CODE          PIC X.
    27              05   FILLER                   PIC X(44).
    28          FD  PRINT-FILE
    29              LABEL RECORDS ARE OMITTED
    30              RECORD CONTAINS 80 CHARACTERS
    31              DATA RECORD IS PRINT-REC.
    32          01  PRINT-REC        PIC X(80).
    33          WORKING-STORAGE SECTION.
    34          01  WORK-AREA.
    35              05   REPLY             PIC X VALUE " ".
    36              05   FILE-STATUS-CODE  PIC XX VALUE "  ".
    37          PROCEDURE DIVISION.
    38          BEGIN-PROGRAM.
    39              OPEN INPUT STUDENT-FILE, OUTPUT PRINT-FILE.
    40          MAIN-LOOP-PROCESSING.
    41              READ STUDENT-FILE AT END GO TO CLOSE-FILE.
    42              MOVE STUDENT-REC TO PRINT-REC.
    43              WRITE PRINT-REC AFTER ADVANCING 1 LINES.
    44              GO TO MAIN-LOOP-PROCESSING.
    45          MAIN-LOOP-EXIT. EXIT.
    46          CLOSE-FILE.
    47              CLOSE STUDENT-FILE.
    48              CLOSE PRINT-FILE.
    49              STOP RUN.
```

Output of program 2

```
ABARA,ROSALIND       1910000010801801
APPLEBAUM,CARLA      1910000020801822
ARNHOLD,DEBORAH      1910000030110833
ATKINSON,TRACEY      1910000040105835
BAILEY,PATRICIA      1910000050110804
BARR,THOMAS          1910000060921815
BELSKY,KATHLEEN      1910000060207817
COHEN,JILL           1910000080223826
```

Program 2 (continued)

```
DESANCTIS,PAUL        1910000090302825
DEVERENT,MICHAEL      1910000100910790
FREDERICO,ALICIA      1910000110402794
FREEDMAN,LAUREEN      1910000121008827
HABER,JEFF            1910000130501822
HARDING,PHEBE         1910000140301817
HATHAWAY,LARRY        1910000150301838
HELLER,KAREN          1910000160207804
HODULIK,DEBORAH       1910000170401814
IACOVELLI,MICHAEL     1910000180918815
MCKNIGHT,GREGORY      1910000190201828
NEBORAK,JOANNE        1910000200501830
PALMER,DOROTHY        1910000210304824
RACCOSTA,CATHY        1910000220920811
ROEBURG,LISA          1910000230520830
SUHOSKEY,VIRGINIA     1910000241019827
SWENK,DIANE           1910000250301835
VENUTO,JOANN          1910000250309813
WOODS,JOAN            1910000270910829
ZOMORIODIAN,ALI       1910000280820823
```

Program 3
List student file with headings

```
     1            IDENTIFICATION DIVISION.
     2            PROGRAM-ID. LISTPROG.
     3            ENVIRONMENT DIVISION.
     4            INPUT-OUTPUT SECTION.
     5            FILE-CONTROL.
     6                SELECT STUDENT-FILE ASSIGN TO DISK
     7                    FILE STATUS IS FILE-STATUS-CODE
     8                    ACCESS IS SEQUENTIAL
     9                    ORGANIZATION IS SEQUENTIAL.
    10                SELECT PRINT-FILE ASSIGN TO PRINTER.
    11            DATA DIVISION.
    12            FILE SECTION.
    13            FD  STUDENT-FILE
    14                LABEL RECORDS ARE STANDARD
    15                VALUE OF FILE-ID "STUDENTS.MST"
    16                RECORD CONTAINS 80 CHARACTERS
    17                DATA RECORD IS STUDENT-REC.
    18                COPY STDREC.COB.
    19            01  STUDENT-REC.
    20                05  STUDENT-NAME          PIC X(20).
    21                05  STUDENT-SSN           PIC 9(9).
    22                05  ADMISSION-DATE.
    23                    10  ADMIT-MONTH       PIC 99.
    24                    10  ADMIT-DAY         PIC 99.
    25                    10  ADMIT-YEAR        PIC 99.
    26                05  CURRICULUM-CODE       PIC X.
    27                05  FILLER                PIC X(44).
    28            FD  PRINT-FILE
    29                LABEL RECORDS ARE OMITTED
    30                RECORD CONTAINS 80 CHARACTERS
    31                DATA RECORD IS PRINT-REC.
    32            01  PRINT-REC      PIC X(80).
    33            WORKING-STORAGE SECTION.
    34            01  WORK-AREA.
    35                05  REPLY          PIC X VALUE " ".
    36                05  FILE-STATUS-CODE  PIC XX VALUE " ".
    37                05  WORK-SSN.
    38                    10 WORK-SSN1-3     PIC 999.
    39                    10 WORK-SSN4-5     PIC 99.
    40                    10 WORK-SSN-REST   PIC 9999.
    41            01  PRINT-LINE.
    42                05  FILLER         PIC X VALUE " ".
    43                05  PRT-NAME       PIC X(30).
    44                05  FILLER         PIC X(10) VALUE SPACES.
    45                05  PRT-SSN1-3     PIC XXX.
    46                05  FILLER         PIC X VALUE "-".
    47                05  PRT-SSN4-5     PIC XX.
    48                05  FILLER         PIC X VALUE "-".
    49                05  PRT-SSN-REST   PIC XXXX.
    50                05  FILLER         PIC X(6) VALUE SPACES.
    51                05  PRT-MM         PIC XX.
    52                05  FILLER         PIC X VALUE "/".
    53                05  PRT-DD         PIC XX.
    54                05  FILLER         PIC X VALUE "/".
    55                05  PRT-YY         PIC XX.
    56                05  FILLER         PIC X(7) VALUE SPACES.
    57                05  PRT-CCODE      PIC X.
    58                05  FILLER         PIC X(6) VALUE SPACES.
    59            01  HDR-1.
    60                05  FILLER         PIC X(33) VALUE SPACES.
    61                05  FILLER         PIC X(15) VALUE
```

Program 3 (continued)

```
LISTPROGCOB                                14:09:14   13-Feb-84   PAGE   2
Line Number Source Line    IBM Personal Computer COBOL Compiler   Version 1.00

   62              "STUDENT LISTING".
   63              05  FILLER          PIC X(32) VALUE SPACES.
   64          01  HDR-2.
   65              05  FILLER          PIC X(62) VALUE SPACES.
   66              05  FILLER          PIC X(6)  VALUE "DATE: ".
   67              05  HDG-DATE        PIC X(8).
   68              05  FILLER          PIC X(5) VALUE SPACES.
   69          01  HDR-3.
   70              05  FILLER          PIC X(39) VALUE SPACES.
   71              05  FILLER          PIC X(16) VALUE
   72              "SOCIAL SECURITY ".
   73              05  FILLER          PIC X(12) VALUE
   74              "  ADMISSION ".
   75              05  FILLER          PIC X(13) VALUE
   76              "  CURRICULUM ".
   77          01  HDR-4.
   78              05  FILLER          PIC X(13) VALUE SPACES.
   79              05  FILLER          PIC XXXX  VALUE "NAME".
   80              05  FILLER          PIC X(27) VALUE SPACES.
   81              05  FILLER          PIC X(6)  VALUE "NUMBER".
   82              05  FILLER          PIC X(10) VALUE SPACES.
   83              05  FILLER          PIC XXXX  VALUE "DATE".
   84              05  FILLER          PIC X(8)  VALUE SPACES.
   85              05  FILLER          PIC X(8)  VALUE "CODE    ".
   86          PROCEDURE DIVISION.
   87          BEGIN-PROGRAM.
   88              OPEN INPUT STUDENT-FILE, OUTPUT PRINT-FILE.
   89              PERFORM HEADING-RTN.
   90          MAIN-LOOP-PROCESSING.
   91              READ STUDENT-FILE AT END GO TO CLOSE-FILE.
   92              MOVE STUDENT-NAME TO PRT-NAME,
   93              MOVE ADMIT-MONTH TO PRT-MM,
   94              MOVE ADMIT-DAY TO PRT-DD,
   95              MOVE ADMIT-YEAR TO PRT-YY,
   96              MOVE CURRICULUM-CODE TO PRT-CCODE,
   97              MOVE STUDENT-SSN TO WORK-SSN,
   98              MOVE WORK-SSN1-3 TO PRT-SSN1-3,
   99              MOVE WORK-SSN4-5 TO PRT-SSN4-5,
  100              MOVE WORK-SSN-REST TO PRT-SSN-REST,
  101              WRITE PRINT-REC FROM PRINT-LINE AFTER ADVANCING 1 LINES.
  102              GO TO MAIN-LOOP-PROCESSING.
  103          HEADING-RTN.
  104              WRITE PRINT-REC FROM HDR-1 AFTER ADVANCING PAGE.
  105              ACCEPT HDG-DATE FROM DATE.
  106              WRITE PRINT-REC FROM HDR-2 AFTER ADVANCING 1 LINES.
  107              WRITE PRINT-REC FROM HDR-3 AFTER ADVANCING 1 LINES.
  108              MOVE SPACES TO PRINT-REC.
  109              WRITE PRINT-REC FROM HDR-4 AFTER ADVANCING 1 LINES.
  110              MOVE SPACES TO PRINT-REC.
  111              WRITE PRINT-REC AFTER ADVANCING 1 LINES.
  112          MAIN-LOOP-EXIT. EXIT.
  113          CLOSE-FILE.
  114              CLOSE STUDENT-FILE.
  115              CLOSE PRINT-FILE.
  116              STOP RUN.
```

Program 3 (continued)

Output of program 3

```
                          STUDENT LISTING
                                              DATE:  840213
                          SOCIAL SECURITY   ADMISSION    CURRICULUM
            NAME              NUMBER          DATE         CODE

ABARA,ROSALIND            191-00-0001       08/01/80          1
APPLEBAUM,CARLA           191-00-0002       08/01/82          2
ARNHOLD,DEBORAH           191-00-0003       01/10/83          3
ATKINSON,TRACEY           191-00-0004       01/05/83          5
BAILEY,PATRICIA           191-00-0005       01/10/80          4
BARR,THOMAS               191-00-0006       09/21/81          5
BELSKY,KATHLEEN           191-00-0006       02/07/81          7
COHEN,JILL                191-00-0008       02/23/82          6
DESANCTIS,PAUL            191-00-0009       03/02/82          5
DEVERENT,MICHAEL          191-00-0010       09/10/79          0
FREDERICO,ALICIA          191-00-0011       04/02/79          4
FREEDMAN,LAUREEN          191-00-0012       10/08/82          7
HABER,JEFF               191-00-0013       05/01/82          2
HARDING,PHEBE             191-00-0014       03/01/81          7
HATHAWAY,LARRY            191-00-0015       03/01/83          8
HELLER,KAREN              191-00-0016       02/07/80          4
HODULIK,DEBORAH           191-00-0017       04/01/81          4
IACOVELLI,MICHAEL         191-00-0018       09/18/81          5
MCKNIGHT,GREGORY          191-00-0019       02/01/82          8
NEBORAK,JOANNE            191-00-0020       05/01/83          0
PALMER,DOROTHY            191-00-0021       03/04/82          4
RACCOSTA,CATHY            191-00-0022       09/20/81          1
ROEBURG,LISA              191-00-0023       05/20/83          0
SUHOSKEY,VIRGINIA         191-00-0024       10/19/82          7
SWENK,DIANE               191-00-0025       03/01/83          5
VENUTO,JOANN              191-00-0025       03/09/81          3
WOODS,JOAN                191-00-0027       09/10/82          9
ZOMORIODIAN,ALI           191-00-0028       08/20/82          3
```

Program 4
Create index sequential file from sequential file

```
INDXSTDTCOB                              14:32:21   13-Feb-84   PAGE   1
Line Number Source Line   IBM Personal Computer COBOL Compiler   Version 1.00

     1           IDENTIFICATION DIVISION.
     2           PROGRAM-ID. BLDINDX.
     3           ENVIRONMENT DIVISION.
     4           INPUT-OUTPUT SECTION.
     5           FILE-CONTROL.
     6               SELECT STUDENT-FILE ASSIGN TO DISK
     7                   FILE STATUS IS FILE-STATUS-CODE
     8                   ACCESS IS SEQUENTIAL
     9                   ORGANIZATION IS SEQUENTIAL.
    10               SELECT STUDENT-INDX-FILE ASSIGN TO DISK
    11                   FILE STATUS IS INDX-FILE-STATUS
    12                   ACCESS IS SEQUENTIAL
    13                   ORGANIZATION IS INDEXED
    14                   RECORD KEY IS STUDENT-SSN-OUT.
    15           DATA DIVISION.
    16           FILE SECTION.
    17           FD  STUDENT-FILE
    18               LABEL RECORDS ARE STANDARD
    19               VALUE OF FILE-ID "STUDENTS.MST"
    20               RECORD CONTAINS 80 CHARACTERS
    21               DATA RECORD IS STUDENT-REC.
    22               COPY STDREC.COB.
    23           01  STUDENT-REC.
    24               05  STUDENT-NAME            PIC X(20).
    25               05  STUDENT-SSN             PIC 9(9).
    26               05  ADMISSION-DATE.
    27                   10  ADMIT-MONTH         PIC 99.
    28                   10  ADMIT-DAY           PIC 99.
    29                   10  ADMIT-YEAR          PIC 99.
    30               05  CURRICULUM-CODE         PIC X.
    31               05  FILLER                  PIC X(44).
    32           FD  STUDENT-INDX-FILE
    33               LABEL RECORDS ARE STANDARD
    34               VALUE OF FILE-ID "STDTINDX.MAS"
    35               RECORD CONTAINS 80 CHARACTERS
    36               DATA RECORD IS NEW-STUDENT-RECORD.
    37           01  NEW-STUDENT-RECORD.
    38               05  STUDENT-NAME-OUT    PIC X(20).
    39               05  STUDENT-SSN-OUT     PIC X(9).
    40               05  ADMIN-DATE-OUT      PIC X(6).
    41               05  CURRICULUM-CODE-OUT PIC X.
    42               05  FILLER              PIC X(44).
    43           WORKING-STORAGE SECTION.
    44           01  WORK-AREA.
    45               05  REPLY           PIC X VALUE " ".
    46               05  FILE-STATUS-CODE  PIC XX VALUE "  ".
    47               05  INDX-FILE-STATUS  PIC XX VALUE "  ".
    48           PROCEDURE DIVISION.
    49           BEGIN-PROGRAM.
    50               OPEN INPUT STUDENT-FILE, OUTPUT STUDENT-INDX-FILE.
    51           MAIN-LOOP-PROCESSING.
    52               READ STUDENT-FILE AT END GO TO CLOSE-FILE.
    53               MOVE STUDENT-REC TO NEW-STUDENT-RECORD.
    54               WRITE NEW-STUDENT-RECORD.
    55               GO TO MAIN-LOOP-PROCESSING.
    56           MAIN-LOOP-EXIT. EXIT.
    57           CLOSE-FILE.
    58               CLOSE STUDENT-FILE.
    59               CLOSE STUDENT-INDX-FILE.
    60               STOP RUN.
```

Program 5 List
Index sequential file

```
INDXLISTCOB                               14:27:00     13-Feb-84    PAGE   1
Line Number  Source Line    IBM Personal Computer COBOL Compiler   Version 1.00

     1          IDENTIFICATION DIVISION.
     2          PROGRAM-ID. LISTPROG.
     3          ENVIRONMENT DIVISION.
     4          INPUT-OUTPUT SECTION.
     5          FILE-CONTROL.
     6              SELECT STUDENT-FILE ASSIGN TO DISK
     7                  FILE STATUS IS FILE-STATUS-CODE
     8                  ACCESS IS SEQUENTIAL
     9                  RECORD KEY IS STUDENT-SSN
    10                  ORGANIZATION IS INDEXED.
    11              SELECT PRINT-FILE ASSIGN TO PRINTER.
    12          DATA DIVISION.
    13          FILE SECTION.
    14          FD  STUDENT-FILE
    15              LABEL RECORDS ARE STANDARD
    16              VALUE OF FILE-ID "STDTINDX.MAS"
    17              RECORD CONTAINS 80 CHARACTERS
    18              DATA RECORD IS STUDENT-REC.
    19              COPY STDREC.COB.
    20          01  STUDENT-REC.
    21              05   STUDENT-NAME            PIC X(20).
    22              05   STUDENT-SSN             PIC 9(9).
    23              05   ADMISSION-DATE.
    24                   10  ADMIT-MONTH       PIC 99.
    25                   10  ADMIT-DAY         PIC 99.
    26                   10  ADMIT-YEAR        PIC 99.
    27              05   CURRICULUM-CODE        PIC X.
    28              05   FILLER                 PIC X(44).
    29          FD  PRINT-FILE
    30              LABEL RECORDS ARE OMITTED
    31              RECORD CONTAINS 80 CHARACTERS
    32              DATA RECORD IS PRINT-REC.
    33          01  PRINT-REC       PIC X(80).
    34          WORKING-STORAGE SECTION.
    35          01  WORK-AREA.
    36              05   REPLY           PIC X VALUE " ".
    37              05   FILE-STATUS-CODE  PIC XX VALUE "  ".
    38              05  WORK-SSN.
    39                  10  WORK-SSN1-3      PIC 999.
    40                  10  WORK-SSN4-5      PIC 99.
    41                  10  WORK-SSN-REST    PIC 9999.
    42          01   PRINT-LINE.
    43              05  FILLER           PIC X VALUE " ".
    44              05  PRT-NAME         PIC X(30).
    45              05  FILLER           PIC X(10) VALUE SPACES.
    46              05  PRT-SSN1-3       PIC XXX.
    47              05  FILLER           PIC X VALUE "-".
    48              05  PRT-SSN4-5       PIC XX.
    49              05  FILLER           PIC X VALUE "-".
    50              05  PRT-SSN-REST     PIC XXXX.
    51              05  FILLER           PIC X(6) VALUE SPACES.
    52              05  PRT-MM           PIC XX.
    53              05  FILLER           PIC X VALUE "/".
    54              05  PRT-DD           PIC XX.
    55              05  FILLER           PIC X VALUE "/".
    56              05  PRT-YY           PIC XX.
    57              05  FILLER           PIC X(7) VALUE SPACES.
    58              05  PRT-CCODE        PIC X.
    59              05  FILLER           PIC X(6) VALUE SPACES.
    60          01  HDR-1.
```

Program 5 (continued)

```
 61              05  FILLER        PIC X(23) VALUE SPACES.
 62              05  FILLER        PIC X(10) VALUE "(INDEXED) ".
 63              05  FILLER        PIC X(15) VALUE
 64              "STUDENT LISTING".
 65              05  FILLER        PIC X(32) VALUE SPACES.
 66          01  HDR-2.
 67              05  FILLER        PIC X(62) VALUE SPACES.
 68              05  FILLER        PIC X(6)  VALUE "DATE: ".
 69              05  HDG-DATE      PIC X(8).
 70              05  FILLER        PIC X(5) VALUE SPACES.
 71          01  HDR-3.
 72              05  FILLER        PIC X(39) VALUE SPACES.
 73              05  FILLER        PIC X(16) VALUE
 74              "SOCIAL SECURITY ".
 75              05  FILLER        PIC X(12) VALUE
 76              "  ADMISSION ".
 77              05  FILLER        PIC X(13) VALUE
 78              "  CURRICULUM ".
 79          01  HDR-4.
 80              05  FILLER        PIC X(13) VALUE SPACES.
 81              05  FILLER        PIC XXXX  VALUE "NAME".
 82              05  FILLER        PIC X(27) VALUE SPACES.
 83              05  FILLER        PIC X(6)  VALUE "NUMBER".
 84              05  FILLER        PIC X(10) VALUE SPACES.
 85              05  FILLER        PIC XXXX  VALUE "DATE".
 86              05  FILLER        PIC X(8)  VALUE SPACES.
 87              05  FILLER        PIC X(8)  VALUE "CODE     ".
 88          PROCEDURE DIVISION.
 89          BEGIN-PROGRAM.
 90              OPEN INPUT STUDENT-FILE, OUTPUT PRINT-FILE.
 91              PERFORM HEADING-RTN.
 92          MAIN-LOOP-PROCESSING.
 93              READ STUDENT-FILE AT END GO TO CLOSE-FILE.
 94              MOVE STUDENT-NAME TO PRT-NAME,
 95              MOVE ADMIT-MONTH TO PRT-MM,
 96              MOVE ADMIT-DAY TO PRT-DD,
 97              MOVE ADMIT-YEAR TO PRT-YY,
 98              MOVE CURRICULUM-CODE TO PRT-CCODE,
 99              MOVE STUDENT-SSN TO WORK-SSN,
100              MOVE WORK-SSN1-3 TO PRT-SSN1-3,
101              MOVE WORK-SSN4-5 TO PRT-SSN4-5,
102              MOVE WORK-SSN-REST TO PRT-SSN-REST,
103              WRITE PRINT-REC FROM PRINT-LINE AFTER ADVANCING 1 LINES.
104              GO TO MAIN-LOOP-PROCESSING.
105          HEADING-RTN.
106              WRITE PRINT-REC FROM HDR-1 AFTER ADVANCING PAGE.
107              ACCEPT HDG-DATE FROM DATE.
108              WRITE PRINT-REC FROM HDR-2 AFTER ADVANCING 1 LINES.
109              WRITE PRINT-REC FROM HDR-3 AFTER ADVANCING 1 LINES.
110              MOVE SPACES TO PRINT-REC.
111              WRITE PRINT-REC FROM HDR-4 AFTER ADVANCING 1 LINES.
112              MOVE SPACES TO PRINT-REC.
113              WRITE PRINT-REC AFTER ADVANCING 1 LINES.
114          MAIN-LOOP-EXIT. EXIT.
115          CLOSE-FILE.
116              CLOSE STUDENT-FILE.
117              CLOSE PRINT-FILE.
118              STOP RUN.
```

Program 5 (continued)

Output of program 5

(INDEXED) STUDENT LISTING

| | | DATE: 840213 | |
NAME	SOCIAL SECURITY NUMBER	ADMISSION DATE	CURRICULUM CODE
ABARA, ROSALIND	191-00-0001	08/01/80	1
APPLEBAUM, CARLA	191-00-0002	08/01/82	2
ARNHOLD, DEBORAH	191-00-0003	01/10/83	3
ATKINSON, TRACEY	191-00-0004	01/05/83	5
BAILEY, PATRICIA	191-00-0005	01/10/80	4
BARR, THOMAS	191-00-0006	09/21/81	5
COHEN, JILL	191-00-0008	02/23/82	6
DESANCTIS, PAUL	191-00-0009	03/02/82	5
DEVERENT, MICHAEL	191-00-0010	09/10/79	0
FREDERICO, ALICIA	191-00-0011	04/02/79	4
FREEDMAN, LAUREEN	191-00-0012	10/08/82	7
HABER, JEFF	191-00-0013	05/01/82	2
HARDING, PHEBE	191-00-0014	03/01/81	7
HATHAWAY, LARRY	191-00-0015	03/01/83	8
HELLER, KAREN	191-00-0016	02/07/80	4
HODULIK, DEBORAH	191-00-0017	04/01/81	4
IACOVELLI, MICHAEL	191-00-0018	09/18/81	5
MCKNIGHT, GREGORY	191-00-0019	02/01/82	8
NEBORAK, JOANNE	191-00-0020	05/01/83	0
PALMER, DOROTHY	191-00-0021	03/04/82	4
RACCOSTA, CATHY	191-00-0022	09/20/81	1
ROEBURG, LISA	191-00-0023	05/20/83	0
SUHOSKEY, VIRGINIA	'191-00-0024	10/19/82	7
SWENK, DIANE	191-00-0025	03/01/83	5
WOODS, JOAN	191-00-0027	09/10/82	9
ZOMORIODIAN, ALI	191-00-0028	08/20/82	3

Program 6
File maintenance for index sequential file

```
INDXMAINCOB                           14:33:04    27-Feb-84    PAGE   1
Line Number Source Line    IBM Personal Computer COBOL Compiler   Version 1.00

     1          IDENTIFICATION DIVISION.
     2          PROGRAM-ID. INDXMAIN.
     3          ENVIRONMENT DIVISION.
     4          INPUT-OUTPUT SECTION.
     5          FILE-CONTROL.
     6              SELECT STUDENT-FILE ASSIGN TO DISK
     7                  FILE STATUS IS FILE-STATUS-CODE
     8                  ACCESS IS DYNAMIC
     9                  RECORD KEY IS STUDENT-SSN
    10                  ORGANIZATION IS INDEXED.
    11          DATA DIVISION.
    12          FILE SECTION.
    13          FD  STUDENT-FILE
    14              LABEL RECORDS ARE STANDARD
    15              VALUE OF FILE-ID "STDTINDX.MAS"
    16              RECORD CONTAINS 80 CHARACTERS
    17              DATA RECORD IS STUDENT-REC.
    18              COPY STDREC.COB.
    19          01  STUDENT-REC.
    20              05  STUDENT-NAME            PIC X(20).
    21              05  STUDENT-SSN             PIC 9(9).
    22              05  ADMISSION-DATE.
    23                  10  ADMIT-MONTH     PIC 99.
    24                  10  ADMIT-DAY       PIC 99.
    25                  10  ADMIT-YEAR      PIC 99.
    26              05  CURRICULUM-CODE         PIC X.
    27              05  FILLER                  PIC X(44).
    28          WORKING-STORAGE SECTION.
    29          01  WORK-AREA.
    30              05  REPLY           PIC X VALUE " ".
    31              05  FILE-STATUS-CODE  PIC XX VALUE "  ".
    32              05  WORK-SSN.
    33                  10 WORK-SSN1-3      PIC 999.
    34                  10 WORK-SSN4-5      PIC 99.
    35                  10 WORK-SSN-REST    PIC 9999.
    36              05  SSN-WORK        PIC X(9).
    37              05  NAME-WORK       PIC X(30).
    38              05  ADMDT-WORK      PIC 9(6).
    39              05  CURCDE-WORK     PIC X.
    40          SCREEN SECTION.
    41          01 STUDENT-SCREEN.
    42              05 BLANK SCREEN.
    43              05 LINE 3 COLUMN 2 VALUE
    44                 'ENTER NAME (QUIT TO END)'.
    45              05 LINE 3 COLUMN 30 PIC X(30) TO NAME-WORK AUTO.
    46              05 LINE 5 COLUMN 2 VALUE
    47                 'SOCIAL SECURITY NUMBER'.
    48              05 LINE 5 COLUMN 30 PIC X(9) TO SSN-WORK AUTO.
    49              05 LINE 7 COLUMN 2 VALUE
    50                 'ADMISSION DATE'.
    51              05 LINE 7 COLUMN 30 PIC X(6) TO ADMDT-WORK AUTO.
    52              05 LINE 9 COLUMN 2 VALUE
    53                 'CURCULUM CODE'.
    54            05 LINE 9 COLUMN 30 PIC X TO CURCDE-WORK AUTO.
    55          PROCEDURE DIVISION.
    56          BEGIN-PROGRAM.
    57              OPEN I-O STUDENT-FILE.
    58          MAIN-LOOP-PROCESSING.
    59              DISPLAY STUDENT-SCREEN.
    60              ACCEPT STUDENT-SCREEN.
    61              IF NAME-WORK = "QUIT" GO TO CLOSE-FILE.
```

Program 6 (continued)

```
INDXMAINCOB                          14:33:04    27-Feb-84    PAGE   2
Line Number Source Line    IBM Personal Computer COBOL Compiler   Version 1.00

    62              MOVE SSN-WORK TO STUDENT-SSN.
    63              READ STUDENT-FILE RECORD KEY IS STUDENT-SSN.
    64              IF FILE-STATUS-CODE = "10" GO TO ADD-ROUTINE.
    65              IF FILE-STATUS-CODE = "23" GO TO ADD-ROUTINE.
    66              IF NAME-WORK = "REMOVE" GO TO REMOVE-ROUTINE.
    67              IF NAME-WORK = SPACES NEXT SENTENCE ELSE
    68              MOVE NAME-WORK TO STUDENT-NAME.
    69              IF ADMDT-WORK = SPACES NEXT SENTENCE, ELSE
    70              MOVE ADMDT-WORK TO ADMIT-MONTH.
    71              IF CURCDE-WORK = SPACES NEXT SENTENCE, ELSE
    72              MOVE CURCDE-WORK TO CURRICULUM-CODE.
    73              REWRITE STUDENT-REC.
    74              GO TO MAIN-LOOP-PROCESSING.
    75          ADD-ROUTINE.
    76              MOVE NAME-WORK TO STUDENT-NAME,
    77              MOVE SSN-WORK TO STUDENT-SSN,
    78              MOVE ADMDT-WORK TO ADMISSION-DATE,
    79              MOVE CURCDE-WORK TO CURRICULUM-CODE,
    80              WRITE STUDENT-REC.
    81              GO TO MAIN-LOOP-PROCESSING.
    82          REMOVE-ROUTINE.
    83              DELETE STUDENT-FILE RECORD.
    84              GO TO MAIN-LOOP-PROCESSING.
    85          CLOSE-FILE.
    86              CLOSE STUDENT-FILE.
```

Output of list program after file maintenance performed

(INDEXED) STUDENT LISTING

NAME	SOCIAL SECURITY NUMBER	ADMISSION DATE	CURRICULUM CODE
		DATE: 840227	
ABARA,ROSALIND	191-00-0001	08/01/80	1
APPLEBAUM,CARLA	191-00-0002	08/01/82	2
ARNHOLD,DEBORAH	191-00-0003	01/10/83	3
ATKINSON,TRACEY	191-00-0004	84/05/83	4
BAILEY,PATRICIA	191-00-0005	01/10/80	4
COHEN,JILL	191-00-0008	02/23/82	6
DESANCTIS,PAUL	191-00-0009	03/02/82	5
DEVERENT,MICHAEL	191-00-0010	09/10/79	0
FREDERICO,ALICIA	191-00-0011	04/02/79	4
FREEDMAN,LAUREEN	191-00-0012	10/08/82	7
HABER,JEFF	191-00-0013	05/01/82	2
HARDING,PHEBE	191-00-0014	03/01/81	7
HATHAWAY,LARRY	191-00-0015	03/01/83	8
HELLER,KAREN	191-00-0016	02/07/80	4
HODULIK,DEBORAH	191-00-0017	04/01/81	4
IACOVELLI,MICHAEL	191-00-0018	09/18/81	5
MCKNIGHT,GREGORY	191-00-0019	02/01/82	8
NEBORAK,JOANNE	191-00-0020	05/01/83	0
PALMER,DOROTHY	191-00-0021	03/04/82	4
RACCOSTA,CATHY	191-00-0022	09/20/81	1
ROEBURG,LISA	191-00-0023	05/20/83	0
BUHOSKEY,VIRGINIA	191-00-0024	10/19/82	7
SWENK,DIANE	191-00-0025	03/01/83	5
WOODS,JOAN	191-00-0027	09/10/82	9
ZOMORIODIAN,ALI	191-00-0028	08/20/82	3
PAUL A DESANCTIS	191-00-0031	02/27/84	3
WILLIAM J ATKINSON,	191-00-0041	02/27/84	4

Program 7
Index sequential file listing using table for processing

```
indxtab1COB                                    15:46:14   27-Feb-84   PAGE   1
Line Number  Source Line   IBM Personal Computer COBOL Compiler   Version 1.00

   1            IDENTIFICATION DIVISION.
   2            PROGRAM-ID. LISTPROG.
   3            ENVIRONMENT DIVISION.
   4            INPUT-OUTPUT SECTION.
   5            FILE-CONTROL.
   6                SELECT STUDENT-FILE ASSIGN TO DISK
   7                    FILE STATUS IS FILE-STATUS-CODE
   8                    ACCESS IS SEQUENTIAL
   9                    RECORD KEY IS STUDENT-SSN
  10                    ORGANIZATION IS INDEXED.
  11                SELECT PRINT-FILE ASSIGN TO PRINTER.
  12            DATA DIVISION.
  13            FILE SECTION.
  14            FD  STUDENT-FILE
  15                LABEL RECORDS ARE STANDARD
  16                VALUE OF FILE-ID "STDTINDX.MAS"
  17                RECORD CONTAINS 80 CHARACTERS
  18                DATA RECORD IS STUDENT-REC.
  19                COPY STDREC.COB.
  20            01  STUDENT-REC.
  21                05   STUDENT-NAME            PIC X(20).
  22                05   STUDENT-SSN             PIC 9(9).
  23                05   ADMISSION-DATE.
  24                    10   ADMIT-MONTH         PIC 99.
  25                    10   ADMIT-DAY           PIC 99.
  26                    10   ADMIT-YEAR          PIC 99.
  27                05   CURRICULUM-CODE         PIC X.
  28                05   FILLER                  PIC X(44).
  29            FD  PRINT-FILE
  30                LABEL RECORDS ARE OMITTED
  31                RECORD CONTAINS 132 CHARACTERS
  32                DATA RECORD IS PRINT-REC.
  33            01  PRINT-REC        PIC X(132).
  34            WORKING-STORAGE SECTION.
  35            01  WORK-AREA.
  36                05   REPLY          PIC X VALUE " ".
  37                05   FILE-STATUS-CODE  PIC XX VALUE "  ".
  38                05 WORK-SSN.
  39                    10 WORK-SSN1-3     PIC 999.
  40                    10 WORK-SSN4-5     PIC 99.
  41                    10 WORK-SSN-REST   PIC 9999.
  42                05   INDX        PIC 999 VALUE ZERO.
  43            01  CURRICULUM-TABLE.
  44                05 FILLER        PIC X(19) VALUE "0UNKNOWN           ".
  45                05 FILLER        PIC X(19) VALUE "1MARKETING         ".
  46                05 FILLER        PIC X(19) VALUE "2MANAGEMENT        ".
  47                05 FILLER        PIC X(19) VALUE "3NURSING           ".
  48                05 FILLER        PIC X(19) VALUE "4FASHON DESIGN     ".
  49                05 FILLER        PIC X(19) VALUE "5DATA PROCESSING   ".
  50                05 FILLER        PIC X(19) VALUE "6SCIENCE           ".
  51                05 FILLER        PIC X(19) VALUE "7ACCOUNTING        ".
  52                05 FILLER        PIC X(19) VALUE "8BUS ADMINISTRATION".
  53                05 FILLER        PIC X(19) VALUE "9GENERAL STUDIES   ".
  54            01  TABLE-CURRICULUM REDEFINES CURRICULUM-TABLE.
  55                05 FILLER OCCURS 10 TIMES.
  56                    10 TABLE-CODE        PIC X.
  57                    10 TABLE-DESCRIPTION  PIC X(18).
  58            01  PRINT-LINE.
  59                05   FILLER        PIC X VALUE " ".
  60                05   PRT-NAME      PIC X(30).
  61                05   FILLER        PIC X(10) VALUE SPACES.
```

Program 7 (continued)

```
( indxtab1COB                              15:46:14    27-Feb-84    PAGE    2
Line Number Source Line    IBM Personal Computer COBOL Compiler   Version 1.00

    62              05  PRT-SSN1-3     PIC XXX.
    63              05  FILLER         PIC X VALUE "-".
    64              05  PRT-SSN4-5     PIC XX.
    65              05  FILLER         PIC X VALUE "-".
    66              05  PRT-SSN-REST   PIC XXXX.
    67              05  FILLER         PIC X(6) VALUE SPACES.
    68              05  PRT-MM         PIC XX.
    69              05  FILLER         PIC X VALUE "/".
    70              05  PRT-DD         PIC XX.
    71              05  FILLER         PIC X VALUE "/".
    72              05  PRT-YY         PIC XX.
    73              05  FILLER         PIC X(7) VALUE SPACES.
    74              05  PRT-CDESC      PIC X(18).
    75              05  FILLER         PIC X(6) VALUE SPACES.
    76         01  HDR-1.
    77              05  FILLER         PIC X(23) VALUE SPACES.
    78              05  FILLER         PIC X(10) VALUE "(INDEXED) ".
    79              05  FILLER         PIC X(15) VALUE
    80              "STUDENT LISTING".
    81              05  FILLER         PIC X(32) VALUE SPACES.
    82         01  HDR-2.
    83              05  FILLER         PIC X(62) VALUE SPACES.
    84              05  FILLER         PIC X(6)  VALUE "DATE: ".
    85              05  HDG-DATE       PIC X(8).
    86              05  FILLER         PIC X(5) VALUE SPACES.
    87         01  HDR-3.
    88              05  FILLER         PIC X(39) VALUE SPACES.
    89              05  FILLER         PIC X(16) VALUE
    90              "SOCIAL SECURITY ".
    91              05  FILLER         PIC X(12) VALUE
    92              "  ADMISSION ".
    93              05  FILLER         PIC X(13) VALUE
    94              "  CURRICULUM ".
    95         01  HDR-4.
    96              05  FILLER         PIC X(13) VALUE SPACES.
    97              05  FILLER         PIC XXXX  VALUE "NAME".
    98              05  FILLER         PIC X(27) VALUE SPACES.
    99              05  FILLER         PIC X(6)  VALUE "NUMBER".
   100              05  FILLER         PIC X(10) VALUE SPACES.
   101              05  FILLER         PIC XXXX  VALUE "DATE".
   102              05  FILLER         PIC X(8)  VALUE SPACES.
   103              05  FILLER         PIC X(8)  VALUE "CODE    ".
   104         PROCEDURE DIVISION.
   105         BEGIN-PROGRAM.
   106             OPEN INPUT STUDENT-FILE, OUTPUT PRINT-FILE.
   107             PERFORM HEADING-RTN.
   108         MAIN-LOOP-PROCESSING.
   109             READ STUDENT-FILE AT END GO TO CLOSE-FILE.
   110             MOVE STUDENT-NAME TO PRT-NAME,
   111             MOVE ADMIT-MONTH TO PRT-MM,
   112             MOVE ADMIT-DAY TO PRT-DD,
   113             MOVE ADMIT-YEAR TO PRT-YY,
   114             PERFORM SEARCH-TABLE THRU TABLE-SEARCH-EXIT,
   115             MOVE STUDENT-SSN TO WORK-SSN,
   116             MOVE WORK-SSN1-3 TO PRT-SSN1-3,
   117             MOVE WORK-SSN4-5 TO PRT-SSN4-5,
   118             MOVE WORK-SSN-REST TO PRT-SSN-REST,
   119             WRITE PRINT-REC FROM PRINT-LINE AFTER ADVANCING 1 LINES.
   120             GO TO MAIN-LOOP-PROCESSING.
   121         HEADING-RTN.
   122             WRITE PRINT-REC FROM HDR-1 AFTER ADVANCING PAGE.
   123             ACCEPT HDG-DATE FROM DATE.
```

Program 7 (continued)

```
indxtab1COB                          15:46:14    27-Feb-84    PAGE   3
Line Number Source Line    IBM Personal Computer COBOL Compiler   Version 1.00

124              WRITE PRINT-REC FROM HDR-2 AFTER ADVANCING 1 LINES.
125              WRITE PRINT-REC FROM HDR-3 AFTER ADVANCING 1 LINES.
126              MOVE SPACES TO PRINT-REC.
127              WRITE PRINT-REC FROM HDR-4 AFTER ADVANCING 1 LINES.
128              MOVE SPACES TO PRINT-REC.
129              WRITE PRINT-REC AFTER ADVANCING 1 LINES.
130          MAIN-LOOP-EXIT. EXIT.
131          SEARCH-TABLE.
132              MOVE 1 TO INDX.
133          SEARCH-LOOP.
134              IF CURRICULUM-CODE = TABLE-CODE (INDX)
135                  MOVE TABLE-DESCRIPTION (INDX) TO PRT-CDESC
136                  GO TO TABLE-SEARCH-EXIT.
137              ADD 1 TO INDX.
138              IF INDX = 11 MOVE "** INVALID CODE **" TO PRT-CDESC
139                  GO TO TABLE-SEARCH-EXIT.
140              GO TO SEARCH-LOOP.
141          TABLE-SEARCH-EXIT.
142              EXIT.
143          CLOSE-FILE.
144              CLOSE STUDENT-FILE.
145              CLOSE PRINT-FILE.
```

Output of program 7

```
                      (INDEXED) STUDENT LISTING

                                           DATE: 840227
                          SOCIAL SECURITY  ADMISSION  CURRICULUM
              NAME           NUMBER          DATE       CODE


     ABARA,ROSALIND          191-00-0001   08/01/80   MARKETING
     APPLEBAUM,CARLA         191-00-0002   08/01/82   MANAGEMENT
     ARNHOLD,DEBORAH         191-00-0003   01/10/83   NURSING
     ATKINSON,TRACEY         191-00-0004   84/05/83   FASHON DESIGN
     BAILEY,PATRICIA         191-00-0005   01/10/80   FASHON DESIGN
     COHEN,JILL              191-00-0008   02/23/82   SCIENCE
     DESANCTIS,PAUL          191-00-0009   03/02/82   DATA PROCESSING
     DEVERENT,MICHAEL        191-00-0010   09/10/79   UNKNOWN
     FREDERICO,ALICIA        191-00-0011   04/02/79   FASHON DESIGN
     FREEDMAN,LAUREEN        191-00-0012   10/08/82   ACCOUNTING
     HABER,JEFF              191-00-0013   05/01/82   MANAGEMENT
     HARDING,PHEBE           191-00-0014   03/01/81   ACCOUNTING
     HATHAWAY,LARRY          191-00-0015   03/01/83   BUS ADMINISTRATION
     HELLER,KAREN            191-00-0016   02/07/80   FASHON DESIGN
     HODULIK,DEBORAH         191-00-0017   04/01/81   FASHON DESIGN
     IACOVELLI,MICHAEL       191-00-0018   09/18/81   DATA PROCESSING
     MCKNIGHT,GREGORY        191-00-0019   02/01/82   BUS ADMINISTRATION
     NEBORAK,JOANNE          191-00-0020   05/01/83   UNKNOWN
     PALMER,DOROTHY          191-00-0021   03/04/82   FASHON DESIGN
     RACCOSTA,CATHY          191-00-0022   09/20/81   MARKETING
     ROEBURG,LISA            191-00-0023   05/20/83   UNKNOWN
     SUHOSKEY,VIRGINIA       191-00-0024   10/19/82   ACCOUNTING
     SWENK,DIANE             191-00-0025   03/01/83   DATA PROCESSING
     WOODS,JOAN              191-00-0027   09/10/82   GENERAL STUDIES
     ZOMORIODIAN,ALI         191-00-0028   08/20/82   NURSING
     PAUL A DESANCTIS        191-00-0031   02/27/84   NURSING
     WILLIAM J ATKINSON,     191-00-0041   02/27/84   FASHON DESIGN
```

Sample program to sort the student file placing the sorted results in a line sequential file.

```
IDENTIFICATION DIVISION.
PROGRAM-ID. SORT.

ENVIRONMENT DIVISION.
INPUT-OUTPUT SECTION.
FILE-CONTROL.
    SELECT STUDENT-FILE ASSIGN TO DISK
        ORGANIZATION IS INDEXED
        ACCESS MODE IS DYNAMIC
        RECORD KEY IS STUDENT-ID.

    SELECT XREF-FILE ASSIGN TO DISK
        ORGANIZATION IS INDEXED
        ACCESS MODE IS DYNAMIC
        RECORD KEY IS XREF-NAME.

    SELECT SORT-FILE ASSIGN TO DISK
        ORGANIZATION IS LINE SEQUENTIAL.

DATA DIVISION.
FILE SECTION.
FD  STUDENT-FILE
    LABEL RECORDS ARE STANDARD
    VALUE OF FILE-ID "B:STUDENTS.MST"
    RECORD CONTAINS 80 CHARACTERS
    DATA RECORD IS STUDENT-REC.
01  STUDENT-REC.
    05  STUDENT-ID          PIC X(5).
    05  STUDENT-NAME        PIC X(20).
    05  STUDENT-ADDRESS     PIC X(30).
    05  STUDENT-SSN         PIC 9(9).
    05  ADMISSION-DATE.
        10  ADMIT-MONTH     PIC 99.
        10  ADMIT-DAY       PIC 99.
        10  ADMIT-YEAR      PIC 99.
    05  CURRICULUM          PIC X(10).

FD  XREF-FILE
    LABEL RECORDS ARE STANDARD
    VALUE OF FILE-ID "B:XREF.FILE"
    RECORD CONTAINS 28 CHARACTERS
    DATA RECORD IS XREF-REC.
01  XREF-REC.
    05  XREF-NAME.
        10  STUD-NAME       PIC X(20).
        10  SEQ-NUMB        PIC 999.
    05  STUD-ID             PIC X(5).

FD  SORT-FILE
    LABEL RECORDS ARE STANDARD
    VALUE OF FILE-ID "B:SORT.FILE"
    RECORD CONTAINS 80 CHARACTERS
    DATA RECORD IS SORT-REC.
01  SORT-REC                PIC X(80).

WORKING-STORAGE SECTION.

PROCEDURE DIVISION.
100-MAIN-PROCESSING.
    MOVE 0 TO SEQ-NUMB.
    PERFORM 200-OPEN-FILES.
    PERFORM 250-START-STUD-FILE.
    PERFORM 400-READ-FILE THRU 400-PROCESS-EXIT.
    PERFORM 450-START-XREF-FILE.
    PERFORM 500-WRITE-SORT THRU 500-SORT-EXIT.
```

```
        PERFORM 600-CLOSE-FILES.
        STOP RUN.

    200-OPEN-FILES.
        OPEN I-O STUDENT-FILE  XREF-FILE
            OUTPUT SORT-FILE.

    250-START-STUD-FILE.
        MOVE SPACES TO STUDENT-ID.
        START STUDENT-FILE KEY > STUDENT-ID
            INVALID KEY
            DISPLAY "CANNOT START STUDENT FILE"
            PERFORM 600-CLOSE-FILES
            STOP RUN.

    400-READ-FILE.
        READ STUDENT-FILE NEXT RECORD AT END
            GO TO 400-PROCESS-EXIT.
        MOVE STUDENT-NAME TO STUD-NAME.
        ADD 1 TO SEQ-NUMB.
        MOVE STUDENT-ID TO STUD-ID.
        WRITE XREF-REC INVALID KEY
         PERFORM 700-ERROR.
        GO TO 400-READ-FILE.

    400-PROCESS-EXIT.
        EXIT.

    450-START-XREF-FILE.
        MOVE SPACES TO XREF-NAME.
        START XREF-FILE KEY > XREF-NAME
            INVALID KEY
            DISPLAY "CANNOT START XREF FILE"
            PERFORM 600-CLOSE-FILES
            STOP RUN.

    500-WRITE-SORT.
        READ XREF-FILE NEXT RECORD AT END
            GO TO 500-SORT-EXIT.
        MOVE STUD-ID TO STUDENT-ID.
        READ STUDENT-FILE  INVALID KEY
            PERFORM 800-ERROR.
        WRITE SORT-REC FROM STUDENT-REC.
        GO TO 500-WRITE-SORT.

    500-SORT-EXIT.
        EXIT.

    600-CLOSE-FILES.
        CLOSE STUDENT-FILE, XREF-FILE, SORT-FILE.

    700-ERROR.
        DISPLAY "CANNOT WRITE XREF-REC" XREF-NAME.

    800-ERROR.
        DISPLAY "CANNOT READ STUDENT-FILE" STUDENT-ID.
```

INDEX